Assessing and Treating Culturally Diverse Clients

THIRD EDITION

MULTICULTURAL ASPECTS OF COUNSELING AND PSYCHOTHERAPY SERIES

SERIES EDITOR

Paul B. Pedersen, Ph.D.,
Professor Emeritus, Syracuse University
Visiting Professor, Department of Psychology, University of Hawaii

EDITORIAL BOARD

VOLUMES IN THIS SERIES

Assessing and Treating Culturally Diverse Clients

A Practical Guide

THIRD EDITION

Freddy A. Paniagua

University of Texas Medical Branch at Galveston

Multicultural Aspects of Counseling and Psychotherapy Series 4

SAGE Publications
Thousand Oaks ▪ London ▪ New Delhi

For information:

Sage Publications, Inc.
2455 Teller Road
Thousand Oaks, California 91320
E-mail: order@sagepub.com

Sage Publications Ltd.
1 Oliver's Yard
55 City Road
London EC1Y 1SP
United Kingdom

Sage Publications India Pvt. Ltd.
B-42, Panchsheel Enclave
Post Box 4109
New Delhi 110 017 India

Printed in the United States of America

Library of Congress Cataloging-in-Publication Data

Paniagua, Freddy A.
Assessing and treating culturally diverse clients: A practical guide/Freddy A. Paniagua. — 3rd ed.
    p. cm. — (Multicultural aspects of counseling and psychotherapy; v. 4)
Includes bibliographical references and indexes.
ISBN 1-4129-1008-0 (pbk.)
    1. Cross-cultural counseling—United States. I. Title. II. Series.
BF637.C6P264 2005
361′.06′089—dc22   2004024601

This book is printed on acid-free paper.

06   07   08   09   10   9   8   7   6   5   4   3   2

Acquisitions Editor:	Arthur T. Pomponio
Editorial Assistant:	Veronica K. Novak
Production Editor:	Beth A. Bernstein
Copy Editor:	Judy Selhorst
Typesetter:	C&M Digitals (P) Ltd.
Proofreader:	Liann Lech
Indexer:	Teri Greenberg
Cover Designer:	Glenn Vogel

Contents

Series Editor's Foreword

The continuing theme of the Sage Publications book series **Multicultural Aspects of Counseling and Psychotherapy** has been the importance of providing practical information of immediate value to readers. This contribution to the series is an excellent example of how a book can be practical and still not oversimplify complex issues.

This third edition of *Assessing and Treating Culturally Diverse Clients: A Practical Guide* continues Freddy Paniagua's impressive contribution to the research literature on culture and counseling therapy. This edition breaks new ground in its expanded coverage of contemporary and controversial topics. It helps to prepare clinical and counseling providers for a future in which the standards of multicultural competence will become more important than ever before.

This edition provides the first extensive discussion in the multicultural literature of the significance for the clinical context of the demographic trends found in the 2000 U.S. Census. By covering the demographic changes that have taken place both within and among the four ethnic groups discussed here relative to the majority culture, this book helps to prepare clinical and counseling providers for the clients they can expect to see in the future.

This edition also includes expanded coverage of acculturation issues that encompasses discussion of four different models of acculturation and their applicability in clinical contexts. The problems associated with varying levels of acculturation are particularly relevant to clinical and counseling providers, who will be expected in the near future to provide services to a rapidly increasing number of clients who do not speak English. At present, few of those providers are prepared for this future.

The solid chapters found in the first two editions providing guidelines for the assessment and treatment of African Americans, Hispanics, Asians, and American Indians have been updated and refocused with regard to demographic trends and the complexity of within-group differences. Practical suggestions for dealing with hot-button issues in each ethnic context are specified in ways that will help providers avoid and prevent unnecessary problems.

This edition also includes discussion of the use of the mental status exam along with case vignettes that illustrate the practical value of providers' attending to issues of cultural competence. Each component of this exam is illustrated with culturally appropriate examples. Another feature of this volume is an extensive discussion of recent empirical findings that support arguments concerning racism's influence on the reported prevalence and incidence of mental disorders among clients from the four ethnic groups addressed here.

All three editions of this book have made very successful contributions to the multicultural counseling literature. Large numbers of providers and consumers have benefited from the practical suggestions offered in each edition, and each edition has clarified complex issues of assessment, diagnosis, and treatment in multiethnic contexts with minimal rhetorical, theoretical, or philosophical complications. The immediate, practical importance of multicultural competence has been a prominent theme in all three editions. Perhaps that is why this book is listed among the 100 best-selling books in counseling for 2004.

Of all the books in the **Multicultural Aspects of Counseling and Psychotherapy** series, Freddy's book does the best job of helping clinicians use diagnostic tools in practical and meaningful ways. This book reaches out to well-intentioned clinicians who are seeking to become more intentional in providing mental health services to their culturally diverse clients. It is with great pride that we include this third edition of *Assessing and Treating Culturally Diverse Clients* among the other books in this series.

— Paul Pedersen

Professor Emeritus
Syracuse University,
Visiting Professor,
University of Hawaii
Department of Psychology

Preface

Why This Book Was Written

Four of the major cultural groups that mental health practitioners see in the United States are African Americans, American Indians, Asians, and Hispanics. An important task for practitioners across all mental health disciplines (psychology, psychiatry, social work, family therapy, and the like) is to learn and apply skills that indicate that they are culturally competent in the assessment and treatment of clients from these groups (Pope-Davis & Coleman, 1997). Relevant questions concerning the mental health assessment, diagnosis, and treatment of multicultural clients include the following:

- What should a practitioner do during the first meeting or session with an African American client versus an Asian client?
- Should a practitioner treat an American Indian client with the same therapeutic approach used with a Hispanic client?
- What exactly should a practitioner do differently in assessing and treating members of different cultural groups?
- What are some examples of cross-cultural skills a practitioner should display to minimize bias in the assessment of clients from different cultural groups?

Not only are questions such as these clinically relevant, but a practitioner's failure to answer them and to demonstrate knowledge of the answers in clinical practice may be considered an example of a lack of cultural competence and a violation of ethical principles (LaFromboise, Foster, & James, 1996). For example, the American Psychological Association's (1992) code of ethics states that mental health professionals "must be aware of cultural, individual, and role differences, including those due to age, gender, *race, ethnicity, national origin, religion, . . . language,* and *socioeconomic status*" (pp. 3–4; emphasis added). Violations of this principle may be considered to be cases of "unfair discriminatory practices" (p. 3). In addition, the written and oral exams required for licensure in the practice of psychology, psychiatry, social work, and other mental health professions include items designed to measure test takers' understanding and application of cultural variables that might have impacts on their assessment, diagnosis, and treatment of individuals from multicultural groups seeking mental health services.

An excellent literature is available to help mental health practitioners in the development and application of cross-cultural skills in their clinical contacts with multicultural clients (e.g., Bamford, 1991; Berry, Poortinga, Segall, & Darsen, 1992; Comas-Diaz & Griffith, 1988; Dana, 1993b; Gaw, 1993a; Ho, 1992; Koslow & Salett, 1989; Lefley & Pedersen, 1986; McAdoo, 1993b; Pedersen, 1987, 1997; Ponterotto, Casas, Suzuki, & Alexander, 1995; Seijo, Gomez, & Freidenberg, 1991; Sue & Sue, 2003; Tharp, 1991). In many cases, however, practical guidelines concerning the assessment and treatment of individuals from various cultural groups are either dispersed across the literature (e.g., Comas-Diaz, 1988; Dana, 1993b; Koslow & Salett, 1989) or mixed with discussions of related philosophical, political, and theoretical issues (e.g., Berry et al., 1992; Sue & Sue, 2003). Practitioners interested in self-training to improve their cultural competence in the assessment, diagnosis, and treatment of multicultural groups previously have not had available one comprehensive text that takes an integrative approach and summarizes existing guidelines. In addition, the discussion of multicultural issues in mental health practice (particularly in the areas of assessment and treatment) has been evolving rapidly; practitioners may have a difficult time keeping up with this discussion while engaging in their routine clinical practices. My main goal in this volume is to provide mental health practitioners with an integrative and practical source that will help them understand exactly what they should do or not do to demonstrate cultural competence and avoid unfair discriminatory practices during the assessment, diagnosis, and treatment of African American, American Indian, Asian, and Hispanic clients.

Overview

It is important to note that the descriptions of cultural variables provided in this book reflect generalizations; any given characterization may not be true for all members of a group or for all subgroups within a given group (e.g., in the case of Hispanics, the subgroup of Cubans versus the subgroup of Mexican Americans). As Sue and Sue (2003) note, it is erroneous to believe that all African Americans are the same, that all Hispanics are the same, that all Asians are the same, or that all American Indians are the same. Differences within these groups and across subgroups exist in terms of primary language (particularly among Asians), generational status (e.g., early versus later immigrants), acculturation, and socioeconomic status (Sue & Sue, 1987, 2003). The members of these groups, however, do share some cultural variables that are often considered to be relevant in the assessment, diagnosis, and treatment of all members of non-Anglo-American cultural groups, regardless of group identity (e.g., all tend to place special importance on family relationships and to emphasize the extended family rather than the nuclear family). Such shared cultural variables across diverse groups and subgroups might be termed "cultural commonalities" (Chung, 1992). In this volume, I provide summaries of the cultural commonalities that exist across groups (Chapters 2, 7, 8, 9, and 10) and within subgroups (Chapters 3, 4, 5, and 6) that practitioners can use to guide their clinical practices with African American, Hispanic, Asian, and American Indian clients.

Chapter 1 offers a tentative explanation for the growing use of the terms *multicultural* and *diversity* and the decreasing use of the term *minority* in the literature. Data gathered in the most recent U.S. Census serve to illustrate this point. Chapter 1 also includes a brief discussion of the distinction between race and ethnicity.

Chapter 2 presents an overview of general guidelines regarding the development of a therapeutic relationship with regard to the four culturally diverse groups discussed in this text. Chapter 2 has been enhanced in this new edition with the introduction of new materials in several sections. For example, the chapter now includes a summary of four models of acculturation (the assimilation, separation, integration, and marginalization models) and their applications in clinical contexts. In addition, a section has been added concerning the use of information from the 2000 U.S. Census in clinical contexts. This section addresses the difficulty that clinicians may encounter when dealing with clients who self-identify as members of more than one race, as permitted by the latest U.S. Census. Box 2.1 and Tables 2.1 and 2.2 have been added to illustrate how clinicians might apply their knowledge of census data in their clinical practices. Another area in which census data are relevant for practitioners concerns the numbers of multicultural clients whose native language is not English. Table 2.3 is intended to assist clinicians in estimating how many clients they are likely to encounter in their practices who might report that they speak English "not well" or "not at all" or who say that they speak English less than "very well." The table illustrates this point with U.S. Census data on individuals whose native languages are Spanish, other European languages, and Asian/Pacific Island languages.

Chapters 3, 4, 5, and 6 provide updated overviews of the demographic characteristics of African Americans, Hispanics, Asians, and American Indians, respectively, as well as three sets of practical guidelines for each group: guidelines on cultural variables that may affect assessment, diagnosis, and treatment; guidelines for the first session; and guidelines for conducting psychotherapy in subsequent sessions. In the case of Chapter 4, the section on terminology has been significantly enhanced in this edition with a discussion of the various terms currently used to identify Hispanic clients or Hispanics as a group, such as *Chicano, La Raza, Latinegro,* and *Nuyorican,* and guidelines concerning the use of these terms in clinical contexts. Chapter 4 also includes a new section on different types of Hispanic families (e.g., intact versus bicultural families) that includes some guidelines that clinicians serving such families will find useful.

Chapter 7 presents a summary of practical guidelines to help practitioners understand and prevent attrition among clients from the target multicultural groups. Chapter 8 is intended to assist practitioners in the critical review and evaluation of the epidemiological research that has been conducted concerning the prevalence and incidence of mental disorders among members of the four groups discussed throughout this text. An important addition to Chapter 8 in this new edition is a discussion of the emotional problems that clients may experience as a result of their perceptions of racial discrimination.

Chapter 9 makes an obvious point: that most of the measures, or assessment instruments, that mental health practitioners use today with African American, American Indian, Asian, and Hispanic clients are culturally biased. For various practical reasons, however, it may not be advisable to recommend that practitioners stop using these measures. A better alternative would be to train practitioners to use culturally biased measures in ways that will not harm their multicultural clients. Practitioners need to know how to recognize the biases that exist in the measures they use and how to evaluate the data they gather accurately and appropriately, so that it is meaningful and helpful to them in their work with culturally diverse clients. In this edition, the section in Chapter 9 on examining biases and prejudices has been revised to include a discussion of preliminary empirical findings that support the utility of the Brief Acculturation Scale, an instrument that I developed and that was originally published in the first edition of *Assessing and Treating Culturally Diverse Clients* (see Paniagua, 1994, 1998). Also in Chapter 9, the discussion of the effects of racism as an explanation for the prevalence and incidence of mental disorders in members of some cultural groups has been expanded with the inclusion of recent empirical findings on this topic. In addition, the section dealing with culture-related and culture-bound syndromes now includes an extensive discussion of the importance of distinguishing between culture-bound syndromes and cultural variations in the diagnosis of mental disorders. Another section of Chapter 9 that has been revised extensively is the one that addresses the use of the mental status exam in a cultural context. This section now includes a brief case vignette, a summary of major components of that exam, and additional examples illustrating the administration of the mental status exam in a culturally sensitive context.

The latest edition of the *Diagnostic and Statistical Manual of Mental Disorders,* known as *DSM-IV-TR* (American Psychiatric Association, 2000), has made a major contribution in terms of the inclusion of specific cultural variables across most psychiatric disorders. The *DSM-IV-TR* strongly encourages practitioners to use these variables during the assessment and diagnosis of such disorders. These cultural variables, however, are dispersed across the *DSM-IV-TR,* and they are not recommended across all psychiatric disorders. Chapter 10 summarizes these variables, and the tables in the chapter provide practitioners with a rapid overview. The section in Chapter 10 that addresses cultural considerations when other conditions may be the focus of clinical attention has been expanded in this edition, particularly with the addition of a subsection that encourages practitioners to consider clients' difficulties in dealing with their own cultural identities. Examples of assessment tools that clinicians might use to explore their clients' cultural identities are also provided.

Acknowledgments

I am indebted to many individuals whose support and advice have played a major role in the preparation of this book. I want to thank F. M. Baker (University of Maryland) and Sharon Nelson Le-Gall (University of Pittsburgh) for their review of Chapter 3 and for their valuable suggestions. (The affiliations mentioned here, and those below, reflect the affiliations of these individuals at the time of the publication of the first edition of this book in 1994.) Richard H. Dana (Portland State University) reviewed the guidelines involving the use of the epidemiology of mental health literature with multicultural groups (Chapter 8) and the guidelines concerning the use of culturally biased instruments (Chapter 9). He sent me an extensive commentary regarding ways to improve these chapters, and I am grateful to him for his suggestions. Derald W. Sue (California State University, Hayward) and Anh Nga Nguyen (University of Oklahoma Health Sciences Center) assisted me with Chapter 5, and I also want to thank them for their comments. Derald W. Sue also reviewed Chapter 2; I thank him especially for his help in updating the references on Asian Americans. I thank Stanley Sue (University of California, Los Angeles) for reviewing portions of Chapters 1 and 2, particularly in relation to the discussion on cultural mismatch and racial mismatch.

Arthur McDonald (president of Dull Knife Memorial College in Lame Deer, Montana) reviewed Chapter 6, and I wish to thank him for making me aware of several sensitive issues in the assessment and treatment of American Indian clients. Lillian Comas-Diaz (independent practice, Washington, D.C.) made substantial revisions to the guidelines for the assessment and treatment of Hispanic clients in Chapter 4, including translation of terms from English into Spanish, a better interpretation of the acknowledgment of spiritual issues by Hispanic clients during the first session, and improvement of the references dealing with the assessment and treatment of Hispanic clients. I thank her for her effort and time in revising these materials.

Sylvia Z. Ramirez (University of Texas at Austin) and Sylvia Linares were clinical fellows under my supervision at the time I was organizing my thoughts to write this book. I discussed many of the topics in this text with them, and I thank them for their suggestions. I also want to thank Sylvia Ramirez for reviewing Chapters 4 and 8 as well as for her suggestion to include additional cultural variables to contribute to a better understanding of the assessment and treatment needs of Hispanic clients. Victor L. Tan and Angela S. Lew were clinical fellows under my supervision at the time I wrote Chapter 10, and I want to thank them for their comments and suggestions to improve this chapter.

I have spent many hours over the past 15 years discussing cross-cultural issues with Israel Cuéllar (University of Texas–Pan American). Cuéllar was the first person (as far as I can remember) who encouraged me to write this book. He reviewed Chapters 4, 8, and 9. I thank him deeply for his comments and suggestions on how to improve these chapters.

I have also spent a significant number of hours over the past 20 years discussing cultural issues with Charles E. Holzer III, and his expertise in psychiatric epidemiology has been extremely valuable to me, particularly during the preparation of Chapter 8. I especially thank Holzer for his suggestions regarding the new section in Chapter 2 on practitioners' use of information from the 2000 U.S. Census in clinical contexts.

I thank Paul Pedersen, series editor, who was instrumental in the final preparation of this book for publication. He spent many hours reading each chapter and making sure that the book reflects practical guidelines for clinicians interested in the assessment and treatment of multicultural groups and that it contains minimal rhetoric about multiculturalism.

I also want to thank the staff of Sage Publications for their time and effort in the preparation of this edition. I particularly thank Arthur Pomponio, Veronica K. Novak, Beth A. Bernstein, and Judy Selhorst for their assistance and technical advice. Reviews of the first two editions of this book have been very encouraging, and I have used the critiques that have been offered to correct several points in the present edition. I want to thank the reviewers for their comments. Several readers have taken the time to send to me letters clarifying particular issues, and I have also integrated their clarifications into this edition; I thank these readers for their letters of encouragement.

I want especially to thank my spouse, Sandra A. Black (Sam), and my son, Robert Alexander Paniagua (Rap), for their support and patience throughout the completion of this book.

Finally, I want to note that I recognize that the topics addressed in this volume are extremely sensitive and that I am responsible for any errors or misunderstandings readers may find in the text. I will deeply appreciate any comments and suggestions that readers may send me, and I will consider all reader feedback as I prepare future editions of this book. Please send your comments to me care of Sage Publications, 2455 Teller Road, Thousand Oaks, California 91320.

1

Minority, Multicultural, Race, and Ethnicity Concepts

Minority Groups Versus Multicultural Groups

Many Americans use the term *minority* to refer both to certain cultural groups' numbers in the population and to disadvantages in terms of socioeconomic status (Ho, 1987, 1992; Sue & Sue, 2003; Wilkinson, 1993). Thus, in the United States, Anglo-Americans, or Whites, are not considered a "minority group" because there are too many of them (approximately 211 million in 2000), and as a group, their socioeconomic status is higher than that of other racial/ethnic groups (U.S. Bureau of the Census, 2000). African Americans and Hispanics are often referred to as minority groups because they number approximately 34.6 and 35.3 million, respectively (U.S. Bureau of the Census, 2000), and their socioeconomic status, at the group level, is lower than that of the "majority" group (i.e., Whites). Other examples of "minority groups" in the United States, in terms of numbers and socioeconomic status, include American Indians, Asians, and Pacific Islanders (U.S. Bureau of the Census, 2000). Use of the term *minority* in regard to these groups, however, may not be appropriate for three reasons: discrepancies in income levels across these groups, the impact that these groups can have on other groups, and the connotation of "inferiority" that the term *minority* has in the minds of some members of these groups.

Discrepancies in Income Levels Across "Minority" Groups

Comparisons of the median income levels across "minority" groups (e.g., Asians versus African Americans) reveal discrepancies. For example, in

1

2001, the median income for the Asian and Pacific Islander population in the United States (persons of Japanese, Chinese, Filipino, Hawaiian, and other Asian/Pacific Island heritage) was $53,635, whereas the median income for African Americans in the same year was $29,470. At that time, the national U.S. median income was $42,228 (U.S. Bureau of the Census, 2002a). Thus, although both Asians/Pacific Islanders and African Americans are examples of "minority" groups in terms of their numbers (and in comparison with Anglo-Americans), Asians and Pacific Islanders have a median income far above the national average.

A similar point can be made through a comparison of income levels across subgroups within the same ethnic group. For example, in 2002, the median household income for the Mexican-origin population (a subgroup of Hispanics) residing in the United States was $33,574, whereas the median income for Puerto Ricans (another subgroup of Hispanics) was $27,564 (U.S. Bureau of the Census, 2002b). Although both of these groups are part of the Hispanic "minority" group, it is evident that, as a group, Mexican Americans have a better standard of living than do Puerto Ricans in the United States.

Thus, the term *minority* might be accurate regarding an individual's being a member of a group with a smaller number of people in it than the "majority" group, but it may not be an appropriate way to describe that person in terms of income level (which can vary both between "minority" groups and between subgroups within the same racial or ethnic group).

Impact of "Minority" Groups on Other Groups

Another problem with the use of the term *minority* is that it does not take into consideration the impact that the population size of a "minority" group can have on other groups (Wilkinson, 1986). For example, many African Americans and Hispanics reside in Florida. Currently, a major problem confronting African Americans in Florida is that in several areas of the state (e.g., Miami) they constitute a minority of the population, whereas Hispanics constitute a "majority" group. Both Hispanics and African Americans are examples of minority groups in relation to the total number of people in the United States, but in certain parts of Florida, Hispanics take on majority status. A similar situation exists in the Lower Rio Grande Valley of Texas, which is concentrated around the border between the United States and Mexico. In this region, Mexican Americans are in the majority; other Hispanics (e.g., Puerto Ricans, Cubans), Asians, African Americans, and American Indians are "minority" groups.

In addition, it should be noted that among all "minority" groups in the United States, the Hispanic population is now the largest; for the first time, the 2000 U.S. Census counted more Hispanics (35.3 million) than African Americans (34.6 million) (U.S. Bureau of the Census, 2000).

The Concept That "Minority" Equals "Inferiority"

Mental health practitioners should be aware that some people object to being referred to as *minorities* or as *members of minority groups* because they feel that these terms imply inferiority and a sense of superiority on the part of those in the majority (i.e., Anglo-Americans). For example, in a letter to the editor of the *San Antonio Express News,* one Hispanic person wrote that "when an individual labels me a 'minority,' I feel small, weak and irrelevant. On the other hand, 'ethnically diverse American' is empowering and more accurate" (R. E. Martinez, 1993, p. 5B). McAdoo (1993a) points out that a major reason she advises others to avoid the term *minority* is that "it has an insidious implication of *inferiority*. . . . A sense of superiority is assumed by those of the implied superior status" (p. 6; emphasis added).

Thus, the term *minority* may not be applicable when one considers issues of income level or the size of particular minority groups in relation to other groups, and it may be undesirable given the potential use of the term as synonymous with "inferiority" (Kim, McLeod, & Shantzis, 1992; McAdoo, 1993a; Wilkinson, 1986). Perhaps terms such as *multicultural* and *diverse* are more appropriate to describe the many different populations or groups that make up the U.S. population. These terms emphasize the differences among groups in terms of cultural values rather than the relative sizes of the groups. The use of such terms has been increasing gradually in the literature since I initially presented the reasons noted above in arguing that mental health practitioners and scholars should eliminate the use of the term *minority* (Paniagua, 1994; see, e.g., Ancis, 2003; Cuéllar & Paniagua, 2000; Gibbs, Huang, & Associates, 2003).

In the assessment and treatment of people with mental disorders, a practical guideline for practitioners is that, rather than focusing on the "minority" group per se, they should emphasize the ways in which individuals from diverse groups express their cultural values, their views of the world, and their views of their place in this society. For example, in the multicultural society of the United States, African Americans and Anglo-Americans are two examples of cultural groups. Other groups whose members mental health practitioners may see with less frequency include subgroups of Anglo-Americans, such as Greek, Italian, Irish, and Polish Americans, and West Indian Islanders (Allen, 1988; Jalali, 1988). This book summarizes practical guidelines for the assessment and treatment of four diverse groups often seen in mental health services: African Americans, American Indians, Asians, and Hispanics.

Race Versus Ethnicity

Many people use the terms *race* and *ethnicity* interchangeably, although this practice is somewhat controversial (Phinney, 1996). The two terms may be understood to apply to two different processes (Berry et al., 1992; Betancourt & Lopez, 1993; Borak, Fiellin, & Chemerynski, 2004; Garza-Trevino, Ruiz, & Venegas-Samuels, 1997; Wilkinson, 1993). An understanding of these processes is important for mental health practitioners who are involved in the assessment and treatment of individuals from multicultural groups. As Wilkinson (1993) defines these terms, *race* "is a category of persons who are related by a common heredity or ancestry and who are perceived and responded to in terms of external features or traits," whereas *ethnicity* often refers to "a shared culture and lifestyle" (Wilkinson, 1993, p. 19; see also Borak et al., 2004, p. 242; Casas & Pytluk, 1995, p. 162). Thus, an individual may belong to a particular race without sharing ethnic identity with others of that race. For example, the fact that two African American clients (or two American Indian, Asian, or Hispanic clients) share a common heredity or ancestry does not mean that they necessarily also share the same ethnic identity (i.e., their cultures, values, lifestyles, beliefs, and norms may be very different). Differences in ethnic identities across clients of the same race may be explained in terms of the processes of internal and external acculturation (described in Chapter 2), which can have important implications for the assessment and treatment of the members of many diverse groups. Practitioners should not assume that two clients who share the same racial group will also share the same ethnicity.

2

General Guidelines for the Assessment, Diagnosis, and Treatment of Culturally Diverse Clients

This chapter summarizes the general guidelines and recommendations found in the literature concerning mental health practitioners' assessment, diagnosis, and treatment of clients from all of the culturally diverse groups discussed in this book (e.g., Ancis, 2003; Cuéllar & Paniagua, 2000; Dana, 1993b; Ho, 1987, 1992; Ivey, Ivey, & Simek-Morgan, 1996; Pedersen, 1997; Pedersen, Draguns, Lonner, & Trimble, 1996; Ponterotto et al., 1995). Clinicians working with clients from the various communities described in this book are also strongly encouraged to review the American Psychological Association's (2003) "Guidelines on Multicultural Education, Training, Research, Practice, and Organizational Change for Psychologists," particularly Guideline 5, which deals with the need for culturally appropriate skills in clinical practice (see pp. 390–391). Although the APA guidelines address the clinical practice of psychologists in a multicultural context, they are also relevant for the practice of mental health professionals and administrators of mental health services from other disciplines (e.g., psychiatrists, social workers, marriage and family therapists, licensed professional counselors). Training programs in counseling, marriage and family therapy, school psychology, social work, general psychiatry, and child and adolescent psychiatry should also use those guidelines to enhance their curricula regarding the culturally appropriate skills that students (e.g., doctoral students in clinical psychology) and residents (e.g., residents in general psychiatry) are expected to demonstrate after completion of their training. (It should be noted that the current APA guidelines are scheduled to expire in 2009, in accordance with the association's policy;

after that date, clinicians can inquire about the status of the guidelines by contacting the APA Public Interest Directorate.)

Development of a Therapeutic Relationship

In mental health practice, the therapeutic relationship appears to be of paramount importance to clients from all cultural groups (Ho, 1992; Sue & Sue, 2003). In general, the development of this relationship involves three levels: conceptual, behavioral, and cultural.

The *conceptual* level includes such issues as the client's and the therapist's perceptions of sincerity, openness, honesty, motivation, empathy, sensitivity, inquiring concerns, and credibility in their relationship. The *behavioral* level includes the client's perception of the therapist as competent in his or her profession, which may involve issues such as the therapist's training as well as evidence of the therapist's specialization in the assessment and treatment of particular mental health problems (e.g., expertise in the assessment and treatment of depression; Fuertes & Brobst, 2002). The behavioral level also reflects the therapist's perception of the client as competent in terms of the client's ability to follow directions and to use skills learned in therapy to self-implement the treatment plan as the therapist and client have discussed.

The *cultural* level generally includes two hypotheses (Lonner & Ibrahim, 1996; Paniagua, 1996; Paniagua, Wassef, O'Boyle, Linares, & Cuéllar, 1993; Tharp, 1991). The *cultural compatibility hypothesis* suggests that the assessment and treatment of clients from multicultural groups are enhanced when any racial and ethnic barriers between the client and the therapist are minimized. As racial and ethnic differences between the client and the therapist approach zero, the therapist is more effective in terms of providing culturally sensitive assessment and treatment to the client (Dana, 1993b; Lopez, Lopez, & Fong, 1991; Paniagua, 1996; Sue & Sundberg, 1996; Sue & Sue, 2003). This hypothesis suggests, for example, that the assessment and treatment of an African American client is enhanced if the therapist is also an African American. Racial/ethnic similarity between client and therapist reinforces the therapeutic relationship.

Cultural compatibility between client and therapist may not always improve the therapeutic relationship, however. For example, in a test of this hypothesis, Sue, Fujino, Hu, Takeuchi, and Zane (1991) found that racial "match failed to be a significant predictor of treatment outcome, except for Mexican Americans" (p. 539). (The other groups in their study were Asian American, African American, and White.) These researchers also found that racial match "appears to have a much greater impact on length of treatment [defined as number of sessions] than on outcome" (p. 539). In addition, Maramba and Hall (2002) conducted a meta-analysis of ethnic match as a predictor of treatment dropout, utilization of services, and functioning, and found that although the client-therapist racial/ethnic match in therapy resulted in fewer dropout cases, more utilization of services (i.e., attending more therapy sessions), and improved level of functioning (as measured by the Global Assessment Scale [GAS]; Endicott, Spitzer, Fleiss, & Cohen, 1976), at the termination of therapy the effect sizes of the client-therapist racial/ethnic match on dropout, utilization, and levels of functioning were very small. As the authors note, these findings suggest that this particular type of matching "is not a clinically significant predictor of a decrease in the probability of a client's failure to return to therapy after the first session or an increase in the number of sessions attended by a client" (p. 294). Similarly, Maramba and Hall did not find a significant effect size of client-therapist racial/ethnic match on the GAS (a general measure of a client's level of functioning) at the termination of therapy, suggesting that racial/ethnic match "is not a predictor of improvement in psychotherapy" (p. 294).

Many culturally diverse groups (particularly African Americans) have been included in treatment outcome research conducted by White investigators; the overall conclusion of such studies has been that the race/ethnicity of therapists in relation to clients has no effect on outcomes (Sue, 1988). This is particularly evident in the case of behavioral treatment approaches (including behavior analysis, behavior therapy, and cognitive-behavioral modification; Paniagua & Baer, 1981), which are currently the dominant approaches used by White clinicians. The research subjects included in many studies of these approaches have been selected from a wide range of cultural groups, and the results clearly show the effectiveness of such approaches in the treatment of clients from all races and ethnic backgrounds (see, e.g., Kolko, 1987). In fact, many culturally diverse clinicians and researchers believe that behavioral approaches are probably the most effective strategies for the assessment and treatment of clients from the four cultural groups discussed in this volume (Boyd-Franklin, 1989; Walker & LaDue, 1986; Yamamoto, Silva, Justice, Chang, & Leong, 1993). This is because these strategies are authoritative and concrete, and they emphasize learning focused on the immediate problem—all characteristics of treatment that members of these groups generally prefer (Boyd-Franklin, 1989; Walker & LaDue, 1986).

Sue (1988) notes that client-therapist racial match may lead to cultural mismatch, but racial "mismatches do not necessarily imply cultural mismatches, because therapists and clients from different [racial] groups may share similar values, lifestyles, and experiences" (p. 306). That is, in terms of the distinction between race and ethnicity discussed in Chapter 1, the therapist and the client may share the same racial group (e.g., both Hispanics) but they may not share the same ethnicity (e.g., they have different values and lifestyles). For example, when a highly acculturated Hispanic therapist works with a less acculturated Hispanic client, the result may be a cultural mismatch (i.e., the therapist and the client do not share similar lifestyles and values) regardless of the fact that the therapist and client share the same racial group. Similarly, a White therapist working with a highly acculturated Hispanic client may be a cultural match (if the two share particular Western cultural values and traditions) regardless of the racial mismatch.

In addition, research indicates that because of a history of hostile relations between and among some Asian nations (e.g., wars between China and Japan, Japan and Korea, China and Vietnam), the applicability of the cultural compatibility hypothesis to Asian clients and therapists may be questionable (Yamamoto et al., 1993). For example, if a therapist of Chinese heritage is assigned to assess and treat an older client of Japanese heritage, the therapist-client relationship may be characterized by tension and mistrust, leading to potential failure in treatment. Before an Asian therapist takes on the assessment and treatment of an Asian client, it may be appropriate for the therapist to explore the potential impacts of historical events on the client's reaction to the therapist.

Because of the problems noted above concerning the cultural compatibility hypothesis, as well as researchers' arguments that "little evidence exists . . . to directly demonstrate that the quality of care provided is better when [culturally diverse] patients and their providers are of the same racial or ethnic group" (Smedley, Stith, & Nelson, 2003, p. 134), some scholars have proposed a second hypothesis known as the *universalistic argument* (Dana, 1993b; Paniagua, 1996; Tharp, 1991). According to this argument, assessment and treatment are equally effective across all multicultural groups, independent of the issue of client-therapist racial/ethnic differences or similarities. This hypothesis probably explains the current emphasis in the mental health professions on training Anglo-American therapists in how best to assess and treat clients belonging to the four major cultural groups discussed in this book. The universalistic hypothesis proposes that what is relevant in the assessment and treatment of members of multicultural groups is evidence that the therapist can display both *cultural sensitivity* (i.e., awareness of cultural variables that may affect assessment and treatment) and *cultural competence* (i.e., translation of this awareness into behaviors that result in effective assessment and treatment; see Atkinson & Wampold, 1993, p. 247; Baker, 1988, p. 157).

According to the universalistic hypothesis, White therapists are as effective as African American therapists in assessing and treating African American clients as long as the therapists manifest cultural sensitivity and cultural competence in their clinical practice. This hypothesis also suggests that just because a therapist and his or her client share the same race and ethnicity (e.g., a Hispanic therapist and Hispanic client who share similar values and lifestyles), that does not guarantee the effectiveness of assessment and treatment; the therapist must still demonstrate cultural sensitivity and cultural competence, regardless of his or her sharing the client's race and ethnicity.

Two additional concepts that are part of the universalistic hypothesis are those of credibility and giving (Sue & Sundberg, 1996; Sue & Sue, 2003; Sue & Zane, 1987). The therapist's *achieved credibility* lies in the client's perception that the therapist is effective and trustworthy (Sue & Zane, 1987). As Okazaki (2000) describes it, this form of credibility arises from "what the clinician actually does to instill faith, trust, confidence, or hope in their clients. . . . Credibility must be . . . achieved in early sessions for the client to stay in treatment long enough to gain therapeutic benefits" (p. 178). Sue and Sue (1987) suggest that another form of credibility is also important: *ascribed credibility.* I discuss this kind of credibility in Chapter 5. The concept of the therapist's *giving* involves the client's recognition that the therapist has provided something of value in the client-therapist relationship.

In summary, the universalistic hypothesis states that the therapist's ability to communicate with a client from any cultural group in a giving, culturally sensitive manner and to exhibit cultural competence during assessment and treatment is more important than similarity of race or ethnicity between therapist and client (Baker, 1988; Tharp, 1991). The remainder of this chapter addresses how practitioners from any racial group (including Anglo-Americans) can enhance or develop cultural sensitivity and cultural competence in the assessment and treatment of African American, American Indian, Asian, and Hispanic clients, regardless of racial/ethnic differences or similarities between the practitioners and their clients.

Acculturation

Acculturation is one of the variables that practitioners must consider in the assessment and treatment of clients from the four cultural groups discussed in this book (Cuéllar, 2000; Dana, 1993b; Ho, 1992; Sue & Sue, 2003). In general, acculturation may be defined in terms of the degree to which an individual integrates new cultural patterns into his or her original cultural patterns (Buki, Ma, Strom, & Strom, 2003; Dana, 1993b; Grieger & Ponterotto, 1995; Moyerman & Forman, 1992). As Buki et al. (2003) observe, "The concept of acculturation generally refers to the process by which immigrants adapt to a new culture" (p. 128). In this book, I term this process *external* acculturation; it differs from the *internal* process of acculturation, examination of which is generally absent from the acculturation literature (Casas & Pytluk, 1995; Cuéllar, 2000).

In the *external process of acculturation,* a person moves from his or her country of origin to another country. Examples include immigrants who move to the United States from the Caribbean islands (e.g., Dominican Republic, Cuba); Central America (e.g., Panama, El Salvador); South America (e.g., Bolivia, Colombia); and Asia (e.g., Japan, China, Vietnam). The effects of the external acculturation process are less dramatic when immigrants settle in cities that resemble their home cities in norms, cultural patterns, and values. This is the case, for instance, for most Hispanic immigrants from Cuba, the Dominican Republic, and Puerto Rico who reside in New York City and Miami, as well as for Mexicans who move to U.S. cities located on the U.S.-Mexico border. Hispanic immigrants who live in such U.S. cities not only encounter people who understand their native language, they also find people from their countries of origin who share many of their cultural values (e.g., folk beliefs, customs, music). The effects of the external acculturation process are more dramatic for immigrants who arrive in the United States and settle immediately in cities that bear little similarity to their home cities.

In the *internal process of acculturation,* changes occur in individuals' cultural patterns when the individuals move from one U.S. region to another (e.g., from the South to the Midwest) or from one kind of area to another (e.g., from a rural setting to a city). For example, when American Indians who have been living on reservations in Arizona or New Mexico move from their reservations to densely populated cities, they are exposed to societal expectations and ways of living that are quite different from what they knew previously. Competition and individualism are two values with little relevance among American Indians who reside on reservations. These values, however, are extremely important for most Americans residing outside of reservations. The assimilation of new values and lifestyles is a function of the process of internal acculturation. A minimal internal process of acculturation takes place if a person moves from one area of the United States to another that is similar to the first in terms of values and lifestyle (e.g., if an American Indian moves from one reservation to another reservation).

The internal process of acculturation is further illustrated by the case of Hispanics who reside in certain areas of New York City and then move to certain areas in Florida (e.g., Miami). For these individuals, the impact of acculturation is minimal, whereas for Hispanics who move from New York City to Lawrence, Kansas—or any other city where they share few cultural patterns with the existing residents—the impact is great. Mexican Americans who reside on the U.S.-Mexico border (particularly in the Lower Rio Grande Valley of Texas) and then move from this region to another region of the United States where they find few familiar cultural patterns (e.g., Washington, D.C.) are likely to experience a difficult internal acculturation process. In contrast, Mexican Americans who move from the U.S.-Mexico border into San Antonio, Texas, do not experience much in the way of an internal process of acculturation because they already share many similar cultural patterns with San Antonio residents.

Levels of Acculturation

It is important for practitioners who work with multicultural clients to determine the potential impacts of different levels of acculturation on the clients' assessment and treatment. Acculturation level can be defined in terms of the number of years the client has been involved in the internal or external acculturation process, the age at which the client began the acculturation process, and the client's country of origin. The general assumption is that younger individuals are more easily acculturated than older individuals, and that acculturation level increases the longer a person is involved in the process. Regarding country of origin, individuals from some countries tend to show higher levels of acculturation than do individuals from others. For example, an immigrant from the Dominican Republic who resides in New York City is more easily acculturated than an immigrant from Vietnam in the same city because most Dominicans receive a great deal of exposure to U.S. culture and cultural values in the Dominican Republic, including attitudes, trends in clothing styles, music, and language (many Dominican immigrants learn to speak English before they enter the United States).

Table 8.1 (in Chapter 8) provides a list of the acculturation scales recommended for use with clients from the various groups discussed in this book. For therapists who do not have enough time to conduct thorough acculturation screenings with their clients, Figure 2.1 presents a brief scale for the assessment of three significant variables in the process of acculturation: generation, language preferred, and social activity (Burnam, Hough, Karno, Escobar, & Telles, 1987; Cuéllar, Harris, & Jasso, 1980; Suinn, Rickard-Figueroa, Lew, & Vigil, 1987). For example, family members in the fifth generation are considered highly acculturated in comparison with members in the first generation. In terms of language preferred, when using the Brief Acculturation Scale, the therapist should ask the client about what language he or she prefers to use by framing a general question that covers most situations (e.g., when speaking with children, with parents, with coworkers, and so on). In the case of social activity, a similar approach is recommended. For example, the practitioner might ask a Mexican American client, "When you listen to music and go to a restaurant to eat, do you prefer to do these things with Mexican Americans only, mostly with Mexican Americans, with Mexican Americans and people from other racial groups (e.g., African Americans, Whites, Asians, American Indians), mostly with people from other racial groups (e.g., Whites), or only with people from other racial groups?"

The client's level of acculturation is indicated by his or her score on the Brief Acculturation Scale as follows (Burnam et al., 1987):

1 to 1.75 = low acculturation

1.76 to 3.25 = medium acculturation

3.26 to 5 = high acculturation

To obtain a client's score, the therapist adds all the values checked across variables and divides that total by the total number of items checked. For example, if the client checked 1 (or the first item) on each variable, the client's acculturation score would be 1 (3/3 = 1), which indicates low

Instruction: Please check only one item from the group of Generation items, Language Preferred items, and Social Activity items.				
My generation is:				
First	Second	Third	Fourth	Fifth
(1)	(2)	(3)	(4)	(5)
The language I prefer to use is:				
Mine Only	Mostly Mine	Both Mine and English	Mostly English	Only English
(1)	(2)	(3)	(4)	(5)
I prefer to engage in social activity with:				
Only Within Racial Group	Mostly Within Racial Group	Within/ Between Racial Groups	Mostly With a Different Racial Group	Only With a Different Racial Group
(1)	(2)	(3)	(4)	(5)
Total Score: _____				
Number of Items Checked: _____				
Acculturation Score (Total Score/Number of Items Checked): _____				
The Level of Acculturation for this client is (circle one): Low Medium High				

Figure 2.1   Brief Acculturation Scale

acculturation. If the client checked Items 2, 2, and 3 on the generational, language, and social activity variables, respectively, his or her overall acculturation score would be 2.3, which indicates a medium level of acculturation.

It should be noted that the Brief Acculturation Scale is intended as a tool for quickly determining level of acculturation with clients from all of the four cultural groups discussed in this book, whereas the acculturation scales listed in Table 8.1 have been developed for use with specific groups. For example, the Abbreviated Multidimensional Acculturation Scale (Zea, Asner-Self, Birman, & Buki, 2003) is designed to measure the acculturation levels of Hispanic clients who were born in Central and South American countries, Caribbean countries, or the United States. In contrast, the Acculturation Rating Scale for Mexican Americans is designed for use mostly with Mexican American clients (Cuéllar, Arnold, & Maldonado, 1995), and the Suinn-Lew Asian Self-Identity Acculturation Scale is recommended for use with Chinese, Japanese, and Korean clients (Buki et al., 2003; Suinn, Ahuna, & Khoo, 1992; Suinn et al., 1987).

Models of Acculturation

Clinicians should also be aware of the four main models of acculturation in the current literature and how each of these models may affect the assessment, diagnosis, and treatment of mental disorders among culturally diverse clients (Berry, 1990; Berry, Trimble, & Olmedo, 1986; Cuéllar, 2000; Gurung & Mehta, 2001; Kim-ju & Liem, 2003).

In the *assimilation* model of acculturation, a highly acculturated client strongly identifies only with the dominant or host culture. This client does not share the values, behaviors, and beliefs of the members of his or her culture of origin. For example, the client does not take part in such behaviors as listening to native music, participating in native forms of dance, preparing food in the ways prescribed in the culture of origin, and observing the native culture's dating processes. The client does not hold the beliefs of his or her native culture, including beliefs about the role of evil spirits and unnatural events in explaining medical complications or emotional problems; the belief that women should be submissive to the authority of men in marital relationships; the belief that certain cultural traditions must be observed in the celebration of significant events in the family (such as birthdays and marriages); and beliefs about seeking instrumental support (e.g., child care, money) and emotional support (e.g., counsel and advice; see the section headed "Extended Family" below for further discussion of this concept). A clinician who is not aware of the assimilation model of acculturation might conclude that the behaviors and beliefs displayed by a client who is fully assimilated into the host culture are symptoms suggestive of such *DSM-IV-TR* (American Psychiatric Association, 2000) diagnoses as oppositional defiant disorder (e.g., the client refuses to follow the cultural norms of his or her family's traditional culture but agrees to follow the norms of the host culture), avoiding personality disorder (e.g., the client demonstrates a pattern of avoiding behaviors across years when he or she is expected to display behaviors and beliefs culturally sanctioned by the traditional culture), and adjustment disorder (e.g., the client reports great difficulty in adjusting to behaviors and beliefs expected in his or her own culture).

In the *separation* model of acculturation, the client values only the behaviors and beliefs of his or her traditional culture. The client maintains his or her cultural/ethnic identity, refusing to adapt to or identify with elements of the host (dominant) culture in his or her work environment and social interactions. Practitioners should particularly explore this model of acculturation in those cases where conflicts arise between children and parents; parents from some cultures may bring their adolescent children in for treatment because they are upset that the children are not displaying the behaviors and beliefs of their home cultures (see Chapter 10 for further discussion on this topic). In such a case, a culturally effective clinician is likely to conclude that the conflict between adolescent and parents is the result of the parents' demands that the adolescent value only the behaviors and beliefs expected in the traditional culture, rejecting adaptation to the host culture (see Sue & Sue, 2003, pp. 160–161).

In the *integration* model of acculturation, the client displays behaviors and beliefs found in both his or her traditional culture and the host (dominant) culture. This client maintains his or her cultural and/or ethnic identity and at the same time integrates into his or her identity many values from the host culture. This process of acculturation is also termed *biculturalism,* because the individual combines behaviors, beliefs, and values from two different cultures in his or her social interactions with persons from both of those cultures (see Sue & Sue, 2003, pp. 160–161). This form of acculturation may result in conflicts between the integrated client and individuals from his or her home culture who reject the idea of mixing elements of their own culture with elements in the dominant culture. It is particularly important for the practitioner to explore the nature of such conflicts with the client when the client reports specific problems (e.g., marital conflicts, conduct problems among children and adolescents) that involve either family members who are fully assimilated into the dominant culture (i.e., practicing and valuing only the behaviors and beliefs of the host culture) or family members who are separated from the host culture (i.e., adhering only to the behaviors, beliefs, and norms of the traditional culture and rejecting all elements of the host culture). That is, a client whose acculturation follows the integration model feels comfortable displaying behaviors and beliefs from both the traditional and the dominant cultures, but he or she is likely to experience conflicts (e.g., concerning rituals and traditions associated with marriage, celebration of significant anniversaries) and may have emotional difficulties (e.g., depression) as a result of interacting with family members who are either fully assimilated into the host culture or who accept only the behaviors and values of the traditional culture.

In the *marginalization* model of acculturation, the client rejects the behaviors and beliefs associated with both his or her traditional culture and the host (dominant) culture. During the initial clinical assessment of such a client, the clinician finds it very difficult to identify the client's cultural origins or ethnicity because the client does not report behaviors, beliefs, or cultural norms generally associated with any particular nondominant culture or with the host culture. As Cuéllar (2000) notes, marginalized clients are more "susceptible to psychological and adjustment disorders than persons who have adopted . . . assimilated, integrated or separation modes of adjustment" (p. 52). In regard to clients who are going through the process of acculturation, Gurung and Mehta (2001) describe the life of a person with relatively low susceptibility to psychological and adjustment disorders as "one in which he or she lives a comfortable existence in the host culture, retaining as much of the home culture as he or she likes, together with parts of the host culture's values and behaviors" (p. 141). That is, the acculturated individual most likely to report minimal conflicts or emotional difficulties in a clinical setting is one who displays behaviors and beliefs corresponding with the integration or biculturalism model of acculturation and avoids cultural/ethnic identification with only one culture (i.e., either the traditional or the host culture).

Use of Translators

Mental health practitioners in the United States often need to employ the services of translators when dealing with clients who have limited English proficiency. This is particularly true in the assessment and treatment of Asian Americans, Southeast Asian refugees, and Hispanics (Musser-Granski & Carrillo, 1997). Some scholars, however, recommend that clinicians avoid the use of translators. Martinez (1986), for example, makes two main arguments against the use of translators. First, the translator introduces a third person into the psychotherapy process, and this can lead to distortion and misinterpretation of the client's verbalizations. Omissions, additions, and substitutions are examples of common distortions or errors associated with the process of translation in the practice of psychotherapy (Bamford, 1991; Musser-Granski & Carrillo, 1997). Second, the client may find communicating through a translator to be a disagreeable experience. Other scholars opposed to the use of translators cite the inability of translators to express the original speakers' thoughts, which can lead to clinicians' attempting to work with confusing and misleading information. In addition, research indicates that psychiatric diagnoses tend to be more severe when clients are not interviewed in their own languages and that both clients' noncompliance with therapists' recommendations and therapy dropout rates tend to be higher among clients who are unable to understand English (Seijo, Gomez, & Freidenberg, 1991).

Despite such negative findings, however, many practitioners may find the use of translators unavoidable. If a clinician must use a translator, he or she should keep in mind the following guidelines (Bamford, 1991; Gaw, 1993b; Ho, 1987; Westermeyer, 1993):

1. The clinician should try to employ a translator who shares the client's racial and ethnic background (e.g., a Mexican American translator for a Mexican American client, a Cuban translator for a Cuban client), and the translator should have an understanding of the variability in linguistic expressions within the client's racial/ethnic group (e.g., *mal puesto* among Mexican Americans and *brujeria* among Cubans).

2. The clinician should employ a translator who has training in mental health problems and culture-related syndromes (see Chapter 9 for discussion of such syndromes).

3. The clinician should use a sequential mode of translation (i.e., the client speaks, the translator translates the client's words into English, the therapist speaks, the translator translates the therapist's words into the client's language, and so on) rather than concurrent translation (which can lead to fatigue).

4. The clinician should introduce the translator to the client and then ensure that the translator has some time alone with the client during which the two can talk about interests they may have in common (e.g., their country of origin, music). This reassures the client that the translator can understand him or her and so facilitates the therapeutic alliance between client and therapist.

5. Clinicians should introduce the translator to the client, and assure that the translator spends time alone with the client, talking about events they have in common (e.g., their country of origin, music, etc.). This will provide the message that the translator can understand the client and facilitate the therapeutic alliance between the client and the therapist.

6. The clinician should have the translator provide a sentence-by-sentence translation to avoid the possibility that the translator will leave out any details.

7. The clinician should avoid using technical terms (e.g., "You probably have what we call *dysthymia*") and should ask the client to describe in her or his own words the problem that has led the client to seek treatment (e.g., "Tell me what exactly happened in the last 2 years when you say that you have been feeling very sad").

8. The clinician should recognize that a clinical interview with translation takes twice as long as an interview conducted entirely in English and plan ahead for the extra time needed. If the interview must be terminated abruptly because the clinician has not planned for enough time, the client may infer that the therapist is not interested in his or her case.

9. When interpreting clinical data, the clinician should consider the potential effect of the translator (i.e., the translator may function as a *mediating*

variable, affecting the relationship between the client's reports of symptoms and the clinician's clinical diagnosis).

10. The clinician should consider the translator's level of acculturation in relation to the client's level of acculturation. The fact that a translator and a client share the same racial group is extremely helpful in the evaluation process, but a major discrepancy between translator and client in level of acculturation can create problems. For example, a highly acculturated Hispanic translator who accepts the American way of dating may not be able to appreciate the conflicts experienced by Hispanic parents who believe that it is not appropriate for their daughter to go on dates without a chaperone or to engage in a sexual relationship without being married.

11. The clinician should avoid employing a relative or friend of the client as a translator. An individual who has a prior relationship with the client is often not objective, and this lack of objectivity could lead to distortions that either minimize or maximize the client's psychopathology, depending on the context of therapy.

12. The clinician should avoid asking the client's bilingual child to serve as a translator (particularly when the client's problem involves the child). Employing a client's child in this way can dramatically reverse the hierarchical roles in the family when the parent is monolingual or has a limited command of English. It is particularly important to avoid such role reversal in the assessment and treatment of Hispanic and Asian clients, as the authority of parents (especially the father) in Hispanic and Asian families is extremely important.

13. In the case of an Asian client, the clinician should take care to determine what dialect the client speaks before engaging a translator.

Overdiagnosis of Multicultural Clients

Clinicians should always keep in mind the possibility of overdiagnosing (i.e., mistakenly ascribing "pathology" or mental problems to) clients who are members of any of the four cultural groups discussed in this book (Chapter 9 includes further discussion on this issue). The tendency of some practitioners to "see" pathology or mental health problems in members of these groups has generally been explained in two ways. First, the psychometric properties of the instruments commonly used to screen clients for mental health problems are not generally appropriate for the assessment of such problems among non-Anglo-American groups (Dana, 1993b). Two important problems with such assessment instruments are their use of inappropriate norms for the members of various cultural groups and their lack of cross-cultural validity (i.e., an instrument that was developed to measure a given mental health problem among members of one cultural group may not measure the same problem accurately in members of another cultural group).

The second explanation for overdiagnosis of individuals from non-Anglo-American cultural groups involves a lack of understanding on the part of practitioners concerning the impacts of cultural variables, norms, and values on the development of behaviors that resemble mental health problems (Dana, 1993b; Ramirez, Wassef, Paniagua, & Linskey, 1993). For example, it is not uncommon for Hispanic clients to report that they have *facultades espirituales* (spiritual faculties), meaning that they can communicate with "spirits" who live in an invisible world. Clients with strong religious beliefs may claim that they can communicate with the saints through burning candles, praying, and so on. In addition, it is not uncommon for Hispanic clients to report having "conversations with the saints" or "receiving verbal commands from the Virgin Mary." Asian and African American clients may report that they are possessed by spirits. Clinicians who are unfamiliar with their multicultural clients' culture-related beliefs are likely to interpret such reports as examples of "severe psychopathology" when, in fact, they are only reflections of their clients' belief systems (Bernal & Gutierrez, 1988; Dana, 1993b; Martinez, 1988).

Extended Family

The extended family plays a major role in the lives of the members of all four of the cultural groups discussed in this volume (Ho, 1987; McAdoo, 1993a; Pumariega et al., 1997; Sue & Sue, 2003). What constitutes an extended family? The answer to this question should be provided by the client, not by the therapist. An important guideline for clinicians is to remember that they should *never assume* that their clients' definitions of extended family are the same as their own. For example, a therapist should not assume that an African American client views an aunt as a member of the client's extended family simply because the aunt is biologically related to the client. According to Anderson, Eaddy, and Williams (1990), an African American client is likely to include an aunt in his or her definition of extended family only if the aunt provides the client with two types of support: instrumental support (e.g., money, clothing, child care) and emotional support (e.g., counsel and advice).

The therapist can gain insight into the client's definition of extended family by listening to the client's descriptions of the instrumental and emotional supports he or she receives from any members of the community. The therapist should consider any person the client describes as having a fundamental role in the provision of support as a member of the client's extended family. Thus the individuals in a given client's "extended family" might include the client's brother (but not the client's sister), the client's priest (but not the client's grandfather), a friend (but not an uncle), and the case manager assigned to the client's family by a welfare agency (but not the director of the agency).

The therapist should expect the client to bring both biologically related (e.g., uncles, aunts, sisters) and nonbiologically related (e.g., friends, minister) members of his or her extended family into the treatment setting. In the case of Hispanic clients, the nonbiologically related extended family members who play an active role in the process of psychotherapy often include the clients' godparents (*compadres* and *comadres*) (Comas-Diaz & Griffith, 1988). Among American Indian clients, tribal elders (particularly heads of the clients' tribes) and traditional medicine men and women are often seen as integral parts of the extended family (Dana, 1993b; Ho, 1992; Richardson, 1981).

In the case of African American clients, church membership is an essential element of family life, and fellow church members as well as clergy are often involved in the solution of family issues (Baker, 1988; Dana, 1993b). Grandparents, sisters, and brothers also often play major roles in the extended families of African Americans (Boyd-Franklin, 1989). Asian and Pacific Islander clients, in contrast, usually do not include in their extended families individuals who are not biologically related to them, because of cultural taboos concerning the admission of problems (including mental health problems) to anyone outside the biological family unit (Sue & Sue, 2003). Many clients who are refugees from Southeast Asian countries (Vietnamese, Cambodians, and Laotians) may be exceptions to this rule, however. These clients may emphasize the availability of nonbiologically related persons (e.g., friends) and social agencies (e.g., welfare agencies, community support organizations) in their definitions of extended family rather than nuclear family members (e.g., parents) because they may have had to leave their families behind in their countries of origin or their family members have been killed during war (Mollica & Lavelle, 1988).

Implicit in the above discussion is a distinction between the concepts of the extended family and the family tree. The description of a client's family tree is generally limited to the client's biological relationships (e.g., parents, siblings, uncles). The formulation of a client's genogram usually involves the depiction of his or her family tree (see Ho, 1987, p. 159). In clinical practice, however, when the goal of the genogram is to clarify the client's definition of his or her extended family, the genogram may include all those biologically and nonbiologically related persons the client considers essential as providers of instrumental and emotional supports. The formulation of the genogram in terms of an "extended family tree" may assist the practitioner in understanding who provides such supports to the client during times of crisis. For example, in the case of a Hispanic client, the extended family tree might include the client and the client's children, parents, grandparents, godfather, godmother, priest, and close friends. In the case of an American Indian client, the tree might include a medicine man or medicine woman. In the case of a client who is a refugee from Southeast Asia, the extended family tree is likely to include more friends, social agencies, and case managers than relatives, for the reasons noted above.

Foster Homes and the Extended Family

Boyd-Franklin (1989) has pointed out that when therapists fail to ask their clients about their extended families, sometimes the result is that the clients' children are placed in foster homes when the biological parents are not able to take care of them (e.g., because of hospitalization or because of severe father-mother marital conflicts that may put the children at risk). It is important for the mental health practitioner to ask any client who is a parent to name a member of his or her extended family (as defined by the client) who may be willing to take care of the client's child (or children) if the parent is not able to do so.

The client might select a member of his or her extended family who is not biologically related to the client or the client's child (e.g., friend, godfather), someone who may not share the client's and child's racial/ethnic background. If that is the case, the therapist can help to preserve the racial and ethnic identity of the child by making sure that the foster parent understands the cultural norms, values, and beliefs that are part of the child's racial/ethnic background and that the foster parent can apply that understanding in real-life situations. For example, in the case of an African American child placed with White foster parents, the therapist can advise the foster parents to make special arrangements for the child to participate in activities involving other African American children (Jackson & Westmoreland, 1992). Similar arrangements are recommended for Hispanic, Asian, and American Indian children placed with foster parents from different racial/ethnic backgrounds. In the case of American Indian children, therapists should take care to follow an additional guideline: They should not attempt to handle foster care issues concerning American Indians without first gaining an understanding of the Indian Child Welfare Act (see Chapter 6 for discussion of this act).

Modality of Therapy

In general, African American, American Indian, Hispanic, and Asian clients prefer therapeutic approaches that are directive (i.e., they want to know what the problem is and what they need to do to solve the problem), active (i.e., they want to play a role in the process of psychotherapy), and structured (i.e., they want to know exactly what the therapist recommends to solve the problem) (Sue & Sue, 2003). The forms of psychotherapy most often recommended for members of the various cultural groups discussed in this text are behavioral approaches (e.g., social-skills training) and family therapy (Ho, 1987; Tanaka-Matsumi & Higginbotham, 1996). Chapters 3 through 6 present examples of specific therapeutic approaches recommended for clients in each of the groups addressed in this book.

Individual psychotherapy (i.e., intervention with only the client) is generally recommended for members of all four of the groups discussed here prior to the scheduling of family therapy (a preferred form of intervention across groups, in comparison with individual psychotherapy) in those cases when the phenomenon of acculturation seems to play a major role in the manifestation of the clinical problem. Family therapy is particularly appropriate when the clinical problem involves either marital conflicts (e.g., conflicts based in discrepancies in the values, norms, and worldviews held by marital partners when one partner is less acculturated than the other) or family problems involving children and adolescents with high levels of acculturation relative to their less acculturated parents. For example, Jones (1992) notes that some African American adolescents are referred for therapy because "their parents think they are mimicking maladaptive white adolescent behaviors (such as the wearing of punk-style haircuts or interest in heavy metal rock music)" (p. 34). The assumption of the parents is that these African American adolescents may lose their racial/ethnic identity because of the impact of acculturation (i.e., the adoption of many of the behaviors of White adolescents). Jones recommends that in such cases, practitioners conduct individual psychotherapy sessions "before initiating productive conjoint family therapy" (p. 34).

How Much Information Is Necessary?

Another general guideline for mental health professionals who work with multicultural clients is to avoid collecting very large amounts of information in any one session. It is particularly important that the therapist emphasize the presenting problem during the first therapeutic contact with the client and avoid giving the impression that he or she needs too much additional information to understand the problem. Most clients in the four cultural groups discussed in this volume (particularly Hispanics) tend to view clinicians who try to collect massive amounts of information as incompetent—both in technical terms (i.e., they see such therapists as poorly trained in collecting significant clinical data) and in cultural terms (i.e., they see the therapists as unfamiliar with their particular cultural group) (Seijo et al., 1991).

Of course, it is often essential for the therapist to collect extensive information in order to understand the client's problem. A great deal of information is particularly necessary for the formulation of the client's extended family tree. The guideline that the therapist needs to remember in this context is to plan to collect data *gradually,* across several sessions, rather than attempt to learn everything about the client in a 45-minute session. Factors that can facilitate the therapist's collection of extensive clinical data after the first session with an African American, Hispanic, Asian, or American Indian client include (a) the client's belief that the therapist has identified the client's essential problem, (b) the therapist's provision of concrete recommendations aimed at solving the problem, and (c) the client's favorable perception of the therapist's credibility. In the absence of such factors, a therapist will find it difficult to gather clinical data beyond those collected during the first session (which typically consist of an overview of the problem and perhaps some information about other family members).

The Meaning of *Therapist* Across Multicultural Groups

Mental health professionals should be familiar with the meanings attached to the term *therapist* across different cultural groups. For example, many Asians and African Americans view therapists as "physicians," American Indians often see therapists as medicine men or medicine women, and many Hispanics view therapists as "folk healers" (Comas-Diaz & Griffith, 1988; Ho, 1992; Sue & Sue, 2003).

Understanding the client's definition of *therapist* can greatly enhance the clinician's ability to help the client manage his or her problem. For example, American Indian clients may expect therapists to recommend herbal or other natural substances rather than synthetic medications as part of the treatment of their mental problems. In contrast, many Asian and African American clients would expect their therapists to discuss with them how synthetic medications can control their problems. These differences in expectations are based in differences in the perceptions of therapists across cultural groups (Baker, 1988; Richardson, 1981; Sue & Sue, 2003).

Using Data From the 2000 U.S. Census in the Clinical Context

Clinicians who serve clients from the four culturally diverse groups discussed in this book should be aware of several findings of the most recent

U.S. Census that may have clinical implications for the assessment, diagnosis, and treatment of such clients (Borak, Fiellin, & Chemerynski, 2004; Grieco & Cassidy, 2001; C. E. Holzer III, personal communication, March 2004). For example, in 2000, the U.S. Bureau of the Census modified the questions used in the 1990 census related to race and Hispanic or Latino origin to reflect the latest Office of Management and Budget (OMB) interpretation of "Hispanic" and "race" as two distinct concepts (for a summary of historical events leading to these modifications, see Borak et al., 2004). In the 2000 census, "the question on Hispanic origin asked respondents if they were Spanish, Hispanic, or Latino" (Grieco & Cassidy, 2001, p. 2). In this context, an individual who identified as Hispanic could be of any race, and the terms *Hispanic* and *Latino* were used interchangeably. Five response choices were offered for the question "Is this person Spanish/Hispanic/Latino?": (a) "No, not Spanish/Hispanic/Latino"; (b) "Yes, Mexican, Mexican American, Chicano"; (c) "Yes, other Spanish/Hispanic/Latino" (e.g., individuals from Central and South American countries); (d) "Yes, Puerto Rican"; and (e) "Yes, Cuban." Thus, clinicians serving this population would be wise to stop using the generic terms *Hispanic* and *Latino* when reporting their clinical findings and instead specify the terms their clients have used to identify themselves based on the new classifications derived from this census question.

Also in the 2000 census, respondents were asked to "report the race or races they considered themselves to be" by choosing among five race categories established by the OMB (see Grieco & Cassidy, 2001, p. 2). (These race categories are summarized in Box 2.1.) Respondents who were unable or unwilling to identify themselves using one or more of these categories were asked to check a box marked "Some other race" and then write in their race (respondents who provided write-in entries mentioned such "races" as Belizean, Moroccan, South African, and Hispanic origin).

The most important change in the 2000 U.S. Census was that it allowed respondents to select more than one race from the categories offered to indicate their racial identities. For the first time, individuals who consider themselves biracial or multiracial were able to identify themselves as such. Because of this change in the Census Bureau's general survey methodology, clinicians who are interested in tracking their clients in terms of race should consider noting in their clinical records how their clients self-identify racially using the census categories, whether they identify as members of a single race (e.g., clients who consider themselves to be Black or African American only), as biracial (e.g., Black or African American plus White), or as multiracial (e.g., Black or African American plus White plus American Indian and Alaska Native).

Box 2.1   Race Categories in the 2000 U.S. Census

- *White:* Individuals descended from any of the original peoples of Europe, North Africa, or the Middle East. This group also includes individuals who self-identified as "White" on the census survey or who wrote in "Arab," "Lebanese," "German," "Irish," "Italian," or "Near Easterner."
- *Black or African American:* Individuals descended from any of the Black racial communities of Africa. This group also includes individuals who self-identified as "Black, African, or Negro" on the census survey or who wrote in "African American," "Afro-American," "Haitian," or "Nigerian."
- *American Indian and Alaska Native:* Individuals descended from any of the original peoples of North, South, and Central America, and who have tribal affiliation or attachment to these communities. This group also includes individuals who self-identified as "American Indian and Alaska Native" on the census survey or who wrote in the names of their enrolled or principal tribes, such as Chippewa, Navajo, or Rosebud Sioux.
- *Asian:* Individuals descended from any of the original peoples of the Far East, Southeast Asia, or the Indian subcontinent. This group also includes individuals who self-identified as "Asian Indian," "Chinese," "Filipino," "Korean," "Japanese," "Vietnamese," or "other Asian" on the census survey or who wrote in "Burmese," "Hmong," "Pakistani," or "Thai."
- *Native Hawaiian and other Pacific Islander:* Individuals descended from any of the original peoples of Hawaii, Guam, Samoa, or other Pacific islands. This group also includes individuals who self-identified as "Hawaiian," "Guamanian," "Chamorro," "Samoan," or "other Pacific Islander" on the census survey or who wrote in "Chuukese," "Mariana Islander," or "Tahitian."
- *Some other race:* This category was included to allow individuals who were unable or unwilling to self-identify using any of the five categories listed above. Among the "other races" respondents wrote in were "Belizean," "Cuban," "Hispanic origin," "Mexican," "Moroccan," and "South African."

SOURCE: Adapted from Grieco and Cassidy (2001).

In the 2000 U.S. Census, the majority of respondents self-identified as members of only one race (97.6%; see Grieco & Cassidy, 2001, p. 3). This suggests that most current mental health clients also likely consider themselves to be members of only one race, and that issues related to biracial or multiracial identification of clients may not be of great concern for clinicians practicing in the United States. Practitioners should consider this conclusion with caution, however, for two reasons (see Sue & Sue, 2003, chap. 15; Wehrly, Kenney, & Kenney, 1999). First, in the 2000 census, 2.4% of the total respondents (i.e., more than 6.8 million people) identified themselves as members of two or more races, and some individuals selected all five of the offered race categories plus "Some other race" in self-identifying. Table 2.1 presents a summary of the numbers and percentages of individuals who self-identified as biracial or multiracial in the 2000 U.S. Census. Table 2.2 displays data on the population of the United States in 2000 by race, showing the numbers and percentages of respondents self-identifying as members of each race alone and in combination with other races. (The Hispanic population is not included in Table 2.2 because in 2000, the U.S. Bureau of the Census considered Hispanic to be an ethnicity rather than a race; an ethnicity can occur within any of the five races established by the OMB. For data on the numbers of individuals in the Hispanic population, see Table 4.1 in Chapter 4.)

The second reason clinicians should be careful about underestimating the likelihood that they may encounter clients who consider themselves biracial or multiracial is that in some areas of the country, biracial and multiracial families are more common than in others. Clinicians who provide services in such areas should expect to serve a significant number of biracial or multiracial clients. In the 2000 U.S. Census, the 10 states reporting the highest percentages of individuals who self-identified as biracial or multiracial were as follows (in order of rank): Hawaii (ranked first), Alaska, California, Oklahoma, Nevada, New Mexico, Washington, New York, Oregon, and Arizona. It should be noted that New Jersey (rank = 13), Texas (14), Florida (15), and Illinois (25) were among the 10 states with the highest percentages of Hispanic or Latino population in the 2000 U.S. Census (see Table 4.3 in Chapter 4), but these states did not rank in the top 10 in percentages of biracial and multiracial respondents. The 10 states with the lowest percentages of respondents self-identifying as biracial or multiracial in the 2000 census were Tennessee (rank = 42), Iowa (43), Louisiana (44), New Hampshire (45), Kentucky (46), South Carolina (47), Alabama (48), Maine (49), West Virginia (50), and Mississippi (51).

The number of individuals self-identifying as members of two or more races was relatively low in the 2000 U.S. Census, probably because the

Table 2.1   Population of Two or More Races, Including All Combinations, for the United States: 2000

Race	Number	Percentage
Two races	6,368,075	93.3
Three races	410,285	6.0
Four races	38,408	0.6
Five races	8,637	0.1
Six races	823	—
Total two or more races	6,826,228	100.0

SOURCE: Adapted from Grieco and Cassidy (2001, p. 4).

Table 2.2   Race Alone or in Combination

Subject	Number	Percentage
White		
Total population (all races)	281,421,906	100.0
White alone or in combination[a]	216,930,975	77.1
White alone	211,460,626	75.1
White in combination[a]	5,470,349	1.9
Not White alone or in combination[a]	64,490,931	22.9
Black or African American		
Total population (all races)	281,421,906	100.0
Black or African American alone or in combination[a]	36,419,434	12.9
Black or African American alone	34,658,190	12.3
Black or African American in combination[a]	1,761,244	0.6
Not Black or African American alone or in combination[a]	245,002,472	87.1
American Indian and Alaska Native		
Total population (all races)	281,421,906	100.0
American Indian and Alaska Native alone or in combination[a]	4,119,301	1.5
American Indian and Alaska Native alone	2,475,956	0.9
American Indian and Alaska Native in combination[a]	1,643,345	0.6
Not American Indian and Alaska Native alone or in combination[a]	277,302,605	98.5
Asian		
Total population (all races)	281,421,906	100.0
Asian alone or in combination[a]	11,898,828	4.2
Asian alone	10,242,998	3.6
Asian in combination[a]	1,655,830	0.6
Not Asian alone or in combination[a]	269,523,078	95.8
Native Hawaiian and other Pacific Islander		
Total population (all races)	281,421,906	100.0
Native Hawaiian and other Pacific Islander alone or in combination[a]	874,414	0.3
Native Hawaiian and other Pacific Islander alone	398,835	0.1
Native Hawaiian and other Pacific Islander in combination[a]	475,579	0.2
Not Native Hawaiian and other Pacific Islander alone or in combination[a]	280,547,492	99.7
Some other race		
Total population (all races)	281,421,906	100.0
Some other race alone or in combination[a]	18,521,486	6.6
Some other race alone	15,359,073	5.5
Some other race in combination[a]	3,162,413	1.1
Not some other race alone or in combination[a]	262,900,420	93.4

SOURCE: U.S. Bureau of the Census (2000, Summary File 1, Matrices P7 and P9).

a. In combination with one or more of the other races listed. The six numbers for race "alone or in combination" may add to more than the total population, and the six percentages for race "alone or in combination" may add to more than 100% because individuals may report more than one race.

opportunity to select more than one race was a novelty. Also, although respondents were given information (as in Box 2.1) to help them understand what constitutes being a member of a particular race, many probably did not understand the distinctions between some race categories. Further confusion may have arisen from the question about ethnicity involving the terms *Hispanic* and *non-Hispanic* (see Borak et al., 2004, p. 243). In the next U.S. Census, respondents will probably be given more information regarding how to make their choices among the OMB race categories, and this will probably lead to a substantial increase in the number of people self-identifying as members of two or more races. In addition, the numbers of children born to interracial couples have been increasing over the past 20 years (Gibbs, 2003)—a factor that should result in a parallel increase in the numbers of respondents who self-identify as biracial or multiracial in future U.S. Census surveys.

Although the percentage of individuals who self-identified as biracial or multiracial in the 2000 U.S. Census was quite low, clinicians should not infer that they do not need to enhance their cultural competence in regard to biracial or multiracial clients and their families (see Sue & Sue, 2003, pp. 363–376). As noted above, in 2000, more than 6.8 million individuals in the United States self-identified as members of more than one race, and this number will likely be significantly higher in the 2010 census. Two important guidelines for mental health professionals in this context are as follows: First, when a client self-identifies as biracial or multiracial, the clinician should determine that individual's most dominant culture (S. A. Black, personal communication, March 2004). Second, clinicians who serve clients who self-identify as biracial or multiracial need to develop skills that will help them to integrate cultural variables from the groups with which their clients identify. That is, clinicians must design and develop strategies for assessment, diagnosis, and treatment that emphasize the needs of their biracial or multiracial clients. As an example of the application of these two guidelines, consider a client who self-identifies as both "Black or African American" and "American Indian and Alaska Native." The clinician first must determine the client's dominant culture; in this case, the client identifies most strongly with the African American culture in the United States. The clinician must then design and implement assessment, diagnosis, and treatment strategies for this client by using a combination of the cultural variables that have been shown to be important in mental health practice with both African American and American Indian clients (e.g., Chapters 3 and 6 in this book; see also Gibbs, Huang, & Associates, 2003; Sue & Sue, 2003).

Another area of clinical relevance reflected in the data from the 2000 U.S. Census is the issue of translation (see the discussion above). Table 2.3 presents a summary of census data regarding the languages respondents reported speaking at home as well as their ability to speak English. As the table shows,

Table 2.3   Language Spoken at Home and Ability to Speak English

Subject	Number	Percentage
Population 5 years and over by language spoken at home and ability to speak English		
Population 5 years and over	262,375,152	100.0
Speak only English	215,423,557	82.1
Speak a language other than English	46,951,595	17.9
Spanish	28,101,052	100.0
Speak English "very well"	14,349,796	51.1
Speak English "well"	5,819,408	20.7
Speak English "not well"	5,130,400	18.3
Speak English "not at all"	2,801,448	10.0
Other Indo-European languages	10,017,989	100.0
Speak English "very well"	6,627,688	66.2
Speak English "well"	2,091,447	20.9
Speak English "not well"	1,078,930	10.8
Speak English "not at all"	219,924	2.2
Asian and Pacific Island languages	6,960,065	100.0
Speak English "very well"	3,370,041	48.4
Speak English "well"	2,023,303	29.1
Speak English "not well"	1,260,264	18.1
Speak English "not at all"	306,457	4.4
All other languages	1,872,489	100.0
Speak English "very well"	1,283,663	68.6
Speak English "well"	399,398	21.3
Speak English "not well"	151,125	8.1
Speak English "not at all"	38,303	2.0
Ability to speak English		
Population 5 years and over	262,375,152	100.0
Speak a language other than English	46,951,595	17.9
5 to 17 years	9,779,766	3.7
18 to 64 years	32,756,989	12.5
65 years and over	4,414,840	1.7
Speak English less than "very well"	21,320,407	8.1
5 to 17 years	3,493,118	1.3
18 to 64 years	15,486,421	5.9
65 years and over	2,340,868	0.9
Ability to speak English in household		
Linguistically isolated households[a]	4,361,638	NA
Population 5 years and over in households	254,620,291	100.0
In linguistically isolated households[a]	11,893,572	4.7
5 to 17 years	2,687,603	1.1
18 to 64 years	7,926,537	3.1
65 years and over	1,279,432	0.5

SOURCE: U.S. Bureau of the Census (2000, Summary File 3, Matrices P19, P20, PCT13, PCT14).

NOTE: NA = not applicable.

a. A linguistically isolated household is one in which no member 14 years old or older (a) speaks only English or (b) speaks a non-English language and speaks English "very well." In other words, all members 14 years old and older have at least some difficulty with English.

of the 28.1 million individuals who speak Spanish, approximately 28.3% (almost 8 million) reported in 2000 that they speak English "not well" or "not at all." In the general population, in a sample of 262.4 million (which includes all races and the Hispanic population), 21.3 million reported that they speak English less than "very well." These findings suggest that the issue of translation will continue to be a critical factor in the assessment, diagnosis, and treatment of clients who do not speak English.

3

Guidelines for the Assessment and Treatment of African American Clients

In the 2000 U.S. Census, approximately 34.6 million individuals (12.3% of the total U.S. population) self-identified as "Black or African American." In addition, 1.8 million defined their race as Black or African American in combination with one or more other races (Grieco & Cassidy, 2001; U.S. Bureau of the Census, 2000). In this mixed-race group, the races most commonly reported in combination with Black or African American were as follows: White (784,764 individuals reported African American–White biracial status), American Indian and Alaska Native (182,494 individuals), White *and* American Indian and Alaska Native (112,207 reported this multiracial status), and Asian (106,782 individuals) (Grieco & Cassidy, 2001). In the same census, approximately 5.5 million persons reported that they were White in combination with one or more other races; the second-most-common combination in this group was White and African American (as noted above, 784,764 individuals reported their race as White and Black or African American; 868,395 described themselves as White and Asian).

These findings suggest that although only approximately 12% of the total U.S. population self-identify as Black or African American only, clinicians should be aware of the possibility that they may serve clients who consider themselves both African Americans and members of other races (e.g., American Indian, Asian). As noted in Chapter 2, clinicians who serve biracial and multiracial clients must use culturally sensitive strategies in the assessment, diagnosis, and treatment of those clients.

Socioeconomic Status

At the time of the 2000 U.S. Census, the median income of African American families was $29,470, far below the national U.S. median of

$42,228. The median among White families at that time was $44,517 (U.S. Bureau of the Census, 2002a). The average income per household member among African American families was $15,007, compared with $12,158 for Hispanics, $22,688 for Asians and Pacific Islanders, and $24,951 for Whites (U.S. Bureau of the Census, 2001, 2002b). Approximately 8.2 million, or 24.9%, of those who self-identified in the census as Black or African American (not in combination with other races) were living below the poverty level, in comparison with 12.4% of the U.S. population as a whole and 9.1% of respondents who self-identified as White (not in combination with other races) (Bishaw & Iceland, 2003).

Cultural Variables That May Affect Assessment and Treatment

Racial Labels

Racial labels have been a concern to African Americans for many years (Smith, 1992). Members of this group have been referred to as *Colored, Negro, Black,* and *African American.* The first three of these terms emphasize skin color, whereas the last emphasizes cultural heritage; *African American* is the term currently recommended most often in the literature (Griffith & Baker, 1993; Smith, 1992). Mental health professionals should not use the terms *Colored* and *Negro,* as these are considered derogatory (Smith, 1992). The terms *Black* and *African American* both seem to be acceptable within particular contexts. For example, in an article published in the *Houston Chronicle,* an interviewee who was asked about both terms responded that "if a brother or sister wants to call me black, that's OK. But I would prefer that Anglos call me African American. . . . It acknowledges our ancestry and where we came from, and I think that use of that term by Anglos is more respectful" (quoted in Karkabi, 1993, p. 5D).

It is appropriate for therapists to explore with their African American clients which term (*Black* or *African American*) the clients prefer. A practical strategy is for the clinician to ask the client directly about this matter. Whether the client states a preference for *Black* or *African American,* the therapist should honor the client's wishes and stay neutral with respect to any controversy that may exist regarding the use of either term (for an excellent summary of such controversy, see Smith, 1992).

In addition, clinicians should be aware that in the 2000 U.S. Census, respondents were allowed for the first time to identify themselves as members of more than one race (see Chapter 2 for discussion of this topic). This suggests that a clinician is likely to find it very difficult to determine and label a client's racial status in the absence of the client's own self-designation. For example, a given client may not consider him- or herself to be "Black" or "African American" only, but "African American and White" (i.e., biracial) or "African American and White and American Indian" (multiracial). Again, the best approach for the clinician to follow is to ask the client how he or she would like to be designated in terms of race (particularly if the information requested is needed to track clinical findings across different races or for research purposes).

As noted in Chapter 2 (see Box 2.1), the U.S. Bureau of the Census included the term *Black* (in the designation "Black or African American") in the racial categories used in the 2000 census (categories created by the Office of Management and Budget). Even given that usage, in this new edition I am emphasizing the use of the term *African American,* as I did in earlier editions (see Paniagua, 1994, 1998), because it continues to be the term with the most acceptability in the literature (see, e.g., Dana, 1993b; Gibbs, Huang, & Associates, 2003; Griffith & Baker, 1993; Ho, 1992; Smith, 1992; Sue & Sue, 2003). Among the reasons scholars have given for their preference for the term *African American* are that it is less stigmatizing than *Black* (Dana, 1993b), that it emphasizes cultural heritage rather than skin color (Griffith & Baker, 1993), and that it formalizes the connection between African Americans and the continent of Africa (Fairchild, 1985).

Familism and Role Flexibility

In general, among African Americans, both the nuclear family (parents and children) and the extended family (grandparents, aunts, uncles, and other relatives as well as friends, clergy, and others who provide instrumental and social supports) are important (Boyd-Franklin, 1989; Smith, 1981). Because the concept of *familism* among African Americans generally includes both biologically and nonbiologically related persons, an important guideline for the clinician to follow with a client from this group is to formulate a genogram that emphasizes the client's extended family tree (as defined in Chapter 2) rather than simply the biological family tree. (This guideline holds also for American Indian, Asian, and Hispanic clients.)

Among African American clients, the head of the family is not necessarily the father (Baker, 1988). An important feature of African American families is *role flexibility:* That is, sometimes the mother plays the role of the father as well as the mother, and thus functions as the head of the family, and older children sometimes function as parents, caring for younger children. In fact, it is not uncommon for older African American children to drop out of school so that they can go to work and help their younger siblings secure a good education (Baker, 1988; Ho, 1992; Smith, 1981). Therapists should carefully consider this practice when conducting family therapy with African American families that include adolescents; therapists should not assume that school dropout among adolescents in these families is the result of the problems the parents have brought to the therapists' attention. In addition, as Boyd-Franklin (1989) notes, the concept of role flexibility among African American families can be extended to include the parental role sometimes assumed by grandfathers, grandmothers, aunts, and cousins. Therefore, in assessing an African American client, the therapist should attempt to determine which family member was functioning as the head of the family at the moment of the referral.

Religious Beliefs

For many African Americans, the church (particularly an African American church) is an important part of the extended family (Griffith, English, & Mayfield, 1980; Levin & Taylor, 1993). Therefore, it is important that therapists explore the role that the church plays in the life of each African American client. An initial step is to ask the client whether he or she has a particular church affiliation and, if so, what that is. The majority of church-affiliated African Americans are members of Baptist or African Methodist Episcopal churches (Boyd-Franklin, 1989), but many others worship as Jehovah's Witnesses, Seventh-Day Adventists, Pentecostals, Presbyterians, Lutherans, Episcopalians, and Roman Catholics or as members of the Church of God in Christ or the Nation of Islam.

Despite the central role that the church plays in the lives of many African Americans (Smith, 1981), it is important that mental health practitioners avoid assuming that all of the African American clients they serve have strong church ties. To explore whether a particular client includes the church in his or her extended family, the therapist might ask, "Have you discussed your emotional problems with anyone in your church?" Note that "anyone" here could refer to a fellow church member, a minister, a priest, or anybody else with some connection to the client's church. If the client indicates that members of his or her church are essential in providing the client with instrumental and emotional support, the therapist could ask, "Would you like to include these church members in our discussion of your concerns?"

Folk Beliefs

Some African Americans believe that folk medicine can be effective in the treatment of both medical and mental problems (Baker & Lightfoot, 1993; Wilkinson & Spurlock, 1986). The belief systems of many African Americans include the idea that mental problems can have either physical causes or causes that may be described as occult or spiritual. If an illness has a physical cause, according to such beliefs, it can be cured with herbs, teas, and other natural substances; in such a case, an individual might consult a folk doctor for treatment. If an illness is perceived to have been caused by occult or spiritual factors (including evil spirits, supernatural forces, violation of sacred beliefs, and sin), the individual might consult a folk healer (Dana, 1993b).

Some African Americans might seek help for mental health problems from one of several types of healers. The kind of healer known as the old lady generally deals with common ailments; she provides advice and gives medications (e.g., herbs). The old lady is most often consulted by young mothers. The spiritualist is the most common kind of folk healer consulted by African Americans seeking help in dealing with their problems. The voodoo priest, or *hougan,* has more formal training in the process of healing than do other folk healers (including training in how to select plants to be used for healing purposes and which organs or other parts of certain animals clients should ingest to treat particular problems, as well as training in the skills needed to help clients deal with individual and family problems). In addition to seeking the help of folk healers, many African Americans believe that the solutions to their problems should include involvement with Bible study groups, prayer meetings, and advice from clergy (Dana, 1993a). To enhance their ability to assess and treat African American clients appropriately, therapists need to understand these clients' beliefs regarding the causes of mental health problems and their solutions (Baker & Lightfoot, 1993; Smith, 1981).

Healthy Cultural Paranoia

Slavery and racism are two important factors in the history of African Americans in the United States that have dramatically shaped the social and psychological development of the members of this group over time (Gregory, 1996; Smith, 1981). An important consequence of these factors has been the development of *healthy cultural paranoia* among African Americans (Ho, 1992; Smith, 1981). Many African Americans present themselves as highly suspicious of people of other races and of those who hold values that are different from theirs; such an attitude can interfere with the client-therapist relationship. However, when a therapist perceives that an African American client does not trust him or her, the therapist should avoid asking the client to explain that distrust; asking for an explanation demonstrates a lack of understanding of the phenomenon of healthy cultural paranoia, and the client may then perceive the therapist as culturally insensitive.

The Language of African American Clients

Communicative exchange between client and therapist is an essential element in the process of psychotherapy; this applies to all forms of therapy, not only to what has been termed "talk therapy." Effective communicative exchange may be difficult to achieve when the client uses words, syntax, and phonology with which the therapist is unfamiliar (Wilkinson & Spurlock, 1986). This point is particularly important for practitioners to remember in the assessment and treatment of African American clients, who may use Black English rather than Standard English or street talk during the therapeutic process.

Both Dillard (1973) and Smitherman (1995) provide a wide variety of examples to demonstrate the distinctions between Standard English and Black English. For instance, the two forms of English differ in terms of grammar; the question "Have they gone there?" in Standard English might be phrased "Is they gone there?" in Black English (Dillard, 1973, p. 49). Because of differences between Black English and Standard English, a therapist may misunderstand what an African American client is saying. For example, in Black English, the sentences "My child sick" and "My child be sick" mean two different things: The first sentence indicates that the child is currently sick and the sickness is of short-term duration, whereas the second sentence indicates that the child has been sick for a long time (Dillard, 1973). As Smitherman (1995) explains, in Black English, the verb *be* is used to "indicate continuous action or infrequently occurring activity" (p. 7).

African American clients' use of street talk may also affect the assessment and treatment of members of this group. In using street talk, a client may or may not use Standard English; in either case, the therapist may have problems understanding what the client is saying because the client is using words or phrases with which the therapist is unfamiliar. For example, the sentence "I would like to have plenty of bank to buy a hog to go to Cali" is grammatically correct in Standard English, but the listener cannot understand this sentence unless he or she knows the meanings of the slang words *bank* (money); *hog* (Cadillac or, more generally, any car); and *Cali* (California) (see Dillard, 1973, p. 240; Smitherman, 1995, pp. 54, 75, 135). Additional examples of Black street talk are "I was mad at her because she was not clean" (*clean* in this specific case means dressed up or stylishly dressed); "If I get a gig, I will feel better" (*gig* means job); and "He likes to rap with the dude who lives across the street" (*rap* means talk, *dude* means man).

The basic guideline for the practitioner concerning language is this: If the therapist cannot understand the language of an African American client, the therapist should ask the client directly to clarify what he or she means. Several African Americans with whom I consulted as I was writing this chapter told me that, in many instances, they have problems understanding individuals who use Black English and street talk. Thus, a therapist of any race who cannot understand the language used by an African American client should not feel embarrassed to ask questions that will enhance client-therapist communication. The therapist should be careful, however, not to give the impression that he or she is questioning the correctness of the client's use of Black English rather than Standard English or the correctness of particular words. The therapist must reassure the client, both verbally and nonverbally, that he or she is asking for clarification only to facilitate the verbal exchange between therapist and client, which is crucial to the therapist's understanding of the client's concerns.

The First Session

The therapist's first session with any client sets the tone for a healthy client-therapist relationship in subsequent sessions (Baker, 1988; Ho, 1992; Smith, 1981). The literature suggests specific guidelines concerning the cultural skills a therapist should employ during the first encounter with an African American client.

Discussing Racial Differences

Because of the history of racism and discrimination against African Americans by the dominant Anglo-American culture, an African American client referred to an Anglo-American therapist is likely to come to the first session with the belief that the therapist is an "alien" who will not be able to understand the client's problem because of racial differences. To minimize these feelings, the therapist should begin the first session by acknowledging the racial difference between therapist and client and encouraging the client to talk about his or her feelings concerning this issue. (An exception to this guideline is that if the session is part of a brief or emergency intervention involving a crisis, the therapist should not raise issues of race; Wilkinson & Spurlock, 1986.)

When the therapist is White and the client is African American, the therapist might begin talking about race during the first session by saying, "Some African American clients feel uncomfortable when they are referred to a White therapist. Perhaps we could briefly talk about any feelings you may have regarding our racial differences." Boyd-Franklin (1989) suggests that the therapist simply ask, "How do you feel about working with a white therapist?" (p. 102). Such general comments and questions may not only reduce racial tension between the client and the therapist, they may also help the therapist to look less anxious, more comfortable, and more sensitive to the client's expectations and beliefs (Baker, 1988). In addition, when the therapist discusses racial issues openly with an African American client, the client may feel reassured that he or she is in a safe environment where anything can be discussed.

Another important guideline for the therapist is to avoid further discussion of racial issues in subsequent sessions (unless the client brings them up). By continuing to raise such issues after the first session, a White therapist may convey to an African American client the impression that the therapist is anxious about the potential effects of cross-racial issues and that this anxiety may interfere with his or her ability to assess and treat the client effectively (Boyd-Franklin, 1989).

It should be noted that discussion of racial issues in the first session may also be important when the client and the therapist are both African Americans. Although often African American practitioners assume that it is unnecessary to discuss race with their African American clients because those clients are likely to be less suspicious and guarded, more relaxed, and more open to discussing personal problems with them than they would be with therapists of other races, they may be mistaken in this assumption (Boyd-Franklin, 1989; Wilkinson & Spurlock, 1986). For example, as Boyd-Franklin (1989) points out, because many male African Americans hold beliefs that may be described as "macho," a client from this group may find it difficult to discuss personal matters openly with an African American therapist. In addition, an African American client being treated by a therapist from the same race may "check out" the therapist for nonverbal cues that suggest the therapist is distancing him- or herself from the client; this may result in the client's displaying the same kind of healthy cultural paranoia generally assumed to be part of African American clients' relationships with White therapists.

One important guideline for an African American therapist treating a client from the same race is to avoid thinking that racial similarity will necessarily enhance (or guarantee the success of) the therapist-client relationship. An African American therapist working with an African American client should take care to present both verbal and nonverbal behaviors aimed at establishing the therapist as a peer of the client; the therapist should not assume that the client will consider the therapist a peer simply because he or she is African American. An African American therapist might indicate his or her interest in discussing racial issues with a client of the same race by saying something like the following: "African American [or Black, depending on the client's stated preference] clients sometimes feel uncomfortable discussing mental problems with African American mental health professionals. Because I am an African American, I am wondering if you might have any such feelings." To facilitate a verbal exchange with the client on this particular issue, the therapist should avoid sitting behind a desk; by making sure there are no barriers between therapist and client, the therapist signals that he or she does not want to distance him- or herself from the client and conveys the sense that he or she will take the discussion of racial issues very seriously. This physical arrangement is recommended throughout the entire process of therapy as well, to continue the development of trust between client and therapist (Boyd-Franklin, 1989).

It is important to make a distinction between a discussion of racial issues to facilitate assessment and treatment during the first session and the African American therapist's (explicit or implicit) role as a "protector of the race" (Boyd-Franklin, 1989). African Americans are aware of the history of slavery, racism, and rejection experienced by members of their race in the United States. Thus, an African American client may become suspicious of an African American therapist who, in the process of assessment and treatment, presents him- or herself as a member of this race who has the education and training to "preach and teach" African American clients. Therefore, in addition to scheduling a brief period to discuss racial issues in the first session with an African American client, the African American therapist should avoid mixing any discussion of racial issues intended to help develop the therapist-client relationship with discussions of political and racial problems in society.

Regardless of the race of the therapist, a discussion of racial differences during the first therapy session with an African American client does not necessarily guarantee the enhancement of the therapist-client relationship in subsequent sessions. As Wilkinson and Spurlock (1986) note, "The therapist's openness, sensitivity, and ability . . . , training and experience, are generally more important" in this regard (p. 51).

Exploring the Client's Level of Acculturation

The fact that a client is African American does not necessarily mean that the client identifies as African American (Dana, 1993b; Ho, 1992). Some African American clients identify more strongly with the Anglo-American culture than with African American culture and may display behavior patterns much like those found in the Anglo-American community (e.g., styles of dress, music, language). An African American may acquire such behavior patterns and preferences through the internal acculturation process described in Chapter 2. In the first session with an African American client, the therapist should determine how the client perceives his or her identity: Does the client identify more strongly with the dominant culture or with the culture of his or her own race (Sue & Sue, 2003)? One way in which the therapist might explore this issue is by encouraging the client to talk about his or her past and current experiences with the African American community versus his or her experiences with the Anglo-American community. In addition, the Brief Acculturation Scale may be useful (see Figure 2.1 in Chapter 2).

Avoiding Offering Causal Explanations for Problems

Many African American clients believe that emotional problems are caused by environmental factors. Thus, the therapist should avoid linking an African American client's mental health problems with, for example, the behavior of the client's parents or other members of the client's extended family. The therapist should not offer any possible explanations regarding the origin of the problems during the first session. During this session, an African American client is likely to prefer that the therapist provide concrete suggestions regarding how to solve the mental problems rather than a long and complex explanation of the problems' origin (Baker, 1988).

Including the Church in the Assessment and Therapy Processes

As noted above, the church plays a major role in the lives of many African Americans (Dana, 2002; Griffith et al., 1980; Sue & Sue, 2003; Taylor & Chatters, 1986). It is particularly important that therapists remember this fact when assessing and treating African American women, because they tend to be more involved with church activities than are African American men (Levin & Taylor, 1993). A practical guideline for the therapist is to determine whether the client is a member of a particular church and, if so, how the client perceives the church as a source of economic and emotional supports. If the client indicates an affiliation with a church, the therapist should inform the client that he or she is welcome to bring fellow church members to subsequent sessions to help with the assessment and treatment of the client's concerns. For example, the therapist might say, "If you believe that someone in your church should be invited to discuss this problem with you and me, please let me know, and I will be glad to extend an invitation to that person to join us at our next session."

If the therapist is aware prior to the first session (e.g., because the client has mentioned it when scheduling the session) that the client belongs to one of the churches in the community, the therapist should let the client know in advance, either on the phone or in writing, that he or she is welcome to bring any church member he or she wishes to the first meeting. Therapists should make sure that their support staff members (e.g., secretaries, mental health paraprofessionals) are aware of this guideline as well, because in many instances, the therapist is not the person who makes the first contact with a client.

With an African American client who is a new resident in the community, it is important for the therapist to find out whether the client has already found a church that fulfills his or her religious needs. Of course, the therapist should be familiar with the churches available in that particular community. A good approach is for the therapist to have available for African American clients a list of the names, telephone numbers, and addresses of all of the churches in the community. As Boyd-Franklin (1989) notes, by helping an African American client find a church, a therapist may contribute significantly to the process of psychotherapy (e.g., the client's minister may encourage the client to continue going to therapy sessions or to follow the therapist's recommendations). In addition, this sort of assistance may greatly enhance the therapist-client relationship.

Defining the Roles of Those Accompanying the Client

Many African American clients assume that they may bring members of their extended families to an initial session with a therapist (Baker, 1988). The people they bring with them often include both relatives (e.g., uncles, aunts) and nonrelatives (e.g., friends, godparents, fellow church members). To avoid making false assumptions about the roles of those who accompany a client to the first session, the therapist must clarify the role of each person prior to beginning to assess the case. The therapist's main concern should be to determine whether any of these individuals may be helpful in the evaluation and treatment of the client (Griffith & Baker, 1993). In addition, the therapist should be aware of the importance of the presence of the client's grandmother at the first meeting. Given that the grandmother is probably the second-most-important member of the client's extended family (Boyd-Franklin, 1989), the grandmother's attendance at the first session is often a sign that she offers the client a great deal of social and/or spiritual support.

In many African American families, the primary caretaker of children is not the mother but the grandmother. A grandmother may bring a child to a clinic for assessment and treatment, but she may lack an understanding of the fundamental psychological and developmental processes that are relevant to the assessment and treatment of the child. The therapist must be aware that, despite her lack of understanding, the grandmother is likely to be responsible for making major decisions regarding the child's life. For example, the child's mother may not follow the therapist's recommendations for treatment of the child without the approval of the child's grandmother. For this reason, an important guideline for the therapist who is working with an African American child is to explore quickly in the first session the role of the grandmother in the child's life. If the therapist perceives that the grandmother's role is crucial, he or she should invite the grandmother to attend subsequent therapy sessions and to participate actively in the child's assessment and treatment.

Using an Approach With a Present-Time Focus

During the first session, an African American client might bring up both the *core,* or most essential, problem that he or she feels should be considered first and additional problems that may be handled in later sessions (Baker, 1988). The therapist should be aware that the client probably expects to receive suggestions for a focused, brief intervention to deal with the core problem quickly.

Screening for Depression and Schizophrenia

Griffith and Baker (1993) suggest African Americans may be under-diagnosed for depression because of a common myth that African Americans rarely become depressed. These authors recommend that a therapist screen an African American client concerning the following before concluding that the client does not have major depression:

1. Neurovegetative signs (e.g., weight loss, fatigue)

2. View of the future

3. Past and current sources of pleasure from specific persons

4. Level of productivity

5. Degree of participation in church activities

6. Degree of participation as a caregiver for younger family members

The diagnosis of schizophrenia appears to be more common among African American clients than among White clients (Good, James, Good, & Becker, 2003). Clinicians should be aware of the potential explanations for this finding so that they can avoid misdiagnosing their African American clients. Among the reasons African Americans may be overdiagnosed as schizophrenic are the phenomenon of healthy cultural paranoia, as described above; the belief in spirit possession held by some African American clients; and perceptions of these clients associated with racial stereotyping, such as that they are "dangerous," "aloof," and "argumentative" (e.g., see the definition of paranoid-type schizophrenia in the *DSM-IV-TR;* American Psychiatric Association, 2000, pp. 313–314). (Chapter 9 includes a detailed summary of this topic; see also Good et al., 2003.)

Griffith and Baker (1993) have suggested that the high prevalence of schizophrenia reported among African American clients might be related to substance abuse. Hallucinations and delusions, which are the key symptoms in a diagnosis of schizophrenia, can also result from chronic alcoholism and the use of illicit drugs (e.g., powdered or crack cocaine, heroin). Thus, during the first session with an African American client, the therapist should screen for a history of substance abuse. If a client arrives at a clinic with symptoms of schizophrenia that abate within approximately 2 hours in the absence of treatment (e.g., medication), the client probably has experienced cocaine psychosis. If the therapist fails to screen for substance abuse in such a case, the result might be an erroneous diagnosis of schizophrenia.

Handling Family Secrets With Care

During the first session with an African American client, the therapist should take care to be sensitive to the possibility of family secrets. The key point for the therapist to remember in this respect is to wait for the natural revelation of any family secrets over time, because in most cases, they will eventually be revealed (Boyd-Franklin, 1989). Family secrets can take many forms, including reasons for adoption (e.g., why a child was adopted by an aunt), use of drugs by parents (and other members of the family), past problems with the police that have led to arrests and convictions, and secrets regarding fatherhood (Boyd-Franklin, 1989).

The literature offers therapists specific guidelines regarding methods for identifying the secrets that might exist in the family as well as general guidelines concerning appropriate ways to handle these secrets during the first session. For example, if a grandmother brings her grandchild to the child's first therapy session and states that she has adopted the child without providing a reason for the adoption, the therapist should suspect that the grandmother is protecting a family secret. If an adolescent client asks his parents in the presence of the therapist, "Why do I look different from my brothers?" and the parents avoid answering the question, this could also be a case involving a family secret. The therapist might suspect a family secret if he or she says to a client, "Could you tell me about your life when you were an adolescent?" and the client replies, "I don't feel like talking about that now."

The basic first-session guideline for the therapist regarding suspected family secrets includes three elements: The therapist should listen carefully to what the client says, attend to the amount of silence that follows when the client is questioned about an issue that appears to be sensitive, and avoid asking questions that may imply that there are family secrets or that may lead to their revelation. For example, during the first session with a child client, the practitioner generally expects one or both parents to be present to register the child and sign documents dealing with consent for assessment and treatment. If a parent (either the mother or the father) is not present to fulfill these tasks, the therapist should not ask whoever has accompanied the child (whether a grandparent, an adult brother or sister, an adult aunt or uncle, or someone else), "Why is the child's mother not here today?" Although at first glance this question may seem appropriate, the therapist needs to understand that by asking it, he or she is inviting the premature discussion of a family secret, and the result could be attrition (i.e., the family may not come back for additional sessions).

In circumstances such as those in this example, the therapist should take the following steps. First, he or she should inquire about the relationship between the child and the person seeking help for the child (e.g., a grandparent) to help determine who has legal guardian status in regard to the child. Second, the therapist should clearly state that if the child's legal guardian is not present, the therapist will see the child only to determine whether the child's needs require immediate attention (e.g., suicide attempts). If the person who has brought the child in for treatment states that he or she is not the legal guardian, the therapist should say something like the following: "I am very pleased that you brought Sue to the clinic today; this shows that you care about her. I will see Sue now only to determine that she is not a danger to herself or to others. The next time you bring

Sue to the clinic, it would be helpful if you would also bring her legal guardian to sign consent forms that will allow me to conduct further assessment and therapy." Such a statement not only avoids questions dealing with family secrets, it also provides the individual with an opportunity to mention the child's legal guardian without pressure from the therapist. In addition to taking these two steps, the therapist must be familiar with all laws and regulations in his or her state regarding consent for the assessment and treatment of children and adolescents. For example, in Texas, any adult family member (e.g., a grandparent, an adult brother or sister) may give consent for the treatment of a child "when the person having the power to consent . . . cannot be contacted and actual notice to the contrary has not been given by that person" (Costello & Hays, 1988, p. 87).

Avoiding "Trying Too Hard"

A few years ago, the presenters of a workshop on the assessment and treatment of African American clients offered by the Texas Psychological Association made the following observation: If a therapist tries too hard to understand African Americans, he or she probably does not understand them at all. Boyd-Franklin (1989) makes a similar observation. She gives as an example an Anglo therapist who uses what the therapist thinks are current African American slang terms when talking with African American clients in an "attempt to join with the [African American] family" (p. 100). Therapists should avoid this approach for two reasons: First, they may use the slang inappropriately, which will lead their African American clients to see them as less culturally competent; and second, some African American clients may see such actions as condescending.

Emphasizing Strengths Rather Than Deficits

During the first session with an African American client, it is important that the therapist avoid any suggestion (either verbal or nonverbal) that the client likely comes from a disorganized, unstable, and psychologically unhealthy family. This characterization of African American families, which was prevalent during the 1960s, has been challenged by scholars over the past 40 years. For example, as Boyd-Franklin (1989) notes, the assumption that a stable, organized, and psychologically healthy family "must consist of two parents" (p. 15) suggests that any family lacking two parents is inherently pathological. The fact that many African American families are headed by single mothers led some people to conclude that these families must be disorganized, unstable, and psychologically unhealthy. That conclusion is inaccurate, however (Wilkinson & Spurlock, 1986), because it does not take into consideration the roles that factors such as the involvement of the extended family, role flexibility, strong religious orientation, and strong emphasis on the value of education play in family functioning. These factors are the strengths of the African American family, and therapists should emphasize these strengths in the first and all subsequent therapy sessions to encourage their African American clients' participation in therapy (Boyd-Franklin, 1989).

Many times, an African American mother in her first therapy session will report that she is a single mother. If the therapist does not explore with such a client the importance of extended family and the client's definition of her extended family (as discussed in Chapter 2), the client may not reveal to the therapist the existence of important individuals in her life, such as a person who may be a potential stepfather to her children. Knowing about such a person can be important to the therapist, because a stepfather can play an essential role in the development and maintenance of family functioning during the process of psychotherapy.

Conducting Psychotherapy

During the first therapeutic contact with an African American client, the therapist must collect preliminary clinical data, and there is minimal emphasis on the psychotherapy process. If the client returns for psychotherapy in subsequent sessions (Chapter 7 summarizes guidelines for the prevention of attrition), the therapist should follow the guidelines summarized below, as recommended in the literature (Baker, 1988; Boyd-Franklin, 1989; Dana, 1993b; Griffith & Baker, 1993; Ho, 1992; Lefley & Pedersen, 1986; Smith, 1981).

Emphasizing Empowerment

During the course of therapy with an African American client, it is important that the therapist reinforce the concept of "empowerment," relating this concept to the client's experience of therapeutic changes (see Dana, 2002, p. 11). Empowerment is an important concept in therapy with clients from any cultural background, but it is especially important in the case of African American clients because of the long history of slavery, racism, and discrimination experienced by members of this group. When dealing with the concept of empowerment in psychotherapy, the therapist should seek to accomplish two major goals: (a) to help the client gain the skills he or she needs to be able to make important life decisions, whether for him- or herself or for family members; and (b) to help the client develop the skills he or she needs to feel in control of his or her life.

For example, when an African American client is referred for therapy by a welfare agency, the client may experience a sense of powerlessness related to the fact that he or she had no input into the selection of a therapist.

The therapist's task in such a case is to display sensitivity to the client's feelings of powerlessness (saying to the client, for example, "I understand that you feel your power of choice has been taken away from you regarding the selection of a therapist") and to make it clear to the client that in the process of psychotherapy, he or she will learn specific techniques and skills to deal with such feelings (e.g., problem-solving training and social-skills training).

Recommended Modalities of Therapy

Problem-Solving and Social-Skills Training

The central goal of problem-solving training is to teach an individual how to solve quickly one or more problems in a series of problems (Kratochwill & Bergan, 1990). Because the therapist teaches the client how to resolve his or her own problems, this strategy may help the client to feel that he or she is regaining power (or control) over his or her own behavior or the behavior of other family members. In general, African American clients (like clients from the other cultural groups discussed in this volume) expect therapists to offer quick solutions to the problems the clients identify as most important (among a set of target problems). Therefore, problem-solving training can facilitate development of the client's positive perception of therapist credibility (i.e., the client's feeling that the therapist knows how to treat this particular client and his or her problems) and the client's sense of trust toward the therapist (Boyd-Franklin, 1989).

The main goal of social-skills training is to teach an individual how to be appropriately assertive in social interactions (Lange & Jakubowski, 1976). As Yamamoto, Silva, Justice, Chang, and Leong (1993) note, many members of non-Anglo-American cultural groups "feel they cannot speak up or assert themselves. Despite improving race relations, [members of such groups] often express that they still feel as if they are *second-class citizens*" (p. 116; emphasis added). Social-skills training is recommended for African American clients who are not assertive in their interpersonal relationships (including with family members) because they fear negative consequences (e.g., rejection, verbal reprimands) or because they believe that they do not have the right to express their feelings to people in positions of "power" outside the extended family. As Dana (2002) notes, clinicians working with African American clients should consider modifying the interventions they use that emphasize problem-solving training and social-skills training "on the basis of acculturation and racial identity information" (p. 10) (see Chapter 10).

Family Therapy

As noted above, the extended family plays a major role in the lives of many African American clients. For this reason, several scholars have suggested that practitioners should consider family therapy among the first treatment approaches to use with African American clients. All forms of family therapy are recommended with African American families, but two particular tactics are recommended when any form of family therapy is scheduled with African American clients (Boyd-Franklin, 1989, pp. 141–142). The first of these is for the therapist to assign the family members tasks to carry out at home and then report on in subsequent sessions with the therapist. This not only allows the therapist to deal with the problem in the target setting (i.e., at home), it may also encourage those family members who refuse to come to therapy to participate (or at least be more active) in the process of family therapy. In addition, many African American clients enter treatment looking for a "quick fix" for their problems (Boyd-Franklin, 1989), and family members may see the assignment of tasks as an example of the therapist's interest in dealing with their problems quickly.

The second tactic is the use of role-play scenarios to develop communication among family members. Many African American clients are not familiar with the concept of "family therapy" as something that can help them solve their problems, but only if they elect to communicate with each other. It is recommended that the therapist schedule several sessions in which each family member is encouraged to role-play the way he or she might talk about the target problem at home; through such sessions, the therapist can help all family members understand that they can solve their problems only when they elect to communicate their feelings and concerns to each other. One important consequence of using role playing in family therapy in this way is the reestablishment of a sense of power or control in the family. That is, by learning how to communicate and solve problems through role playing, African American clients can learn that the "powerlessness" or "weakness" they were feeling prior to therapy can gradually be transformed into a sense of empowerment or control. Boyd-Franklin (1989) suggests that the reestablishment of this sense of control should be seen as a fundamental task in the treatment of African American clients with any form of family therapy.

When the goal of family therapy is to deal with the emotional problems of an African American couple (e.g., husband and wife), additional guidelines apply. In general, when a White couple seeks help from a therapist, the partners mutually agree to discuss their problems with the therapist. Among African American couples, in contrast, this level of agreement "is exceedingly rare" (Boyd-Franklin, 1989, p. 225). Boyd-Franklin (1989) suggests that this may be explained by the socialization of African American men, which, influenced by racism and discrimination, has led to the development of the "macho" role, preventing African American men from showing weakness during difficult times. Many African American men may see any admission of emotional problems to people outside the family network as a sign of "weakness."

Thus, even if both partners in an African American couple come to the first therapy session, the therapist will probably need to develop strategies to encourage the man to return for therapy. Boyd-Franklin (1989) provides a series of general guidelines for therapists seeking to engage African American men in therapy with their partners. First, the therapist should signal to the woman that the therapist can see her alone. Second, it is important for the therapist to explore the woman's understanding of her partner's position with respect to therapy for their mutual problems. Third, although the woman's presenting her partner with an ultimatum (e.g., "If you do not come to therapy, I will leave you") may be a good way to get the man to therapy initially, it is important that the therapist help the woman to understand that if the man feels he is being "forced" to come to therapy, he may lose his autonomy and the power to choose his own ways of confronting and resolving the couple's problems. Fourth, it is important for the woman to understand that it may help if the therapist talks to the man *directly;* the therapist might explain that he or she does not want to use the woman as a "messenger." The therapist should consult with the woman to determine a time and day when the therapist can reach the man on the phone; the woman should not inform her partner that the therapist is planning to call him. Because of the generally negative attitude toward therapy among African Americans (which stems in part from the phenomenon of healthy cultural paranoia, discussed above), during their first phone conversation the therapist should tell the man that the therapist has discussed the target problem with the man's partner (e.g., his wife) and that the main purpose of the conversation is to explore the man's ideas, suggestions, and understandings with respect to the problem (*only* the problem the woman has mentioned to the therapist). The therapist should emphasize that he or she needs this information so that he or she can *assist* the couple (avoiding the word *help*) in the solution of their *concerns* (avoiding the word *problem*).

4

Guidelines for the Assessment and Treatment of Hispanic Clients

As of the 2000 census, the total number of Hispanics residing in the United States was approximately 35.3 million (U.S. Bureau of the Census, 2000). As Table 4.1 shows, the majority of these Hispanics were Mexican Americans, who accounted for approximately 20.6 million, or 58.5%, of all Hispanics (this proportion was down slightly from 60% in 1990), followed by Puerto Ricans (3.4 million) and Cubans (1.2 million). In the 2000 census, approximately 1.7 million persons living in the United States reported their heritage as Central American (e.g., Costa Rican, Guatemalan, Panamanian, Salvadoran), and approximately 1.4 million reported South American heritage (e.g., Argentinean, Bolivian, Colombian, Venezuelan). Individuals of Salvadoran (655,165) and Colombian (470,684) heritage made up the largest Central American and South American groups in the total Hispanic population.

It has been estimated that by the year 2020, the U.S. population will include from 47 million to 54.3 million Hispanics (Dana, 1993b; Marin & Marin, 1991). The majority of Hispanics (approximately 86%) live in urban areas (Marin & Marin, 1991; U.S. Bureau of the Census, 2000); Table 4.2 lists the 10 U.S. cities with the highest percentages of Hispanic population in 2000. East Los Angeles, California, with a population that is 97% Hispanic, has the highest proportion of Hispanic population in the United States. The majority of U.S. cities with high percentages of Hispanics are found in two states, California and Texas.

Table 4.3 lists, in order, the 10 U.S. states with the largest Hispanic populations as of the 2000 U.S. Census. Leading this list is California, with approximately 11 million; Texas is second with about 6.7 million, followed by New York with almost 2.9 million. According to the U.S. Bureau of the Census (2000), the 10 states that experienced the largest increases in

Table 4.1   Hispanic or Latino Population by Type, 2000

Subject	Number	Percentage
Hispanic or Latino		
Total population	281,421,906	100.0
Hispanic or Latino (of any race)	35,305,818	12.5
Not Hispanic or Latino	246,116,088	87.5
Hispanic or Latino by type		
Hispanic or Latino (of any race)	35,305,818	100.0
Mexican	20,640,711	58.5
Puerto Rican	3,406,178	9.6
Cuban	1,241,685	3.5
Other Hispanic or Latino	10,017,244	28.4
Dominican (Dominican Republic)	764,945	2.2
Central American (excludes Mexican)	1,686,937	4.8
Costa Rican	68,588	0.2
Guatemalan	372,487	1.1
Honduran	217,569	0.6
Nicaraguan	177,684	0.5
Panamanian	91,723	0.3
Salvadoran	655,165	1.9
Other Central American	103,721	0.3
South American	1,353,562	3.8
Argentinean	100,864	0.3
Bolivian	42,068	0.1
Chilean	68,849	0.2
Colombian	470,684	1.3
Ecuadoran	260,559	0.7
Paraguayan	8,769	0.0
Peruvian	233,926	0.7
Uruguayan	18,804	0.1
Venezuelan	91,507	0.3
Other South American	57,532	0.2
All other Hispanic or Latino	6,211,800	17.6
Spaniard	100,135	0.3
Spanish	686,004	1.9
Spanish American	75,772	0.2
Not elsewhere classified	5,349,889	15.2

SOURCE: U.S. Bureau of the Census (2000, Summary File 1, Matrix PCT11).

numbers of Hispanics from 1990 to 2000 are California (increase of approximately 3.3 million), Texas (2.3 million), Florida (1.1 million), New York (526,000), Illinois (626,000), Arizona (607,000), New Jersey (377,000), Georgia (326,000), Colorado (311,000), and North Carolina (302,000). The majority of the members of four subgroups within the

Table 4.2   U.S. Cities With Highest Percentages of Hispanic Population, 2000

City	State	Percentage
East Los Angeles	California	97
Laredo	Texas	94
Brownsville	Texas	91
Hialeah	Florida	90
McAllen	Texas	80
El Paso	Texas	77
Santa Ana	California	76
El Monte	California	72
Oxnard	California	66
Miami	Florida	66

SOURCE: U.S. Bureau of the Census (2000).

Table 4.3   U.S. States With Largest Hispanic Populations, 2000

State	Number
California	11.0 million
Texas	6.7 million
New York	2.9 million
Florida	2.7 million
Illinois	1.5 million
Arizona	1.3 million
New Jersey	1.1 million
New Mexico	765,000
Colorado	736,000
Washington	442,000

SOURCE: U.S. Bureau of the Census (2000).

Hispanic population (Mexican Americans, Cubans, Puerto Ricans, and Dominicans) reside in four states: California, Texas, New York, and Florida. Most Mexican Americans live in southwestern states (Arizona, California, Colorado, New Mexico, and Texas); the majority of Cubans live in Florida (mainly in Miami); and the majority of Puerto Ricans and Dominicans live in New York and New Jersey. Other Hispanics of Central American and South American heritage reside mostly in New York City and San Francisco (Marin & Marin, 1991).

Socioeconomic Status

The 2000 U.S. Census found that the median household income for all Hispanic families was $33,565, well below the national median of $42,228 and the median for White families of $44,517. The same census revealed that the average annual income per household member in the Hispanic population was $12,158, in comparison with $24,951 for Whites, $22,688 for Asians and Pacific Islanders, and $15,007 for African Americans (U.S. Bureau of the Census, 2001, 2002a).

Among the three largest subgroups of Hispanics, families of Mexican origin residing in the United States reported the highest median household income level in 2002 ($33,574), followed by Puerto Rican families ($28,738) and Cuban families ($27,564). In the same year, the median household income for families of Central and South American origin was $37,512, which was still below the national median (i.e., $42,228) but higher than the median incomes for Mexican, Puerto Rican, and Cuban families (U.S. Bureau of the Census, 2002b). In 1999, approximately 7.8 million Hispanic individuals (22.6% of the total population in the United States) were living below the poverty level, in comparison with 12.4% of the total U.S. population and 9.1% of the White population (Bishaw & Iceland, 2003).

It should be noted that many Hispanic immigrants have come from countries where the proportion of the population living below the poverty level is substantially larger than the proportion of people subsisting at a similar level in the United States (Central Intelligence Agency, 2003). For example, in 1998, almost half (47%) the population of Venezuela was living below the poverty line, and in 1999, Bolivia (70%), El Salvador (48%), and Panama (37%) also had large proportions of their populations living in poverty. In 2000, half of the population of Peru was living below the poverty level; in 2001, the poverty figures for other Latin American countries were as follows: Argentina, 37%; Colombia, 55%; Ecuador, 70%; Nicaragua, 40%; Mexico, 50%; and Paraguay, 36%. In 2002, Guatemala reported that 75% of the country's population was living below the poverty line, the highest proportion among all Latin American countries. In 1997, Uruguay reported the lowest percentage of population below the poverty level (i.e., 6%) in all Latin American countries, followed by Chile (21%), Costa Rica (20.6%), and the Dominican Republic (25%). (It should be noted that the proportion in poverty reported by the Dominican Republic is extremely low in comparison with the 80% of people in Haiti living below the poverty level in 2002; the island of Hispaniola is divided between Haiti and the Dominican Republic.)

Terminology

In general, the term *Hispanic* refers to individuals of Latin American or Spanish heritage living in the United States; a person may be considered Hispanic if he or she speaks Spanish or is descended from a Spanish-language culture, or if he or she has a Spanish surname. Ruiz and Padilla

(1977) define Hispanics as all persons of "Spanish origin and descent." Marin and Marin (1991) provide a more inclusive definition: "individuals who reside in the United States and who were born in or trace the background of their families to one of the Spanish-speaking Latin American nations or Spain" (p. 1). These persons would include immigrants from Spain; Central American countries (e.g., Mexico, Panama, Costa Rica); South American countries (e.g., Venezuela, Colombia); and the Caribbean (e.g., Puerto Rico, Cuba) as well as their descendants.

Additional terms sometimes used to refer to Hispanics, both individually and as a group, include *Latino/a, Hispanic American, La Raza, Hispano/a, Spanish people,* and *Americano/a* (Comas-Diaz, 2001). (In Spanish, nouns are either masculine or feminine, and nouns that refer to persons take masculine or feminine form depending on whether they are applied to males or females. Thus, the noun *Latino* refers to a man and the noun *Latina* refers to a woman. Throughout this chapter, I use *o/a* on the ends of such nouns to indicate the forms for both men and women.) The term *Latino/a* carries the implication that the person referred to is from a Latin American country or of Latin American heritage, and, as Dana (1993b) notes, many Mexican Americans tend to prefer this term because it "does not signify the conqueror Spain" (p. 66). Clinicians who serve Hispanic clients should be aware, however, that in the 2000 U.S. Census, some Hispanics rejected the official adoption of the term *Latino,* arguing that it may be understood to include individuals from all countries with languages that originated in the Latin language, such as France and Italy (Borak, Fiellin, & Chemerynski, 2004). The term *Hispanic American* emphasizes that the person is not only of Latin American or Spanish descent but that he or she was born in the United States.

Currently, the literature suggests that most scholars prefer the term *Hispanic* and define it widely to include any person who labels him- or herself as such because he or she is from, or descended from others who were from, Spain, any South American country, any Central American country, or the Caribbean (Dana, 1993b; Ho, 1992; Marin & Marin, 1991; Ruiz, 1981). Clinicians should be aware that many people who consider themselves Hispanic do not speak Spanish, and that many individuals with Spanish surnames do not identify themselves as Hispanic, whether or not they speak Spanish. A therapist should never assume that someone is Hispanic based on that person's surname. For example, a woman with a Hispanic last name may be a non-Hispanic who is married to a Hispanic man. Also, as Borak et al. (2004) point out, the classification of persons as Hispanic on the basis of surnames has "often confused Hispanics with others who have Italian, Portuguese, or Filipino surnames" (p. 242). To determine a client's racial and ethnic identity, the best approach the therapist can take is to ask the client to describe his or her own identity using one or more of the racial categories described in the U.S. Census (as listed in

Box 2.1 in Chapter 2) and/or the census question about ethnicity (Hispanic versus non-Hispanic) discussed in Chapter 2.

The term *La Raza* (The Race) is used by many Spanish-speaking individuals who identify with or are actively involved in a movement devoted to ensuring equal opportunities and civil rights for Hispanics (Comas-Diaz, 2001). Persons who trace their family heritage to the Spanish *conquistadores* (conquerors) and to the Europeans who arrived in North America in the 15th century and occupied "what is known today as Mexico, California, Texas, Florida, New Mexico, and Arizona" (Comas-Diaz, 2001, p. 117) might describe themselves as *Hispanos/as*. Some may use the term *Spanish people* to describe individuals who speak Spanish, but, as Comas-Diaz (2001) notes, although this term is appropriate in reference to people from Spain (i.e., Spaniards), it is not an accurate way to refer to individuals from Latin American countries and the Caribbean. The term *Americano/a,* although usually used in the past by Spanish speakers to identify individuals "who are not of Hispanic/Latino extraction . . . has been used recently to designate Latinos living in the United States" (Comas-Diaz, 2001, p. 117). In addition, in my own clinical practice with Hispanic clients, I have found that some Hispanics call themselves *Americano/a* because they consider themselves as belonging to the "American continent."

The terms discussed briefly above are generally considered to be "generic" terms that clients from this culturally diverse group might use in describing their racial/ethnic identities. Comas-Diaz (2001, pp. 117–119) suggests that it is also important for practitioners to be aware of "specific or national terms" that Hispanics might use to describe themselves. As is true in the use of the generic terms, members of the culturally diverse group known as Hispanics may apply specific or national terms to themselves based on political and/or psychosocial factors, and clinicians should keep this in mind when providing mental health services to Hispanic clients. Among the specific or national terms that Comas-Diaz identifies are *Mexican, Mexican American, Chicano/a, Boricua, Nuyorican, Rican, Latinegro/a,* and *Caribeño.*

Among Hispanics, the term *Mexican* is usually used to designate an individual from the Republic of Mexico who comes to the United States to visit family members or to work. That is, a person of Mexican descent who was born in the United States or a Mexican immigrant who has become a U.S. citizen would not be called a Mexican; rather, such an individual might describe him- or herself as Mexican American. Therapists should be aware, however, that not all individuals of Mexican descent who were born in the United States identify themselves as Mexican American; as Comas-Diaz (2001) puts it, they may not identify with "a Mexican heritage but rather with a Spanish heritage (such as Hispanos) . . . [and] for those who do not view themselves as 'American' by choice, this designation is problematic" (p. 118). For these reasons, some American-born individuals of Mexican descent prefer to refer to themselves as Mexican rather than Mexican American.

The term *Chicano/a* is generally used to refer to an individual who is descended from poor, rural Mexicans who came to the United States during the 1930s and 1940s as seasonal migrant workers (Comas-Diaz, 2001). For this reason, the term may have negative connotations for some people from the Republic of Mexico and for some Mexican Americans. Some persons of Mexican descent, however, prefer to refer to themselves as *Chicano/a* because they do not consider themselves to be part of the mainstream U.S. culture and want to maintain their own cultural/ethnic identity in the United States.

Some individuals from the island of Puerto Rico, and some descendants of Puerto Ricans, refer to themselves as *Boricua* or *Rican*. *Boricua* is a Taino name that originated from the word *borinquen,* an old name for the island that today is known as Puerto Rico (Comas-Diaz, 2001). (The Taino were Indians who lived on several Caribbean islands, including those now known as Cuba, Hispaniola, and Puerto Rico, at the time Cristóbal Colón [Christopher Columbus] invaded those islands and practically eliminated the Taino during his "discovery of the New World.") Many individuals of Puerto Rican heritage prefer to be called Boricua rather than *Puerto Riqueño* (Puerto Rican) as a gesture of their rejection of Puerto Rico's current colonial status. Some second- and third-generation Puerto Ricans residing in the United States prefer to call themselves Rican, however (Comas-Diaz, 2001). Ricans have developed their own cultural identity by combining elements of the cultures of both Puerto Rico and the U.S. mainland. For example, whereas many Boricuas and *Puerto Riqueños* do not recognize the role of African influences in the history of the island of Puerto Rico, many Ricans emphasize their debt to these influences and identify to some degree with the African American community in the U.S. mainland (Comas-Diaz, 2001).

Nuyoricans are individuals of Puerto Rican descent who are born and grow up in New York City. As Comas-Diaz (2001) notes, the same pattern of naming is used for people of Puerto Rican heritage who are born in other large U.S. cities; for example, a *Chicagorican* is an individual of Puerto Rican ancestry who is born and raised in Chicago.

A *Latinegro/a* is someone of Hispanic heritage who is perceived by members of the Hispanic community as well as by other North Americans as "Black." Latinegros who are substantially involved with the African American community (e.g., through the acculturation phenomenon described in Chapter 2) are also sometimes referred to as *Afro Latinos* (Comas-Diaz, 2001). Finally, *Caribeño/a* is a term generally used to refer to someone of Caribbean island heritage (e.g., a person of Cuban, Dominican, Puerto Rican, or Jamaican descent). *Caribeños* also sometimes call themselves *Islanders*.

Perhaps the most important guideline for the clinician in regard to the above discussion is that he or she should not assume anything about the client's cultural identity or how the client prefers to refer to that identity. Rather, the therapist should ask the client what ethnic or cultural designation he or she prefers and then respect and value the client's self-designation. As Comas-Diaz (2001) notes, "The mediating factors in self-designation are gaining a voice and power to name one's identity and define one's reality" (p. 116).

Cultural Variables That May Affect Assessment and Treatment

Religious and Folk Beliefs

Many Hispanics hold religious and folk beliefs that are similar to those found among African Americans (Dana, 1993b; Ho, 1992; C. Martinez, 1993; Ruiz, 1981). Religious leaders such as priests (for Hispanics who are Roman Catholic) and ministers (for Protestant Hispanics) are key figures in the process of understanding and assisting Hispanic clients in dealing with their mental health problems. Some Hispanic clients may believe that mental health problems are caused by evil spirits, and so believe that the church, rather than a therapist, has the power to treat these problems (Ruiz, 1981). Some Hispanics believe that prayers will cure physical or mental health problems, and so they seek help from health care or mental health professionals only after they have exhausted all religious and folk remedies. In addition, some Hispanics believe that certain forms of behavior—such as *envidia* (envy) and *mal de ojo* (evil eye), which is said to result from excessive admiration and attention—can cause physical and mental health problems in others. Some might consult an *espiritista* (spiritualist), *curandero/a* (folk healer), or *brujo/a* (witch doctor) to resolve such problems. To enhance their ability to assess and treat Hispanic clients effectively, therapists should be familiar with the religious and folk beliefs among the Hispanics in the communities they serve. It is important to note, however, that therapists should not assume that all their Hispanic clients share such beliefs.

Machismo, Respeto, and *Marianismo*

In general, men tend to be dominant in Hispanic families, and this dominance includes direct sexual power over women. Among Hispanic men, the personal quality known as *machismo* is very important; the characteristics that make up *machismo* include physical strength, sexual attractiveness, masculinity, aggressiveness, and the ability to consume an excessive amount of alcohol without getting drunk (Comas-Diaz, 1988;

Comas-Diaz & Duncan, 1985). *Machismo* also denotes a sense of *respeto* (respect) from others. According to Comas-Diaz and Duncan (1985), in general, the term *respeto* among Hispanics refers to "the appropriate deferential behavior toward others on the basis of age, social position, economic status, and sex" (p. 465). In the context of *machismo, respeto* is seen in the submission of women and children to the authority of a man. In the context of interpersonal relationships, a Hispanic who shows *respeto* for authority figures (e.g., parents, elders) is considered *una persona bien educada* (a well-educated person), someone whose parents have taught him or her the importance of conducting social relationships *con respeto y dignidad* (with respect and dignity). If a child is described as *mal educado* (poorly educated), the implication in the Hispanic community is that the child's parents have not properly educated him or her concerning the respect with which others should be treated, particularly persons in positions of authority. As Ho (1992) notes, in the Hispanic community, an individual "could be illiterate and still be considered *una persona bien educada*" (p. 108; emphasis added) if he or she has good skills in human relationships and shows the proper *respeto* in the presence of others, particularly those in authority. Thus, if a Hispanic father tells a therapist, *"Mi hijo no tiene educación"* (literally, "My son does not have education"), he means that his son does not show him and other people in authority the proper amount of respect. A therapist who is unfamiliar with the concept of *respeto* in Hispanic culture is likely to misunderstand the father and emphasize a line of questioning dealing with the son's performance in school rather than begin to address the real issue.

Marianismo is a personal quality in women that is highly valued by many Hispanics; the characteristics that make up *marianismo* are submissiveness, obedience, dependence, timidness, docility, sentimentality, gentleness, and virginity until marriage (Comas-Diaz, 1988; Comas-Diaz & Duncan, 1985; Martinez, 1988; Ruiz, 1981). Under the ideals of *marianismo,* women are expected to devote their time to cooking, cleaning, caring for their children, and other activities that benefit their husbands and families. *Marianismo* is named for the Virgin Mary, the embodiment of *marianismo* characteristics and a highly revered figure among Hispanic Catholics (Comas-Diaz & Duncan, 1985). As some scholars have observed, the phenomenon of *marianismo* illustrates two ideas about women commonly found in Hispanic cultures: that women are spiritually superior to men and that women are the individuals who endure all the suffering caused by men (Comas-Diaz, 1988; Comas-Diaz & Duncan, 1985).

When Hispanic immigrants first arrive in the United States from their countries of origin, where *machismo* and *marianismo* are accepted as defining men's and women's proper social roles, family members' differing attempts to continue the traditions of *machismo* and *marianismo* may lead to conflicts (e.g., marital problems between husband and wife, conflicts between children and parents). In such cases, rather than attempting to change the clients' attitudes through psychotherapy, the most practical approach for the therapist is to present concrete examples that will lead the clients to understand why many of the elements of *machismo* and *marianismo* are not considered socially acceptable in the United States.

Familismo

Among most Hispanics, family relationships are paramount (Ho, 1992; Ruiz, 1981). Thus, therapists should be aware that any attempt to conduct psychotherapy with a Hispanic client without the involvement of the client's family (both nuclear and extended family) is bound to fail. Hispanics generally turn to family members during times of stress and economic difficulties, and those who seek help from mental health professionals often consult first with family members. This is particularly true in the case of more traditional Hispanic families, in comparison with more acculturated families (L. Comas-Diaz, personal communication, January 1994). This consultation with family members sometimes involves individuals in the extended family network who are tied to the person seeking help through special relationships rather than by blood, such as godparents and friends.

Unlike in African American families, role flexibility within the family is generally not rewarded in the Hispanic community. In the traditional Hispanic home, the father is the head of the family, the wife takes care of the children, and children must behave according to the father's rules.

Personalismo

In general, Hispanics value warmth over distance in interpersonal relationships (Bernal & Gutierrez, 1988; Ho, 1992; C. Martinez, 1993), and they tend to expect *personalismo* (personalism) in their interactions with mental health professionals. Hispanic clients may feel uncomfortable if they perceive that they are being treated as "things" or that a therapist views their problems as "abstractions," or if there is too much physical distance between client and therapist. Hispanics in general may sense a lack of warmth from others when a handshake is not accompanied by a hug, or when they feel that someone is avoiding sharing "personal" information in conversation.

Hispanic clients' desire for *personalismo* in the therapeutic relationship may directly affect their selection of therapists and thus indirectly affect the process of psychotherapy with members of this group. For example, a Hispanic client might select a therapist not on the basis of the therapist's professional credentials but rather on the basis of the therapist's ability to share personal information about him- or herself (excluding very intimate information) with the client, such as preferences in food, music, and hobbies. Such sharing by the therapist may enable the Hispanic client to develop a certain level of trust in the therapist and thus confidence in the client-therapist relationship. Therapists should be aware, however, that not all Hispanic clients are concerned mostly with personalism when selecting therapists; many Hispanic professionals, for example, are likely to give equal if not more weight to mental health practitioners' professional credentials (L. Comas-Diaz, personal communication, January 1994).

One expression of *personalismo* that a therapist may experience during the process of psychotherapy with a Hispanic client is the client's offering of gifts as a way of expressing gratitude for the services provided. If the therapist repeatedly rejects such gifts, he or she may fail to meet the client's expectations of *personalismo* in the client-therapist relationship, and this could result in the client's dropping out of therapy. Therapists who work with Hispanic clients need to recognize and explain to their clients who bring them gifts the conditions under which it is appropriate for a therapist to accept such gifts (e.g., at Christmastime, when a Mexican American client presents the therapist with a wooden cup made in Mexico) and the conditions under which it is not (e.g., when the gift is offered as a form of payment for therapy).

Individualismo

The American ideal of individualism emphasizes competition and the ability of the individual to achieve economic and professional success without assistance from other members of the community (Sandoval & De La Roza, 1986). The Hispanic concept of *individualismo,* in contrast, emphasizes what is *unique* about each member of the community and how this uniqueness leads to cooperation among community members rather than to competition (Canino & Canino, 1993). Among Hispanics, *individualismo* means that everyone has something to offer to the community.

The concepts of *individualismo* and *familismo* are related in that an individual is expected to share with all members of the family the characteristic, skill, or talent that makes him or her unique (e.g., a mother's ability to cook traditional dishes is shared by all members of her family). Therapists who work with Hispanic clients should take care to explore these clients' sense of *individualismo.* This is particularly important when a client feels that his or her *individualismo* is threatened by the therapist's suggestions for changes in the client's behaviors.

Fatalismo

Fatalismo (fatalism), or the belief that a divine providence governs the world and that an individual cannot control or prevent adversity, is a common characteristic among Hispanics (Ho, 1992; Neff & Hoppe, 1993). This fatalism might be interpreted in at least two different ways. First, it could indicate a sense of vulnerability and lack of control in the presence of adverse events, as well as the individual's feeling that such events are "waiting" to affect his or her life. This type of *fatalismo* can have a negative effect on the treatment of Hispanic clients, particularly when the goals of therapy compete with the client's fatalistic perception that no protections exist against his or her problems. Second, fatalism may be interpreted as an adaptive response to the uncontrollable life situations that many Hispanics (and members of other non-Anglo-American groups) experience in U.S. society (Neff & Hoppe, 1993). This kind of fatalism is often associated with involvement in religious activities, which provide the individual with both personal and social resources. Thus, in the treatment of a fatalistic Hispanic client, the therapist should screen carefully to determine which type of fatalism the client is displaying. If the client's *fatalismo* is of the first type, the therapist may want to encourage the client to become involved in religious activities to minimize the fatalism's negative impact (in the sense of the client's perceived lack of control in the presence of adverse events) on the treatment process (Neff & Hoppe, 1993).

Perceptions of Skin Color

In the United States, African Americans and Whites constitute the two major racial denominations. Among Hispanics, in contrast, a wide range of racial denominations exists (Ramos-McKay, Comas-Diaz, & Rivera, 1988), particularly in the cases of Puerto Ricans, Cubans, and Dominicans. For example, many Hispanics refer to other Hispanics who have dark skins as *morenos* or *prietos;* those with olive skin or dark complexions are called *trigueños.* Hispanics with light skin or kinky hair are known as *grifos, jabaos,* or *albinos;* people who have Indian features are called *indios.*

Among many Hispanics, a person's position in society is much more a function of class (e.g., low socioeconomic status versus high socioeconomic status) than of color. Many Hispanics often say that "green [i.e., the color of the dollar] is the most important color." Thus, Hispanic immigrants whose socioeconomic status was low in their countries of origin understand that any discrimination they experienced there stemmed from their class status, regardless of their skin color. When these individuals enter the United States, however, they experience a different kind of discrimination in which their skin color is an important variable. For example, many *morenos* or *prietos* do not classify themselves as Black or African American, yet when they enter the United States, they find that they are perceived as Black. Many Hispanic families include both *morenos* or *prietos* and *grifos* or *jabaos* (whose skin color resembles that of Anglo-Americans) among their members, and such families may experience a dramatic crisis of identity when they see how differently their members of varying skin colors are treated in U.S. society.

Given that many Hispanics do not emphasize skin color in making racial/ethnic classifications, therapists who work with Hispanic clients should avoid using traditional race denominations to categorize those clients. The therapist should also explore with the client any preference concerning skin color in the client's family and how this preference may affect the assessment and treatment of the client. For example, as Ho (1992) notes, some Hispanic parents (particularly Mexican American parents) prefer that their children have light skin color because the parents believe that "if one looks and acts European, one is more acceptable" in American society (p. 105). As Ho observes, darker children raised in a family where lighter skin color is considered desirable may experience serious self-identity conflicts. The preference for lighter-skinned children found among some Hispanic parents might be a function of acculturation (S. Z. Ramirez, personal communication, January 1994), thus it is also important that the therapist conduct an assessment of acculturation (e.g., using one of the scales listed in Table 8.1 in Chapter 8) and integrate the information gained into the client's overall assessment and treatment.

Being Insane Versus Being Mentally Ill

As Dana (1993b) notes, many Hispanics distinguish between having a mental disorder (*enfermedad mental*) and being insane (*loco*). The former terminology is used to describe a less severe problem; the person may be said to be suffering from a *crisis nerviosa* or *ataque de nervios* (i.e., a nervous crisis). In contrast, a person who is described as *loco* has more severe symptoms, possibly showing a complete loss of control and/or withdrawal requiring hospitalization (e.g., schizophrenia or major depression). A Hispanic who perceives him- or herself as having a mental disorder or mental illness is likely to seek help from friends, relatives, and folk healers rather than from mental health professionals. Therefore, when a Hispanic brings a relative to a mental health clinic for help, the therapist should keep in mind that other members of the family may consider the client to be *loco*—that is, seriously disturbed.

The First Session

Scholars have offered several specific guidelines for therapists to facilitate their first encounters with Hispanic clients (Bernal & Gutierrez, 1988; Dana, 1993b; Ho, 1992; C. Martinez, 1988, 1993; Ramos-McKay et al., 1988; Ruiz, 1981; Santiago-Rivera, Arredondo, & Gallardo-Cooper, 2002). These guidelines are summarized below.

Exploring the Client's Level of Acculturation

The therapist should always consider conducting an assessment of both internal and external processes of acculturation during the first session with any Hispanic client (Dana, 1993b; Flores, Tschann, Marin, & Pantoja, 2004; Ho, 1992; Norris, Ford, & Bova, 1996; Ramirez, Paniagua, Linskey, & O'Boyle, 1993; Ramirez, Wassef, Paniagua, Linskey, & O'Boyle, 1994). This is particularly important when the clinical case involves conflict between husband and wife or when the identified client is an adolescent (Bernal & Gutierrez, 1988; Flores et al., 2004). For example, in their investigation of the potential effects of acculturation on marital conflicts in a group of Mexican American husbands and wives, Flores et al. (2004) found that "more acculturated husbands and wives experience more direct marital conflicts than [do] less acculturated husbands and wives" (p. 49).

Among traditional Hispanics, an important value is that women should not have the same freedom and autonomy as men; thus, the ideals of *marianismo* and *machismo* are strongly reinforced in many Hispanic families (Comas-Diaz & Duncan, 1985). The process of acculturation may change this value, however, and so the therapist must determine the degree of impact that different levels of acculturation may have on a given marital relationship. A therapist who asserts during the first session with a Hispanic client that a wife should have the same freedom and independence as her husband displays a lack of understanding of the impact this particular value has for Hispanic families; such an error is likely to lead to attrition.

In addition, in many traditional Hispanic families, a female adolescent is expected to introduce a young man to her parents before the parents will consent to her dating the young man. Dating is sometimes a complex process, including the participation of parents or other relatives (e.g., uncles, aunts) as chaperones. American adolescents generally do not accept the kinds of restrictions that traditional Hispanic families impose on the dating process. Thus, an acculturated Hispanic teenager living with family members who hold traditional Hispanic values can create a "family problem" when her dating behavior differs from her parents' expectations (for an illustrative case, see Bernal & Gutierrez, 1988, pp. 250–252). The parents in such a case might report to the therapist that their daughter "became very depressed" (including diminished interest or pleasure in most activities, significant weight loss, and suicidal ideation) when she was told that she would not be allowed to date without formal approval from her parents. At this point, a therapist who is knowledgeable about Hispanic culture should quickly realize that the young woman is not meeting her parents' cultural expectations regarding dating. In this example, the young woman is *more acculturated* to the American way of dating than are her parents (Martinez, 1986). During the first session, the therapist should carefully explore the differences in levels of acculturation among family members before he or she attempts to give any advice regarding how to solve the "family problem" (which could be, in the final analysis, a cultural problem).

Given the potential importance of acculturation in the manifestation of mental problems, the therapist should screen each member of a Hispanic family for acculturation level in the first session (see Chapter 8 for a summary of acculturation scales recommended for use with Hispanic clients). In subsequent sessions, the therapist should emphasize general discussion of the concept of acculturation and how the family interprets this concept. In fact, such discussion may serve as one of the basic elements of a treatment plan for the Hispanic client, with an emphasis on family therapy.

Formalismo Versus *Personalismo*

As noted above, many Hispanics expect *personalismo* in their relationships with others, including personal contacts and personal attention. However, the therapist should avoid personalism during the first session with a Hispanic client and instead emphasize formality. The therapist can signal formal consideration and respect to the Hispanic client in two ways. The first of these is to avoid placing the relationship on an informal, first-name level during the first session. For example, when client Juan Garcia arrives for his first session, the clinician should say, "Good morning, Mr. Garcia," rather than "Hi, Juan." If the clinician is communicating in Spanish, he or she should use formal personal pronouns (e.g., *usted,* the formal *you,* rather than *tú,* the informal *you*) and formal verb forms (Martinez, 1986). For example, the therapist should say to a Hispanic client during the first session, *"¿Cómo está usted?"* or simply *"¿Cómo está?"* (using the formal form of the verb *estar* [to be] in asking, "How are you?") rather than *"¿Cómo estás?"* or *"¿Cómo estás tú?"* (using the informal form of *estar*). English does not make such distinctions between formal and informal modes of address, but clinicians can easily show similar formality when communicating in English by always addressing Hispanic clients by their last names along with the courtesy title of *Mr., Mrs.,* or *Miss* (e.g., "Mr. Garcia, you said that . . ." instead of "Juan, you said that . . ."). If the therapist is communicating with the client in Spanish, he or she should also use the client's last name and address the client as *señor* (Mr.), *señora* (Mrs.), or *señorita* (Miss). Among Hispanics, the title of courtesy *señor* is used with adult males regardless of marital status, and *señora* is generally used to address women who are married. A *señorita* is a woman who is at least 15 years old, not married, and considered a *virgen* (i.e., without any history of a sexual relationship with a man).

The second way in which the therapist can demonstrate during the first session that he or she will pay proper respect to the Hispanic client's concerns is by keeping the conversation formal and strictly related to the mental problem that has brought the client in for treatment. Thus, the therapist should not say something like the following: "Hi, Juan. My understanding is that you feel sad and need help. By the way, Juan, my notes indicate that your birthday was last week. Did you have a good time?" Such remarks may offend the client, both because the therapist's mode of address is inappropriately informal and because they are unrelated to the client's problem. It should be noted, however, that Hispanic clients may expect to engage in this kind of "chat" (*la plática*) after proper formal amenities have been observed (Martinez, 1986).

Exploring Magical Explanations for Mental Problems

Many Hispanics believe that mental problems might be caused by bad spirits or by witchcraft and that such problems may be resolved with the assistance of an *espiritista* or a *curandero/a*. Sometimes, Hispanic clients may combine the expertise of such folk healers with the expertise of mental health professionals when they seek treatment for mental problems (Martinez, 1986). Therapists should be aware that Hispanic clients who believe in spiritualism may not want to acknowledge that they do in the first session with a therapist (L. Comas-Diaz, personal communication, January 1994).

During the first session with a Hispanic client, the therapist needs to explore, understand, and accept the client's magical or spiritual explanatory model of mental problems for two reasons. First, the therapist's willingness to explore, understand, and accept the client's magical or spiritual interpretation may enhance the therapeutic relationship and thus the actual process of psychotherapy. Second, the therapist may find that he or she can use the client's explanatory model to produce positive behavioral changes. For example, the therapist might indicate to a Hispanic client who maintains such beliefs that the therapist will be pleased to invite the *espiritista* or *curandero/a* to subsequent sessions. This is an especially good strategy for a therapist who plans to conduct group therapy with Hispanic clients who share the same beliefs, because such folk healers generally provide their services in group settings (as opposed to treating individual cases).

As Martinez (1986) notes, if a therapist plans to work with Hispanic clients, he or she should understand these beliefs, but, more important, he or she should also be "prepared to function within both systems" (p. 80)— that is, the folk belief system and the scientific system. If the therapist emphasizes the "scientific" explanation of mental problems, this can cause conflict for the client who holds strong beliefs regarding the role of spirits and the function of the *curandero/a* in the solution of his or her problem (Dana, 1993b; Ho, 1992). If the therapist prefers to deal with the problem from a purely scientific standpoint, it would be appropriate for him or her to refer the client to another practitioner with training (and interest) in the delivery of mental health services to Hispanic clients. (For specific guidelines regarding a cross-cultural curriculum for mental health professionals interested in serving Hispanic clients, see Garza-Trevino, Ruiz, & Venegas-Samuels, 1997.)

It should be noted here that Hispanics do not tend to use witch doctors, or *brujos/as* in the same way they use *curanderos/as*. In general, Hispanics believe that *brujos/as* use the power of the devil to resolve problems; *curanderos/as,* in contrast, use the power of God, in a spiritual sense (I. Cuéllar, personal communication, January 1994). Practitioners should keep this distinction in mind when communicating with Hispanic clients.

Interviewing the Father Separately

When the problem that brings a Hispanic family to therapy involves family conflicts in which children are considered (by parents) to be at the center, the therapist should interview the father alone for a few minutes during the first session. By doing so, the therapist demonstrates his or her recognition of the father's authority in the family. Because of the high value Hispanics attach to the father's authority, this brief meeting signals to the family that the therapist is sensitive to cultural variables among Hispanics and that he or she is ready to respect and support those values during the course of therapy. It is important to note, however, that the therapist should not use this approach with an acculturated Hispanic family, as the mother is likely to perceive that she is being left out of the assessment and treatment process (I. Cuéllar, personal communication, January 1994). Clearly, the therapist needs to assess family members' levels of acculturation *before* attempting to implement this particular guideline.

Giving the Impression That Medication Could Be Recommended

Many Hispanic clients expect the therapist to provide them with medication during the first session. The therapist must first explore whether the client believes that medication is an important treatment for his or her problem. If the client believes he or she needs medication but the therapist disagrees, the therapist's next step is to explain to the client the reasons medication is not warranted. The therapist should also inform the client if there is any likelihood that medication may be used later (Bernal & Gutierrez, 1988; Ramos-McKay et al., 1988).

Offering a Tentative Solution to the Presenting Problem

Many Hispanic clients expect that the first session will consist of a combination of assessment ("What is the problem?") and treatment ("Here is what should be done to deal with this problem"); they expect some immediate help from the therapist and at least a tentative solution to their problems (Ho, 1992). Thus, at the end of the first session with a Hispanic client, it is important that the therapist provide suggestions or recommendations that the client can use to deal quickly with the problem at home. If the therapist informs the client at the end of the first session that he or she wants to gather more information before recommending a therapeutic approach, the result may be attrition (i.e., the client may not come back for therapy).

Understanding Different Types of Hispanic Families

In the assessment, diagnosis, and treatment of Hispanic clients, it is particularly important that clinicians remember that not all Hispanic families are the same. Therapists must take cultural variations into consideration as they respond to the individual families seeking mental health services. In relation to this guideline, Santiago-Rivera et al. (2002) have identified at least four kinds of Hispanic families: intact families, single-parent families, bicultural families, and immigrant families (see also Paniagua, 2004).

Clients from *intact families* are often less acculturated relative to other Hispanic clients; these families are patriarchal in structure, and they generally consider the cultural value of *respeto* toward parents and the elderly as crucial to family harmony. When working with clients from this type of family, the therapist needs to consider carefully the levels of acculturation of all family members, because it is likely that not all members share the same view of tradition that might be expected in a family structure viewed as intact (i.e., with zero or little influence from other cultures). For example, adolescents living in intact Hispanic families are generally more acculturated than their parents, and when these adolescents reject their parents' traditional norms (e.g., in areas such as dating), relational conflicts may arise that could result in erroneous diagnoses of the adolescents, particularly diagnoses of oppositional defiant disorder (American Psychiatric Association, 2000; Paniagua, 2000; see also Box 10.1 in Chapter 10). Clinicians who provide mental health services to intact Hispanic families should also expect that these clients will place relatively high emphasis on the cultural variables of *machismo* and *marianismo*. Clinicians who are unfamiliar with Hispanic culture may erroneously diagnose Hispanic women who display the characteristics associated with *marianismo* (e.g., submissiveness; obedience; and dependence on husband, parents, and other significant members of the family) as having a dependent personality disorder (see American Psychiatric Association, 2000, pp. 721–725; Paniagua, 2000).

When working with Hispanic clients from *single-parent families,* clinicians should consider the clients' views of *familismo* (e.g., does the client who is a child of a single parent perceive his or her relationship with the parent as paramount?) and the clients' perceptions of support from their extended families (see Chapter 2). According to Santiago-Rivera et al. (2002, p. 82), in the case of Hispanic single mothers, it is particularly important that therapists screen carefully for symptoms of depression, sense of isolation from the community, poor general health, and sense of guilt related to these women's perceptions that they have failed to achieve the traditional (intact) Hispanic family structure.

The most important guideline for therapists to follow when working with Hispanic clients from *bicultural families* is to consider the clinical ramifications of accurately distinguishing *acculturated* bicultural families from *cross-cultural* bicultural families (Santiago-Rivera et al., 2002). In the case of acculturated bicultural families, different levels of acculturation among family members may result in significant intergenerational and intercultural conflicts. Clients from cross-cultural bicultural families may also report significant conflicts among family members, leading to diagnoses of one or more of the mental disorders defined in the *DSM-IV-TR* (American Psychiatric Association, 2000), but these conflicts may be associated with intermarriages among members within the Hispanic community (e.g., between individuals of Cuban heritage and Puerto Rican heritage) or among ethnic/racial groups (e.g., between African Americans and Mexican Americans) rather than with varying levels of acculturation within the family. In order to provide culturally sensitive mental health services to clients from these two variants of Hispanic bicultural families, the clinician must understand the roles of the specific cultural variables that can lead to conflicts in these relationships.

In the case of Hispanic *immigrant families,* clinicians should distinguish between clients who came to the United States voluntarily and those who came only under pressure from family members (e.g., children and adolescents often immigrate involuntarily, when their parents or other relatives make the decision to move to the United States). Leaving one's country of origin may in itself be a significantly stressful event, even for an individual who immigrates voluntarily, and clinicians should attend to this possibility when serving Hispanic immigrant families, particularly when the clients have entered the United States illegally or as refugees. Involuntary immigration may result in high levels of stress not only for the individuals who have been forced to immigrate, but for their loved ones who made the decision to immigrate. Such stress may result in significant symptoms leading to a diagnosis of one or more of the mental disorders described in the *DSM-IV-TR,* including psychiatric disorders within the categories of anxiety, disruptive, and mood disorders (American Psychiatric Association, 2000). Therapists should be particularly aware of the possibility of high stress in immigrant children and adolescents, who have often been separated from their friends, boyfriends, girlfriends, and other significant persons in their lives by the move to the United States.

Conducting Psychotherapy

The guidelines summarized below are based on recommendations for psychotherapy with Hispanic clients offered by Comas-Diaz and Duncan (1985), Dana (1993b), Bernal and Gutierrez (1988), Ho (1992), Martinez (1986, 1988, 1993), Ramos-McKay et al. (1988), and Ruiz (1981).

Talking About Spiritual Issues

With all forms of therapies, Hispanic clients tend to expect the therapist to talk about "spiritual factors" that may cause emotional problems (including the *susto*, or a magical fright; the *mal puesto*, or hex; and the *mal de ojo*, or evil eye). As noted earlier, during the first session with a Hispanic client, the therapist should explore the client's beliefs about spiritual issues and how these beliefs may control the way the client thinks and acts. When conducting psychotherapy in subsequent sessions, the therapist should use this information to facilitate the client's assessment and treatment.

Using More *Personalismo* and Less *Formalismo*

Although the therapist should emphasize formality in the first session with a Hispanic client, as discussed above, during the psychotherapy process the Hispanic client generally expects less *formalismo* and more *personalismo,* including relatively close physical proximity between client and therapist, handshaking, and discussion of personal issues by the therapist.

Recommended Modalities of Therapy

Family Therapy

Therapists should consider family therapy as the first therapeutic approach with all Hispanic clients, particularly those from immigrant families. Most Hispanics prefer family therapy because of the importance they place on *familismo* and the extended family. Therapists should expect that Hispanic clients will include nonbiologically related members of their extended families (such as close friends and godparents) in family therapy sessions.

When the therapist has determined that differences in the levels of acculturation among family members are relatively great (e.g., as measured by one or more of the acculturation scales discussed in Chapter 8), it is important that he or she discuss this fact with the family members, using examples that all of them can understand. In doing so, the therapist should emphasize that a person's "being acculturated" does not mean that he or she rejects *familismo.* For example, in the case of an acculturated Hispanic daughter who is having "family problems" because of her parents' disapproval of her approach to dating, the therapist might say to her parents, "Mr. and Mrs. Martinez, I understand your concerns. It may help, however, if we talk about the way adolescents date in this country and how this way of dating does not mean that a female adolescent (like your daughter) *is not really concerned* about her family." The therapist should discuss the differences between the values held by traditional Hispanic families and the new values acquired by later generations (e.g., children of recent immigrant parents) during family therapy.

Group Therapy

Group therapy is recommended with Hispanic clients, but therapists who use this form of therapy should emphasize a problem-focused approach. In addition, several guidelines are often recommended in the literature concerning the work therapists should do prior to scheduling group therapy with Hispanic clients (Martinez, 1986). For example, if the therapist is bilingual and decides to conduct group therapy in Spanish, he or she must keep in mind that although the grammar of Spanish is generally shared across those countries in which the native and official language is Spanish (e.g., Puerto Rico, Cuba, Dominican Republic, Mexico), there are many variants in the ways Spanish-speaking people use Spanish in daily conversation. Thus, the therapist should tell the clients that although the group therapy sessions will be conducted in Spanish, in some cases, speakers may need to explain the meanings of particular words, phrases, or sentences they use to other members of the group.

In addition, therapists should be aware that group therapy with Hispanic clients should not necessarily be conducted in Spanish (Martinez, 1986). Acculturated Hispanics may have problems understanding Spanish, either because they never learned it (as is the case with many U.S.-born Hispanics) or because they have not used it for a long time. Thus, it is important that therapists planning to conduct group therapy with Hispanic clients screen those clients for level of acculturation, including proficiency in both English and Spanish (see Table 2.3 in Chapter 2).

The clients in any given therapy group should share the same level of acculturation (Martinez, 1986). Mixing acculturated and nonacculturated clients, who are likely to hold differing values and beliefs, may lead to confusion and conflict as the group members discuss how to handle particular problems. For example, the views of recent nonacculturated immigrants who hold traditional values regarding dating, the role of the mother, *machismo,* and so on, are likely to conflict with the views of more acculturated Hispanics. The therapist may find it helpful to use the Brief Acculturation Scale (described in Chapter 2) to screen Hispanic clients before including them in any therapy group.

Therapists who conduct group therapy (or any other form of therapy) with Hispanic clients should master the pronunciation of Spanish names. As Martinez (1986) observes, when a therapist pronounces the name of a Hispanic client correctly, this simple event can indicate to the client that the therapist is interested in the client and concerned about his or her problems. Therapists who do not speak Spanish should practice saying their Hispanic clients' names aloud *before* the first group therapy session. They should avoid asking, "How do you say your first and last name?" (*"¿Cómo usted pronuncia su nombre y su apedillo?"*) of any client during the first group therapy session.

The therapist should let all members in a Hispanic therapy group know that they can expect a certain amount of flexibility, particularly in the areas of punctuality and attendance (Martinez, 1986). As Sue and Sue (2003) point out, many Hispanic clients emphasize *events* (e.g., social contacts with friends before attending a therapy session) rather than the *clock* (the assumption that clients should arrive "on time" or early for group therapy). Therapists should keep this tendency in mind when programming any interventions with Hispanic clients.

Behavioral Approaches

Behavioral approaches to psychotherapy (e.g., behavior therapy, cognitive-behavior therapy, applied behavior analysis; see Paniagua & Baer, 1981) are characterized by an emphasis on experimental (empirical) analysis of the success of behavioral interventions in producing behavioral changes and the assessment of these changes using reliable measures. Such approaches do not emphasize the potential impacts that race and ethnicity may have during the assessment and treatment of problem behaviors. The overall assumption in behavioral approaches is that the effectiveness of behavioral interventions should be generalizable across racial and ethnic groups. Systematic desensitization and social-skills training are examples of empirically tested behavioral interventions that scholars have recommended in the treatment of Hispanic clients (Jenkins & Ramsey, 1991). Despite empirical findings regarding the effectiveness of these techniques, therapists who use them with Hispanic clients should remember the following guidelines.

The goal of systematic desensitization is to eliminate anxiety that occurs in the presence of certain environmental events (Paniagua & Baer, 1981). The therapist may enhance the effectiveness of this treatment with a Hispanic client by using Hispanic scenes (e.g., "Imagine that you are in a Mexican restaurant") and by speaking with a Spanish accent in describing those scenes (Jenkins & Ramsey, 1991).

The main goal of social-skills training is to teach a client how to be appropriately assertive in social interactions (Lange & Jakubowski, 1976).

In the absence of any attention to cultural variables, this technique may be inappropriate for Hispanic clients when the goal of intervention is to teach family members, for example, to deal with conflicts between an adolescent and parents, conflicts between husband and wife associated with the wife's attempts to be assertive, and other situations in which the authority of the father or husband cannot be questioned. The value that Hispanics place on *respeto, machismo, marianismo,* and *familismo* might *discourage* assertive behaviors in both male and female Hispanic clients (Comas-Diaz & Duncan, 1985; Soto, 1983). For example, in many traditional Hispanic families, children and adolescents are not allowed to argue with their parents, and children are expected to display respect toward their fathers. If a therapist attempts to teach a Hispanic teenage girl assertive behaviors to manage family conflicts between the girl and her parents (e.g., encouraging her to say to her father, "You don't want me to date Juan, but I will date him anyway"), the parents may see this as a violation of one of their fundamental cultural values—namely, that the child must always show properly respectful behavior toward the father.

Similarly, a Hispanic woman who holds beliefs consistent with the ideals of *marianismo* and *machismo* would not feel comfortable (and might drop out of therapy) if the therapist attempts to teach her to use very assertive behaviors toward her husband (e.g., "You should tell your husband exactly what you think about him. You should be able to express your feelings openly"; or "Today, I will teach you how to reject orders from your husband"). Comas-Diaz and Duncan (1985) recommend that therapists who teach assertive behaviors to Hispanic clients should emphasize that it is important that they clearly recognize the authority of the father or husband *before* they express themselves assertively. For example, instead of teaching a woman "how to reject orders from her husband," the therapist might teach her the importance of acknowledging the authority of her husband along with stating her own feelings (e.g., "With all the respect that you deserve, I feel/believe that I would prefer to visit my family this week"; Comas-Diaz & Duncan, 1985, p. 469). In this way, she can demonstrate *respeto* toward her husband and still make her opinions known.

Medication

Mental health professionals who do not like to recommend the use of medications for their clients usually take this stance for one of two reasons. Some simply do not believe in the effectiveness of drug therapy. Others do believe in the therapeutic effects of medication, but they are not physicians (e.g., psychologists, social workers) and so must depend on the schedules and treatment regimens that physicians (e.g., psychiatrists) prescribe for their clients. As noted above, however, many Hispanic clients expect to receive medication for the treatment of their mental problems. This is particularly true in the case of Mexican American clients (Martinez, 1986). If the therapist does not mention medication during the process of psychotherapy, a Hispanic client may assume that the therapist is not a "good healer," and he or she may not come back for subsequent therapy sessions.

Because many (although not all) Hispanic clients expect to receive medication, therapists should be aware that a large set of empirical data is available concerning drugs that may be effective in the management (not necessarily treatment) of certain mental problems, such as tricyclic antidepressants in the management of depression (Joyce & Paykel, 1989). This is particularly true concerning the use of these antidepressants with clients from the four cultural groups discussed in this book (Silver, Poland, & Lin, 1993).

Regardless of therapists' attitudes toward the use of medication, those who work with Hispanic clients should be aware that recommending drugs for clients who are expecting them during therapy may result in a "placebo effect" (i.e., the client perceives a positive change, even when the medication is not actually effective, simply because the client expects the drug to help). Thus, therapists who work with Hispanic clients may want to consider meeting these clients' cultural expectations regarding medication if they believe the placebo effect will be beneficial for the clients (e.g., the mental problems will become less severe over time).

The following are five additional guidelines concerning the use of medication to manage mental disorders in Hispanic clients:

1. The therapist should ask the client directly about how he or she expects to benefit from the medication; that is, does the client expect that the medication will "cure" the problem or help to manage it?

2. If the therapist is not a medical doctor, he or she must be sure to consult with a psychiatrist regarding the most appropriate medication for the target mental disorder. (Psychiatrists have a higher level of training and expertise in this area than do physicians in other specialties or general practice.)

3. The therapist should use a checklist to screen for the possibility of short-term and long-term side effects, and should discuss these effects with the client *each time* he or she returns for therapy. If the client reports side effects, the therapist should discuss them with the person prescribing the medication.

4. The therapist should keep in mind that although medication can help in the management of a mental disorder, it will not cure the disorder.

5. The therapist should be aware of the tendency among clients to rely exclusively on medication and ignore other aspects of therapy.

Music Therapy and Cuento *Therapy*

When a Hispanic client feels uncomfortable discussing particular problems with the therapist, music therapy may allow the client to express him- or herself *indirectly.* The type of Hispanic music known as *plena* can help a client to communicate about current events, *salsa* music emphasizes the struggle for survival, and the *bolero* deals with the nature of relationships. In the case of Hispanic children, *cuento* (storytelling) therapy may be useful. In such therapy, children express themselves by interpreting readings presented by the therapist.

Avoiding Insight-Oriented and Rational-Emotive Therapies

In general, insight-oriented psychotherapy emphasizes internal conflicts and "blames" the client for his or her own problems. This conflicts with the belief of many Hispanics that the problems in their lives emerge because of external conflicts with the environment and other people. Rational-emotive therapy is an argumentative and/or logistical talk therapy that includes concepts that compete with the Hispanic cultural phenomenon of *machismo,* thus it is inappropriate for the treatment of many Hispanic clients.

5

Guidelines for the Assessment and Treatment of Asian Clients

In the 2000 U.S. Census, "Asian" and "Native Hawaiian and other Pacific Islander" were considered two distinct races (Grieco & Cassidy, 2001; for definitions of these races, see Box 2.1 in Chapter 2). Clinicians, however, should be aware that the current literature concerning the assessment, diagnosis, and treatment of clients from culturally diverse groups generally makes no distinction between Asians and Native Hawaiians and other Pacific Islanders. Instead, the generic term *Asian* is used to designate three major subgroups in the U.S. population (Chung, Kim, & Abreu, 2004; Iwamasa, 2003; Kim, Brenner, Liang, & Asay, 2003; Mollica, 1989; Mollica & Lavelle, 1988; Sodowsky, Kwan, & Pannu, 1995; Sue & Sue, 1987, 2003): Asian Americans (Japanese, Chinese, Filipinos, Asian Indians, and Koreans), Asian Pacific Islanders (Hawaiians, Samoans, and Guamanians), and Southeast Asian refugees (Vietnamese, Cambodians, and Laotians). The literature includes guidelines for mental health professionals working with clients from each of these three subgroups, with specific attention to the special needs of Southeast Asian refugees (Iwamasa, 2003; Okazaki, 2000; Paniagua, 2001a; Sue & Sue, 2003). In this chapter, I use the generic term *Asian* in summarizing the guidelines recommended in the literature for the culturally sensitive assessment, diagnosis, and treatment of clients from all these subgroups. I also include a summary of guidelines intended specifically for therapists working with Southeast Asian refugees.

Approximately 10.3 million individuals (or 3.6% of the population of the United States) identified themselves as Asian only (i.e., not in combination with other races) in the 2000 U.S. Census. In the same year, 398,835 persons, or 0.1% of the U.S. population, self-identified as only Native Hawaiian or other Pacific Islander. Approximately 1.6 million individuals reported being Asian in combination with one or more other races (Grieco & Cassidy, 2001; U.S. Bureau of the Census, 2000). In this group, the most common combinations were Asian and White (868,395); Asian and Native Hawaiian and other Pacific Islander (138,802); Asian and Black or African American (106,782); and Asian, White, and Native Hawaiian and other Pacific Islander (89,611) (Grieco & Cassidy, 2001). In total, approximately 1.1 million of the Asians residing in the United States included White among the racial categories they chose to describe themselves (Grieco & Cassidy, 2001; U.S. Bureau of the Census, 2000).

These findings suggest that although the majority of Asians residing in the United States do not consider themselves either biracial or multiracial, clinicians serving the Asian population should be aware that some clients from this race may identify themselves as members of additional races as well (e.g., Asian and Black or African American). As noted in Chapter 2, in the assessment, diagnosis, and treatment of mental disorders among Asian clients (as with clients from any of the four cultural groups discussed in this volume), therapists should take into account the cultural variables associated with all of the races/ethnicities included in their clients' self-designations. This recommendation may also be applied to Native Hawaiian and other Pacific Islander clients, but the 2000 census shows very little biracial or multiracial self-identification among individuals in this group, so it may not be a significant issue for clinicians. For example, only 475,579 individuals reported in the 2000 census that they were Hawaiian and other Pacific Islander in combination with any other races; of these, 112,964 reported that they were also White, 29,876 said that they were also Asian, and 89,811 reported being also Black or African American (see Grieco & Cassidy, 2001, p. 9).

Among Asians, the most numerous groups in the 2000 U.S. Census were those of Chinese heritage (2.4 million, an increase of about 2 million since the 1990 U.S. Census; see Kim, McLeod, & Shantzis, 1992), followed by persons of Filipino (1.8 million, or about 1 million more from 1990 census), Asian Indian (1.7 million), Vietnamese (1.2 million), and Korean (1.1 million) heritage. Individuals of Japanese heritage made up the smallest Asian subgroup in the 2000 census (approximately 796,700, only about 80,700 more than in the 1990 census; see Kim et al., 1992). Among Pacific Islanders, the most numerous groups were Native Hawaiians (140,652), Samoans (91,029), and Guamanians (58,240).

Socioeconomic Status

In 2000, the median annual income for the Asian and Pacific Islander populations was $53,635, somewhat higher than the median income for the entire U.S. population (i.e., $42,228; U.S. Bureau of the Census, 2000). Among Asians and Pacific Islanders, the median annual income per household was $22,951, compared with $12,158 for Hispanics and $24,951 for Whites (U.S. Bureau of the Census, 2001, 2002b). Approximately 1.3 million of those who self-designated as Asian only (i.e., not in combination with other races), or 12.6% of this racial group, were living below the poverty level (Bishaw & Iceland, 2003), in comparison with 12.4% of the total U.S. population, 9.1% of Whites, 22.6% of Hispanics, and 24.9% of African Americans. The number of persons self-identified as Hawaiian and other Pacific Islander only (not in combination with other races) who were living below the poverty level in 2000 was 64,558 (Bishaw & Iceland, 2003), or 17.7% of people from this race—a higher percentage than that found in the total U.S. population (12.4%), the Asian population (12.6%), or the White (9.1%) population (see Bishaw & Iceland, 2003, p. 8).

Cultural Variables That May Affect Assessment and Treatment

Prejudice, Racism, and Discrimination

Asians living in the United States have historically experienced prejudice, racism, and discrimination (Sue & Sue, 2003; Yamamoto, 1986). This was particularly true during the period from the 1850s through World War II, when many Chinese immigrants came to the United States to work in gold mines and to build railroads. Other Asians (Japanese, Filipinos, Koreans) followed the Chinese. Many people considered the Asian immigrant men who served as a source of cheap labor during that period "sneaky and sinister," and laws were passed to prohibit them from owning American land or bringing their wives with them. Discrimination was also apparent in the housing, employment, and educational opportunities available to these immigrants (Yamamoto, 1986). As Yamamoto (1986) has observed, despite significant improvement in the lives of Asians in the United States, "prejudice, racism, and discrimination still persist" against members of this group (p. 92). Mental health professionals who work with Asian clients should be sensitive to the history of racism and discrimination that Asians have experienced in the United States, taking care to avoid any verbal or nonverbal behaviors that Asian clients might interpret as signs of prejudice.

Familism

As is true of all the other cultural groups discussed in this book, Asians tend to place great emphasis on family relationships (Ho, 1992; Sue & Sue, 2003). Among Asians, the family unit, and not the individual, comes first. The kind of individualism associated with Anglo-American society is not rewarded in Asian culture; rather, like Hispanics, Asians tend to view individualism from the standpoint of the individual's peculiarities. Like Hispanics and African Americans, Asians also place great emphasis on the extended family. Among Asians, each family member's role is clear and unchanging; unlike in African American families, "role flexibility" within the family is not rewarded. As in Hispanic families, in Asian families the father is the dominant figure, and his authority is paramount.

Role of Children and Wives

Traditional Asians believe that children's primary duty is to be good and to respect their parents. Parents are expected to determine the course of their children's lives, without consulting the children about their own desires and ambitions, and any failure on a child's part to comply with parents' expectations is seen as a threat to the parents' authority. Asian women are expected to marry, to be obedient helpers to their husbands, to have children, and to respect the authority of their husbands and fathers. These strong cultural expectations may explain why Asian women and children appear less autonomous and assertive, and more conforming, dependent, inhibited, and obedient to authority, than Anglo women and children (Ho, 1992; Sue & Sue, 2003). Therapists who work with Asian clients need to be aware that these are appropriate (or normal) behavior patterns among Asians. A culturally sensitive therapist will avoid suggesting to an Asian family that children and adolescents need to establish their independence from the authority of their parents. Such a therapist will also avoid discussing the "lack" of assertive behaviors and autonomy in an Asian woman during the process of family therapy.

Suppression of Problems Outside the Family

In general, Asians do not encourage family members to express any family problems to people outside the family (Sue & Sue, 2003). All problems (including physical and mental problems) are to be shared *only* among family members, just as all rewards received and successes achieved by individual family members are shared by the entire family. *Shame* and *guilt* are two mechanisms that Asian families use to enforce norms within the family (Dana, 1993b). These mechanisms play a crucial role in preventing Asians from reporting or admitting their problems in public—that is, to anyone outside the family.

If an Asian does not behave as expected within and outside the family, he or she may lose the confidence and support of family members, which could lead him or her to develop a strong sense of shame and guilt. This sense of shame and guilt may lead to considerable anxiety and depression around the fear that family support may be withdrawn. Several Asian scholars have suggested that Asians' desire to avoid this sense of shame and guilt may explain the strong self-control and self-discipline often reported among persons in this cultural group (e.g., Ho, 1992; Sue & Sue, 2003). Thus, an important guideline for therapists working with Asian clients is to explore with them this sense of shame and guilt in order to understand how difficult it is for these clients to talk about their problems in public. A therapist should not expect that an Asian client will report about his or her emotional problems as soon as the therapist says, "Tell me about your problems" (in contrast to many African American and Hispanic clients, who tend to respond quickly to this invitation the first time they interact with a therapist).

Indirect Versus Direct Forms of Communication

Asians often respond to the verbal communications of others by being quiet and passive; they may go to a great deal of effort to avoid offending others, sometimes answering all questions affirmatively to be polite even when they do not understand the questions, and they tend to avoid eye contact (Chung, 1992; Root, Ho, & Sue, 1986). Therapists who work with Asian clients should be aware that this *indirect* form of verbal communication is appropriate for individuals from this cultural group. This communication pattern is very different from the usual Western style of communication, in which both the speaker (e.g., the client) and the listener (e.g., the therapist) must look expressive and active, and the participants generally do not answer questions that they do not understand.

Two forms of indirect communication that may create problems during the assessment and treatment of Asian clients are silence and lack of eye contact. Therapists should be aware that among Asians, silence is a sign of respect and politeness; it also signals an individual's desire to continue speaking after making a point during a conversation (Sue & Sue, 2003). In Western cultures, eye contact during direct verbal communication is understood to imply attention and respect toward others. Among Asians, however, eye contact is considered a sign of lack of respect and attention, particularly to authority figures (e.g., parents) and older people. A therapist who does not understand the meanings that Asians ascribe to silence and eye contact during conversation may feel uncomfortable when speaking with an Asian client and may change the entire content of the conversation on the assumption that the client is not interested in or is not attending to what the therapist is saying. This error may prevent an Asian client from either elaborating on a prior point or demonstrating attention and respect toward the therapist in the way he or she considers appropriate (i.e., through silence and avoiding eye contact).

The First Session

Displaying Expertise and Authority

Many Asian clients come to their first therapy session expecting that the therapist will tell them what is wrong and how to resolve their problems (Sue & Sue, 2003). In addition, many Asian clients see therapists as authority figures. Thus, to ensure that an Asian client will return for therapy, the therapist should demonstrate both expertise and authority during the first session. These qualities correspond to one of the two dimensions of therapist credibility that have been identified as important among Asian and Pacific Islander clients, namely, *ascribed credibility* (Sue & Zane, 1987), which "derives from the position or role that is assigned by others in society. In Asian culture, characteristics that often go with higher ascribed status include older age, male sex, and higher expertise or authority" (Okazaki, 2000, p. 178). Kim (1985) suggests that a therapist can enhance his or her ascribed credibility with an Asian client by demonstrating expertise and authority during the first session in several ways:

1. The therapist can casually mention prior experiences with other clients who have problems similar to the present client's. For example, the therapist might say, "In my experience with many similar cases . . ." (to show expertise), or "In my professional judgment . . ." (to show authority).

2. The therapist can display his or her diplomas and licenses as well as relevant books.

3. The therapist can use his or her professional title when introducing him- or herself to the client (e.g., "I am Dr. Jones" or "I am Professor Smith").

4. The therapist can suggest to the client some possible reasons or explanations for the client's problem.

5. The therapist can give the client the impression that a solution (cure) to the problem is possible.

6. Throughout the session, the therapist can emphasize concrete and tangible goals and avoid comments that suggest the client will need to be in therapy for a long period of time (many Asian clients believe that only an inexperienced "doctor" needs a lot of time to understand and resolve a problem).

Maintaining Formalism and Conversational Distance

In general, Asian clients tend to feel that their role in therapy is to be passive, respectful, and obedient in the presence of the authority, the therapist (Yamamoto, 1986). Thus, these clients expect *formalism* in the therapist-client relationship. The therapist should not expect an Asian client to be very friendly during the first meeting; rather, this initial contact is generally formal. The therapist should avoid making jokes during this session.

Among Asians, the nature of the relationship between the participants in a conversation often determines the physical distance maintained between them. The basic guideline for therapists to remember concerning conversational distance with an Asian client is to allow the client to define the distance with which he or she is comfortable during the process of assessment and treatment. For example, the therapist can sit down first, allowing the client to determine the distance between them. If the client and therapist have not yet built a trusting relationship, the client is not likely to sit very close to the therapist (Chung, 1992).

Waiting Until the Client Is Ready
to Discuss Emotional Problems

In a traditional Asian family, an individual member's emotional problems are seen as bringing shame on the entire family, thus family members are strongly discouraged from reporting such problems to anyone outside the family. This phenomenon probably explains why current epidemiological data indicate that Asian clients have a very low prevalence of emotional disorders in comparison with members of other cultural groups (Sue & Sue, 2003). In the first session with an Asian client, the therapist must show (both verbally and nonverbally) that he or she will wait until the client is ready to discuss his or her mental problems. This waiting period could include more than one session, and the therapist should be sure the client understands this possibility.

Understanding the Expression of
Mental Problems in Somatic Terms

Asians tend to express psychological disorders in somatic terms (Ho, 1992; Hughes, 1993; Sue & Sue, 2003). This phenomenon is associated with the shame, humiliation, and guilt that can result when an individual makes such problems public (Hughes, 1993). Given the choice of talking about physical symptoms (e.g., chest pains, headaches, and fatigue) or talking about psychiatric symptoms (e.g., hallucinations, delusions), an Asian client would probably select the former, because reporting physical complaints is often more acceptable to Asians (i.e., results in less shame, humiliation, and guilt) than reporting emotional or psychiatric problems (Sue & Sue, 2003).

Thus, when an Asian client consults with a therapist for the first time, he or she may spend a great deal of time talking about physical complaints such as headaches, back pain, weight loss, and fatigue. The therapist can handle an Asian client's somatization of psychological or psychiatric disorders during the first session in two ways (Ho, 1992; Sue & Sue, 2003). First, the therapist should always acknowledge these somatic complaints. The therapist should also tell the client that he or she wants to arrange for the client to be clinically assessed for potential physical disorders (particularly by an Asian physician) before the therapist concludes that the client is exhibiting some form of somatization disorder (e.g., conversion disorder, hypochondriasis, somatoform pain disorder). Second, the therapist should introduce statements that allow the client to move gradually from verbalizations of somatic complaints to verbalizations involving mental health problems. For example, the therapist could say, "I will consult with a physician about your headaches. Perhaps you are having headaches because you do not know what to do to handle some conflicts in your life. Would you like to talk about any such conflicts?" The therapist should avoid making any statements that indicate he or she does not believe that the client "really" has a physical (medical) problem, such as "You don't have headaches. You simply want to avoid talking about your mental problems."

Understanding the First Session as a Crisis

Because many Asians believe that mental illness brings shame and humiliation to their entire families, they tend to wait many years (often 5 to 10 years) before seeking professional help for mental problems (Fujii, Fukushima, & Yamamoto, 1993; Gaw, 1993b). Thus, by the time an Asian client is brought to the attention of a clinician, his or her condition is often chronic and severe, and the family is in a state of crisis. For this reason, the therapist should always consider the first session with an Asian client as a potential crisis point. Because of this possibility, the clinician should be prepared to display two emergency responses: (a) immediate assessment of suicide attempts and suicidal thoughts, and (b) immediate attention to the presenting problem and its treatment (including the availability of family support, the possibility of brief inpatient treatment, and consultation with social agencies involved with Asian communities). If the client needs brief psychotherapy, inpatient treatment, and/or medication, the therapist should inform the client's family of this before the termination of the first session.

As Yamamoto (1986) notes, treating the first session as a crisis is particularly important with elderly Asians referred to outpatient mental health clinics, because of the high frequency of suicidal behavior (approximately 27 in 100,000) among elderly Asians living in the United States. In contrast, the frequency of suicidal behavior is extremely low among elderly Asians living in Asian countries.

Avoiding Any Discussion of Hospitalization

Although it is appropriate for the therapist to consider the first meeting with an Asian client as a potential crisis situation, it is also important that he or she avoid making any comments regarding the hospitalization of the client during the first meeting. Many Asian clients consider psychiatric hospitalization to be a last resort, and instead are likely to expect to hear about alternatives to hospitalization (e.g., outpatient treatment and the delivery of treatments by family members at home) during the first session with a therapist. If the therapist determines during the first session that hospitalization of an Asian client is necessary (e.g., because the client is a danger to him- or herself or others), he or she should follow these guidelines (Fujii et al., 1993; Kinzie & Leung, 1993):

1. The therapist must consult with the client's family members, who must approve the hospitalization.

2. The therapist must provide the client and his or her family members with a detailed description of the anticipated length of the hospital stay, recommended tests, and treatment modality.

3. The therapist should inform the client's family members about the hospital's visiting hours and the reasons family members are not encouraged to go to the hospital with the client (e.g., for clinical or administrative reasons).

4. The therapist should inform the client's family members that they may bring ethnic foods to their hospitalized relative to replace or supplement the Western-style foods offered in the hospital to all inpatients.

5. During the entire period of hospitalization, the therapist should never tell the client about his or her diagnosis. The therapist should share this information only with the client's family members, because many Asians believe that if a person who is ill knows "the truth about the illness, he or she might lose hope and deteriorate more quickly" (Fujii et al., 1993, p. 337).

Considering Alternative Care Services

It is a good tactic for the therapist to assume that an Asian client's presenting problem is a chronic problem developed over a long period. Even in severe clinical cases, however, many Asian families may not agree to allow the hospitalization of their relatives. Therefore, prior to the first session with an Asian client, it is important that the therapist determine the availability of alternative care services. For example, the therapist might consider discussing with the client and his or her family the possibility that the client could be cared for at home with some professional assistance; many Asian families would see this as a more acceptable course of action than hospitalization. The therapist should have available a list of the local community mental health services agencies specifically devoted to treating

Asians (see Box 5.1 for some examples of such agencies). These alternatives could facilitate the assessment and treatment of Asian clients whose families refuse to allow hospitalization and may help these clients to avoid the stigma of mental illness that results from hospitalization or inpatient treatment (Yamamoto, 1986, p. 117).

Box 5.1   Examples of Agencies Offering Alternative Services for Asian Clients

- Asian Community Service Center (Los Angeles)
- Pacific/Asian Preventive Program (San Diego)
- Richmond Area Multi-Service Center (San Francisco)
- Asian Counseling and Referral Service (Seattle)
- Asian American Drug Abuse Program (Los Angeles)
- Center for Southeast Asian Refugee Resettlement (San Francisco)
- Asian Counseling and Treatment Center (Los Angeles)
- Korean American Mental Health Service Center (Los Angeles)
- Operation Samahan (San Diego)

Providing Concrete and Tangible Advice

Asian clients often want therapists to deal with their immediate concerns by providing concrete and tangible advice in the first session (Root et al., 1986; Sue & Sue, 2003). The therapist should be careful to avoid prolonged verbal exchange with the client during the first session and should also avoid making any suggestions that appear ambiguous. For example, the statement "Mr. Sue, you need to change your behavior in a positive way if you want your wife to stay with you" tells the client nothing about exactly what he has to do. In addition, the therapist should avoid discussing solutions to problems that involve long-range goals. For example, the following statement is both ambiguous and implies a long-term goal: "Let's talk about what you need to do to change your behavior in the next 6 months. What do you think you should do to improve your relationship with your wife?" A better statement with an Asian client would be as follows: "During the next 5 days, write on a piece of paper the number of times you and your wife hold hands, eat, and take short walks together. When you return for therapy next week, we will talk about what you have written." This statement is concrete (i.e., it tells the client exactly what to do, both to improve the relationship and to provide the therapist with information), and it suggests a short-term goal (i.e., the client will bring the results of the assignment in for discussion the following week).

Understanding That Psychotherapy Is Not Expected

An Asian client is not likely to expect the therapist to conduct psychotherapy to deal with the client's problem in the first session; rather, the client will expect that this session will be spent on what the therapist wants to know about the client in general. In some cases, therapists may need to have several sessions with Asian clients before they can initiate psychotherapy. However, if the therapist determines that the client is in an emergency situation or crisis, he or she must consider recommending inpatient treatment and/or medication.

As noted above, in Asian cultures, individuals are discouraged from discussing problems (particularly mental problems) with anyone outside of their families. Thus, the therapist cannot expect that during the first session an Asian client will share his or her feelings or emotional problems (Sue & Sue, 2003). The best approach the therapist can take in the first session is to let the client know that the therapist is available to listen when the client is ready to talk, and that the therapist understands that it may take several sessions before the client is able to discuss emotional problems openly.

Considering the Client's Organic Explanation of Emotional Problems

Because Asian clients tend to express their emotional problems in somatic terms, as discussed above (Sue & Sue, 2003), these clients generally place a great deal of emphasis on organic variables as explanations for their emotional problems. For this reason, Asian clients often expect to receive medication (to deal with these "organic" problems) during their first contact with a therapist. A practical guideline for the therapist in this regard is to accept the client's interpretation of the origin of his or her mental problems as an example of the client's belief system. This tactic can greatly enhance the therapist-client relationship in future sessions. If the therapist does not recommend medication during the first session, he or she should explain why in concrete terms. For example, the statement "I don't think you need medication" does not offer the client enough information; he or she still needs to know *why* the therapist is not prescribing medication. A better approach would be for the therapist to say, "To improve communication between you and your wife, I would like to recommend a technique based on learning how to solve problems. Medication is another alternative, and I might consider that later, after I have consulted with your physician regarding the medications you are currently taking to prevent complications that can arise from the combination of two or more medications."

Avoiding Trying to Collect Too Much Information

In general, mental health practitioners are trained to conduct a thorough clinical interview (i.e., to get as much information as possible) during the first meeting with a client. This approach is not recommended with Asian clients, however (Gaw, 1993b), because of these clients' reluctance to discuss personal matters with persons outside their families. In the first session, the therapist should avoid asking questions about specific and sensitive issues (e.g., "How is your sexual relationship with your wife?") and instead ask more general questions (e.g., "How is the relationship between you and your wife?"). By emphasizing general questions in the first session, the therapist can enhance the therapist-client relationship and prepare the way for asking the client about more intimate matters in subsequent sessions.

Working With Southeast Asian Refugee Clients

Whereas the guidelines presented above are suggested for use with all Asian clients, the following additional guidelines are strongly recommended for therapists who work with Southeast Asian refugee clients (Cook & Timberlake, 1989; Mollica, 1989; Mollica & Lavelle, 1988). As noted above, these clients have come to the United States with histories of traumatic events unlike those generally reported by other Asian clients (particularly Asian American/Pacific Islander clients). For this reason, the therapist must plan carefully for the first session with a Southeast Asian refugee client. Below, I offer brief discussions of some specific points that therapists should consider when working with clients from this group (Ho, 1992; Mollica & Lavelle, 1988).

Avoiding Questions About Traumatic Events

During the first session with a Southeast Asian refugee client, it is extremely important that the therapist avoid making statements or asking questions that deal with traumatic events the client may have experienced. The therapist must be familiar with the fact that the client comes to therapy with a history of trauma that may include torture, the loss of loved ones through killing or disappearance, the witnessing of killings, and/or sexual abuse perpetrated by enemies during wartime. It is extremely difficult for such a client to discuss these kinds of events during his or her first meeting with a therapist. Given the traumatic events that Southeast Asian refugees have experienced, the therapist should not end the first session before assessing the client for suicide attempts, organic brain syndrome (because of the high potential for head injury among these refugees), and depression.

Avoiding Pressing the Client to Say More

A Southeast Asian refugee client may experience considerable stress if the therapist urges the client to talk about his or her problems during the first session. The therapist should not encourage a client from this group to say any more than what he or she volunteers without prompting. For example, the therapist should avoid asking questions such as the following during the first session: "Are you sure that this is the reason you need help?" or "Do you think that some dreams about very bad events in your life are creating problems for you?"

Reducing the Client's Stress as Quickly as Possible

A Southeast Asian refugee client is likely to expect help from the therapist quickly in terms of lowering the level of stress caused by a lack of resources; many such clients cannot afford housing, food, clothing, and other vital elements for their survival in the United States (Cook & Timberlake, 1989). The therapist should be familiar with the social services agencies (particularly agencies that deal specifically with refugees) operating in the community that can assist the client with his or her needs and thus help to lower the client's level of stress.

Conducting Psychotherapy

The guidelines summarized below are based on recommendations for psychotherapy with Asians offered by Chung (1992), Ho (1992), Iwamasa (2003), Mollica and Lavelle (1988), Murase (1992), Root et al. (1986), Sue and Sue (2003), and Yamamoto (1986).

Educating Clients in the Terms of Psychotherapy

Because many Asian clients are unfamiliar with terms such as *therapy, psychotherapy, verbal therapy, psychodynamic therapy,* and *behavior therapy* and do not understand how various kinds of psychotherapy differ from traditional healing methods, the therapist should begin the psychotherapy process with a brief introduction in which he or she discusses the meanings of relevant terms (Kim, 1993).

Conducting an Assessment of Shame and Humiliation

During the process of psychotherapy with an Asian client, it is important that the therapist conduct an assessment of the persistence of shame and humiliation in the client resulting from the stigma of mental illness.

The therapist should also discuss this issue and the results of the assessment with the client and his or her family members. Conducted after the first meeting (which is often a crisis situation), this assessment should include attention to the following points (Gaw, 1993b), which the therapist may use to *infer* that the client is having problems talking openly about mental problems because of shame and humiliation resulting from the public admission of such problems:

1. Extreme concern on the part of the client or a family member about the therapist's qualifications

2. Excessive worry about confidentiality

3. Refusal to submit claims for coverage of treatment to a private insurance company

4. Difficulty in keeping appointments or frequent late arrival for therapy

5. Refusal of family members to support the client's treatment

6. Insistence on receiving services from an Anglo clinician to avoid Asian therapists

7. Refusal to seek treatment even when a severe mental health problem is evident

Discussing the Duration of Therapy

Most Asian clients expect quick solutions to their mental problems. As noted above, however, by the time Asians seek professional help, they often have chronic psychiatric disorders. Therapists should inform their Asian clients that it is unrealistic to expect quick solutions to chronic mental health problems and should provide estimates of the likely duration of treatment (Yamamoto, Silva, Justice, Chang, & Leong, 1993). It is not generally recommended that therapists working with Asian clients undertake long-term treatment that emphasizes the uncovering of underlying conflicts (Murase, 1992). Relatively short treatment periods (i.e., no longer than 2 or 3 months) are recommended; if the therapist believes treatment should be extended for a longer period, he or she must negotiate this decision with the client.

Avoiding Personalism

Unlike most Hispanic clients, Asian clients do not expect a high level of personalism in the client-therapist relationship during psychotherapy. Therapists working with Asian clients should be aware that they usually expect the formalism of the first session to continue in subsequent sessions.

Recommended Modalities of Therapy

Medication

As noted above, many Asian clients expect to receive medication as part of therapy. Therapists who prescribe medication for Asian clients need to be aware that the drug dosages recommended for Anglo-Americans are not necessarily applicable for Asian clients because of "differences in body weight and possible ethnic differences in drug metabolism and sensitivities" (Gaw, 1993b, p. 276). If medication is used with Asians, the overall recommendation is to keep doses low because Asians have been shown to have a tendency to respond at much lower doses than non-Asians (Fujii et al., 1993; Kinzie & Leung, 1993). Because many Asian clients use herbal remedies to treat physical and mental problems, the therapist should discuss with the client any potential side effects that may result from the consumption of traditional medicines in combination with psychotropic medication.

Behavioral Approaches

Behavioral approaches (e.g., behavior therapy techniques) are recommended for Asian clients because these approaches are concrete and directive. Also, behavioral approaches do not emphasize the exploration of internal conflicts, which can tend to enhance the "shame" that an Asian client may experience as a result of reporting his or her problems to a therapist.

Family Therapy

The use of family therapy is recommended for Asian clients for two reasons (Berg & Jaya, 1993). First, among Asians, the family unit is more important than the individual. Second, because the concept of withholding information among family members is foreign to many Asians (Hughes, 1993; Sue & Sue, 2003), Asian clients generally expect that their family members will be actively involved in their assessment and treatment by mental health professionals. Asian clients expect therapists to share all information regarding treatment issues with all their family members, rather than only with the client. Additional guidelines concerning family therapy with Asian clients include the following (Berg & Jaya, 1993):

1. When the therapist introduces problem-solving techniques to deal with marital problems or conflicts between children and parents, these techniques should emphasize a process of negotiation rather than head-on confrontation. In this process of negotiation, the therapist serves as the mediator, given the clients' view of the therapist as an expert and a person in a position of authority.

2. To enhance the likelihood of peaceful negotiation, the therapist should see the parties who are in conflict separately before seeing the family members together in therapy sessions.

3. The therapist should keep differences in age and status in mind when addressing family members. For example, the therapist should always address the head of the family by his or her last name and the appropriate title of courtesy (e.g., Mr. Sue, Dr. Sue, Mrs. Sue). During the therapy process, an Asian client may ask the therapist to call him or her by first name, but until this happens, the therapist should continue to show proper respect for the client by maintaining the formality of using the client's last name. As Berg and Jaya (1993) note, many Asian clients believe that the respect they receive from a therapist is more important than what the therapist does to help them to solve their problems.

4. Family therapy must be (a) problem focused, (b) goal oriented, and (c) symptom relieving on a short-term basis (Kim, 1985). Therapy that emphasizes internal conflicts, self-assertion, expression of anger, and acquisition of insights is not recommended for Asian clients (Kim, 1985). Such clients generally expect a therapist to define the goals of family therapy in terms of situational changes requiring external solutions.

5. Family therapy aimed at helping Asian children and adolescents to develop independence from their parents is not recommended. In their social contacts with Anglo-American children, Asian children quickly learn that in the typical mainstream American family, the children are allowed to speak and to question authority and are encouraged to be independent. In family therapy with Asian families, the Western model of sharing power among family members may compete with the vertical, hierarchical structure of traditional Asian families, in which parents (particularly fathers) are in a position of unquestionable authority (Kim, 1985). Thus, the therapist must determine whether all Asian family members in therapy share the same values concerning the undisputable leadership and authority of parents before family therapy begins. In this process, the therapist should evaluate the acculturation levels of all family members (see Chapters 2 and 8).

6. Because Asians emphasize the family unit over the individual, the therapist should ask questions concerning family relationships during the process of assessment and treatment (Berg & Jaya, 1993). For example, the following questions do not emphasize the relationships between the client and other family members: "What do you think about your problem?" "If you stop drinking after treatment, how will you feel?" "How does this problem affect you?" Questions aimed at eliciting similar information, however, can be phrased in terms of relationships: "What do you think your father will say is the main problem between you and him?" "If you stop drinking after treatment, what will your family notice you are doing differently?" "How does this problem affect your family?"

7. The therapist should always protect the dignity and self-respect of all members of the family; this includes avoiding embarrassing family

members in front of one another and the therapist. This guideline is often referred to as helping the client "save face" (Berg & Jaya, 1993; Kim, 1993). For example, an Asian father "loses face" during the process of family therapy if the therapist tells him (in the presence of other family members) that he is "wrong" to demand that his son select a profession that is acceptable to his parents. To avoid embarrassing the father, the therapist should reframe the issue in a positive way. For example, the therapist might begin by complimenting the father on his concern for the family: "I understand that you would like your son to have a profession that could help the family's financial situation. But would you agree that your son would be happier if he selects a profession that is rewarding to him *and* to the family?" The therapist can thus preserve the dignity and proper role of the father while suggesting an alternative solution to the problem.

8. If the central issue in family therapy is divorce, the therapist should follow these practical guidelines (Ho, 1987). First, because divorce is not socially acceptable in Asian communities and is seen as a very serious decision, the practitioner should not raise the idea of divorce as a possible solution to the family's problems; instead, he or she should wait until the clients clearly indicate that it is time to discuss this alternative. Second, because many Asian clients are not familiar with the legal process of divorce, the practitioner should make available to the family members the legal information they need as well as the names, addresses, and telephone numbers of lawyers who have expertise in working with Asian clients. Third, because many Asians feel that divorce brings shame on the entire family, Asian clients who decide to divorce may be faced with the withdrawal of social and economic support by relatives and friends. The practitioner should assist such clients in finding new support systems by encouraging them to meet other Asians who have shared the same experiences. To facilitate this, the therapist might schedule a therapy group made up of Asians who have been divorced.

9. Although it is generally assumed that Asian clients are likely to prefer to involve their entire families in the assessment and treatment of their mental disorders, the therapist must carefully evaluate this issue with each Asian client. An assessment of the client's level of acculturation is helpful in this regard (for examples of acculturation scales recommended for use with Asians, see Table 8.1 in Chapter 8). As Yamamoto (1986) notes, highly acculturated Asian clients may or may not want family members to be involved in their psychotherapy.

Avoiding Talk Therapy

The use of talk therapy is not recommended with Asian clients, who generally prefer therapy that is more active (i.e., that deals with problems quickly) (Gaw, 1993b). As Tsui (1985) notes, Asian clients "expect tangible evidence of intervention, not abstract discussion" (p. 360). For this reason, therapies that involve self-exploration and psychodynamic interpretations of symptoms are likely to be ineffective with Asian clients.

Group Therapy

Because of the tendency among Asians to avoid sharing their problems with people outside their immediate families, group therapy is not generally recommended for Asian clients, particularly in cases involving sensitive issues, such as sexual dysfunction and infertility (Tsui, 1985). Group therapy may be appropriate for an Asian client, however, if the client has no support system (relatives and close friends) available and needs an alternative support system quickly. For example, as noted above, Asian clients who elect to divorce may lose the support of relatives and close friends as a result; these clients might benefit from sharing their experiences with other Asian clients who have also lost social support because of similar "misbehavior" (see Ho, 1987, p. 63).

Additional Guidelines for Therapists
Working With Southeast Asian Refugee Clients

In addition to the above guidelines, which are applicable to therapy with all Asian clients, three specific guidelines are suggested concerning the process of psychotherapy with Southeast Asian refugee clients. First, despite the important role of the extended family in Asian cultures, the therapist should consider carefully before suggesting the use of family therapy because many members of the client's family may not be available (e.g., because of death or disappearance).

Second, during the process of psychotherapy, the therapist should be ready to assist the client in the pursuit of many different kinds of services (Flaskerud & Anh, 1988). The therapist should provide the client with information on local mental health centers as resources for treatment and education about mental disorders as well as education about American society (including culture and lifestyle). A client who is a refugee is also likely to need information about financial assistance programs, community resources for assistance with food and housing needs, and vocational and language training opportunities in the community. The therapist should also inform the client about culturally relevant assessment and treatment for mental disorders, family-related problems, and adjustment problems.

Third, given that recent reports indicate that approximately 50% of Southeast Asian refugees in the United States may be suffering from post-traumatic stress disorder, or PTSD (Kinzie & Leung, 1993), the psychotherapy process with clients from this population (i.e., after the first session) should include thorough screening for PTSD and discussions of specific stressful events the clients have experienced. Therapists should keep in mind, however, that these clients may not discuss feelings about such traumatic experiences for many months. Clients from this group may not voluntarily reveal the severe traumas they have been through, either because they simply avoid talking about these events in general or because they do not think that symptoms such as recurrent distressing dreams and irritability (the primary symptoms of PTSD) are related to their presenting problems. In addition, Southeast Asian refugees might not talk about these events because they believe that clinicians do not want to listen "to the terrible stories and the agony endured by the refugees" (Kinzie & Leung, 1993, p. 290).

Social-Skills Training

Social-skills training is particularly recommended for Southeast Asian refugee clients who have severe anxiety about the possibility of deportation or who fear that their behaviors may give a bad reputation to other Asians (Yamamoto et al., 1993).

6

Guidelines for the Assessment and
Treatment of American Indian Clients

American Indians are also known as Native Americans, but this term is not recommended in the literature because it does not include other Indian groups in the United States (e.g., Eskimos, Aleuts) or native peoples from other countries (e.g., Canadian and Mexican Indians) who have settled in the United States (Fleming, 1992). The terms preferred in the current literature are *American Indians* and *Alaska Natives* (Fleming, 1992; Grieco & Cassidy, 2001; LaFromboise & Dizon, 2003; Sue & Sue, 2003; Thompson, Walker, & Silk-Walker, 1993). Thompson et al. (1993) suggest that the term *Indian* should be used to "refer to all American Indians, Alaska Natives, and Canadian and Mexican Indian people" (p. 189). In the continental United States, American Indians constitute the largest Indian group seen in mental health services (Ho, 1992; Richardson, 1981). In addition, historical analyses of the period before Europeans "discovered" the North American continent in 1492 and subsequent periods have emphasized American Indians (Walker & LaDue, 1986). Thus the majority of historical and clinical materials on which this chapter is based are representative of American Indians.

In the 2000 U.S. Census, 2.5 million individuals described their race as American Indian and Alaska Native only (i.e., not in combination with other races) (Grieco & Cassidy, 2001; U.S. Bureau of the Census, 2000). In addition, approximately 1.6 million people described themselves as American Indian and Alaska Native in combination with at least one other race. Within this group, the most common combinations were American Indian and Alaska Native and White (1,082,683); American Indian and Alaska Native and Black or African American (182,494); and American Indian and Alaska Native, White, and Black or African American (112,207) (Grieco & Cassidy, 2001). A total of 52,429 census respondents said that they were American Indian and Alaska Native and Asian (Grieco

& Cassidy, 2001). Approximately 4.1 million people, or 1.5% of the total U.S. population, self-designated as American Indian and Alaska Native alone or in combination with one or more other races (Grieco & Cassidy, 2001; LaFromboise & Dizon, 2003). Therefore, although about 2.5 million people self-identified as only American Indian and Alaska Native in 2000, mental health professionals should expect to see in their practices a modest number of biracial and multiracial families that include American Indian and Alaska Native heritage; in assessing, diagnosing, and treating clients from such families, therapists need to take into account the cultural variables associated with all the relevant races (Sue & Sue, 2003).

Currently, the majority of American Indians and Alaska Natives live in six U.S. states: Alaska, Arizona, California, Oklahoma, New Mexico, and Washington (U.S. Bureau of the Census, 2000). Approximately 37% of the members of this population reside on reservations in the United States (Barcus, 2003); there are 300 reservations, most of which have fewer than 1,000 Indians living within their boundaries (Ho, 1992).

Socioeconomic Status

During the period 2000–2002, the average annual household income for those self-designating as American Indian and Alaska Native only (not in combination with other races) was $32,679 (U.S. Bureau of the Census, 2004). During the same period, average annual household incomes for other racial groups in the United States (not in combination with other races) were as follows: Asians, $55,113; Whites, $45,390; African Americans, $29,982; and Hispanics, $33,946 (U.S. Bureau of the Census, 2004). In 2000, 25.7% of American Indians and Alaska Natives were living below the poverty level, in comparison with 12.4% of the total U.S. population and 9.1% of Whites (Bishaw & Iceland, 2003). Approximately 50% of American Indians residing on or near reservations are unemployed (Sue & Sue, 2003). Of the four groups discussed in this text, American Indians are the most disadvantaged in terms of socioeconomic characteristics, mortality, and life expectancy (Barcus, 2003; Dillard & Manson, 2000; Sue & Sue, 2003).

What Is an "Authentic" Indian?

As Barcus (2003) notes, among the four cultural groups discussed in this book, American Indians constitute the only group with "a legal definition of race" (p. 24). Individuals who want to be considered as American Indians for purposes of gaining assistance from federal aid programs for Indians must prove their Indian status in terms of the definition established by the Bureau of Indian Affairs, which is housed in the U.S. Department of the Interior (Ho, 1992; Jaimes, 1996; Sue & Sue, 2003; Trimble & Fleming, 1989; Wise

& Miller, 1983). This definition states that in order to be considered an Indian, a person must be at least one-quarter Indian by blood and must have proof of tribal status (Harjo, 1993; Ho, 1987; Jaimes, 1996).

It is important to note, however, that the federal government does not have the final word on this issue; the federal government is required also to recognize the sovereign status of each tribe's definition of what constitutes Indian status (A. McDonald, Dull Knife Memorial College, personal communication, January 1994; O'Brien, 1989). Because it is extremely difficult to apply any definition of this kind in clinical practice, practitioners should consult with professionals who work for organizations that assist American Indians (see Box 6.1 for a list of some of these) and with tribal leaders when they have clients who need the assistance of federal programs for Indians but the clients are not sure of their official Indian status. The therapist should never ask a client who self-identifies as American Indian, "Are you sure that you meet the definition of an Indian in this country?" This is an inappropriate question because many American Indians consider the blood quantum formula "pseudoscientific," and, as Jaimes (1996) notes, it "is still viewed as racist by many Indians" (p. 50; see also Barcus, 2003, p. 24).

Box 6.1   Organizations That Assist American Indians

American Indian Child Resource Center
522 Grand Avenue
Oakland, CA 94610
phone (510) 208-1870; fax (510) 208-1886
Web site http://www.aicrc.org

Association on American Indian Affairs
966 Hungerford Drive, Suite 12-B
Rockville, MD 20850
phone (240) 314-7155; fax (240) 314-7159
Web site http://www.indian-affairs.org

Chief Dull Knife College
1 College Drive
Lame Deer, MT 59043
phone (406) 477-6215; fax (406) 477-6219
Web site http://www.cdkc.edu

Indian Health Service
801 Thompson Avenue, Suite 400
Rockville, MD 20852-1627
phone (301) 448-1083
Web site http://www.ihs.gov/index.asp

Box 6.1 (Continued)

National Council of Urban Indian Health
501 Capitol Court, NE, Suite 100
Washington, DC 20002
phone (202) 544-0344; fax (202) 544-9394
Web site http://www.ncuih.org

National Indian Child Welfare Association
5100 SW Macadam Avenue, Suite 300
Portland, OR 97239
phone (503) 222-4044; fax (503) 222-4007
Web site http://www.nicwa.org

Society of Indian Psychologists
c/o Rebecca Foster, SIP President
P.O. Box 1429
Browning, MT 59417
Web site http://www.geocities.com/indianpsych

Urban Indian Health Institute
P.O. Box 3364
Seattle, WA 98114
(206) 812-3030
Web site http://www.uihi.org

Cultural Variables That May
Affect Assessment and Treatment

Impacts of Historical Events

Mental health practitioners who assess and treat American Indians should be familiar with the impacts of critical historical events experienced by American Indians as a group across four time intervals (Barcus, 2003; Walker & LaDue, 1986). Walker and LaDue (1986) describe these periods as follows: (a) the precontact period, prior to 1492; (b) the Manifest Destiny period, 1492–1890; (c) the assimilation period, 1890–1970; and (d) the Indian self-determination period, 1970 to the present.

Precontact Period

American Indians developed many of the cultural rules, roles, values, and beliefs that still exist today among members of this group during the precontact period. An important element of this period is the "survival pact," which includes rules that govern the "symbiotic relationship among the individual, the group, and the earth. . . . [These rules] touched all aspects of life, including marriage and social encounters, food gathering, hunting and fishing, religion, and medicine. . . . As long as tribes followed these rules, they survived and prospered" (Walker & LaDue, 1986, p. 145). Features of the survival pact have been passed from generation to generation through legends, histories, and songs.

An illustration of Indian beliefs about what can happen to an individual or the group if the survival pact is violated is found in the case of a "mystery illness" experienced by the Navajo Nation in 1993. When tribal members contracted this illness, which had flulike symptoms and provoked acute respiratory distress often leading to death, many Navajos explained the origin of the illness in terms of the survival pact. According to a report published in the *Houston Chronicle,* a Navajo who was interviewed said that "the tribal elders . . . feel that the disease is a prophecy of Mother Earth right. . . . The medicine men are saying [the illness occurred] because of something we have done wrong, for not taking better care of the Earth" (quoted in Foreman, 1993, p. 18A). Later, health officials in New Mexico discovered that the illness was caused by the hantavirus, which is present in rodent droppings and urine. On the basis of this information, Western doctors consulted with the Navajo medicine men in an effort to minimize fears and deal with the disease. This example not only illustrates the function of the survival pact among American Indians (exemplified here by a case involving the largest Indian tribe in the United States, i.e., the Navajo Nation), it also shows the role that medicine men play today in moments of crisis as well as the attention and respect they receive from members of the mainstream American scientific community (who are familiar with the role of the medicine man among American Indians).

Manifest Destiny Period

Two important features of the Manifest Destiny period were the occurrence of disease epidemics that affected the lives of many Indians and the further development of racism and discrimination against American Indians that included the creation of reservations and boarding schools for Indian children. A familiarity with both of these can help practitioners to understand why many American Indian clients do not trust Anglo mental health professionals.

Early explorers (White men from other lands) in North America introduced to American Indian populations such "European" diseases as smallpox, cholera, malaria, pneumonia, syphilis, diphtheria, and typhoid fever, resulting in massive numbers of Indian deaths (Brandon, 1989; Walker & LaDue, 1986). One consequence of the devastation brought by these epidemics was a drastic change in many of the features of the survival pact. For example, prior to the epidemics, the job of the medicine man was to cure all diseases regardless of their cause. Medicine men were not able to cure these new diseases, however, and as a result the medicine man became "of little practical or spiritual value to his tribe" (Walker & LaDue, 1986, p. 153). In addition, the epidemics killed many elders and tribal leaders, who had been the ones who taught the rules of the survival pact to younger members of the tribes (e.g., the harmony between the group and the Earth as a measure of stability in the tribe, beliefs in supernatural and spiritual events, values and rules of behavior). Thus, the epidemics led to the loss of much of the meaning of the survival pact in the minds of many American Indians.

In addition to contributing to the loss of many features of the survival pact, the epidemics led to the conversion to Christianity of many Indians. Walker and LaDue (1986) suggest that this occurred for two reasons: First, the epidemics left little hope among the Indians for a "return to the traditional ways," and second, "the Christian promise of a better afterlife must have seemed quite inviting" (p. 156). It is now clear, however, that the intent of the Christian missionaries who converted the Indians during such epidemics was to impose their beliefs and rules of conduct on the tribes, including the elimination of all the cultural values encompassed by the survival pact.

Initially, many American Indians considered the creation of the reservations to be a positive event in their struggle to move away from the influence of Whites on their lives, culture, language, and religion (Walker & LaDue, 1986). The federal government promised American Indians that they would be resettled on vast amounts of land where they would be protected from the influences of Whites. These promises were broken many times, however. Indians were relocated to remote areas as existing reservations were eliminated or reduced in size. In addition, legislation was passed that made it illegal for Indians to use their own languages or to practice their own religions and customs on the reservations, and many tribal leaders were exiled. The reservations were "unhappy and miserable" places (Walker & LaDue, 1986, p. 157).

Also during this period, the federal government, along with various (non-Indian) religious groups, created a system of boarding schools for Indian children (Reyhner & Eder, 1988). The main goal of these schools was to replace the children's practice of Indian languages, modes of dress, beliefs, religions, and customs with the practices of the White civilization. In such schools, Indian "children were punished severely for speaking their own language. . . . [The message was that] to be Indian was to be bad" (Walker & LaDue, 1986, p. 157).

Assimilation Period

During the assimilation period, the development of racism and discrimination against American Indians was reinforced by the continuing existence of the reservations and boarding schools (Barcus, 2003; O'Brien, 1989). During the early years of this period, Indians had two choices: death or assimilation into White culture. Many Indians moved away from their old traditions, not only to avoid death but as a result of the deaths of the Great Chiefs, who were instrumental in the transmission of tribal traditions to younger members (Walker & LaDue, 1986). Despite these negative influences on the lives of many Indians, during the assimilation period many old traditions continued, and American Indians experienced two important victories: They became the last group of people to be recognized as full U.S. citizens with voting privileges, and they received, with the passage of the Indian Reorganization Act, the right to govern themselves according to their traditional cultural values (O'Brien, 1989).

These victories, however, were followed in the 1950s by further efforts on the part of Whites to force Indians to assimilate into (i.e., accept and practice the standards of) the White society. These efforts took the forms of *termination* and *relocation* (Jaimes, 1996; Walker & LaDue, 1986). Termination involved the nullification of all special agreements and relationships that had existed between the federal government and the tribes. Relocation consisted "of an effort in the 1960s to do away with American Indian reservations" (Barcus, 2003, p. 27). American Indians residing on reservations were provided with federal funds and travel assistance to encourage them to move to large cities such as Chicago, Denver, and Los Angeles. This effort led to increases in already existing social (e.g., cultural ambivalence) and behavioral (e.g., depression, alcoholism) problems among Indians, but it failed to accomplish the goal of eliminating traditional Indian cultures and values. It should be noted that American Indians who reside in large U.S. cities are generally referred to as *urban Indians* to differentiate them from Indians who remained on the reservations (see Barcus, 2003, p. 27). In clinical practice, therapists should keep this distinction in mind during the assessment and diagnosis process, because a significant number of urban Indians are marginalized, "meaning that they no longer fit into their own cultural group nor [are they] part of the majority population" (Barcus, 2003, p. 28). As noted in Chapter 2, a severe negative consequence of such marginalization is increased risk for psychological and adjustment disorders (see Cuéllar, 2000, p. 52).

Self-Determination Period

The self-determination period for American Indians, which continues today, has been characterized by an increase in the numbers of Indians in leadership roles in federal Indian programs and the passage of four laws designed to benefit Indians (Goodluck, 1993; O'Brien, 1989; Walker & LaDue, 1986): the Indian Self-Determination Act (1975), the Indian Health Care Improvement Act (1976), the Indian Child Welfare Act (1978), and the Indian Religious Freedom Act (1978). These are, of course, positive events in the history of American Indians, but even given these events, many American

Indians find it very difficult to forget about the ill treatment Indians as a group have received from Whites historically. Many American Indians are thus very suspicious of White people and tend to mistrust anyone outside their society (particularly Whites) who make promises to them concerning socioeconomic, political, and cultural opportunities outside their own lands. Mental health professionals who work with American Indian clients should be familiar with the overall effects of the historical events noted above on the lives of American Indians. This is particularly important for White mental health professionals, who, during the process of assessment and treatment of American Indian clients, may feel that they are being "rejected" or "mistrusted" by these clients without "apparent" reason (see Barcus, 2003, p. 28).

Practitioners involved in the assessment and treatment of Indian children must have "extensive knowledge of the Indian Child Welfare Act [ICWA; passed by the U.S. Congress in 1978] and its implications for the client system" (Goodluck, 1993, p. 222). The ICWA "acknowledged the tribe as *the best agency to determine custody* issues for Indian children. The Act reaffirmed that *tribes possessed jurisdiction over child-custody proceedings* for all Indian children living on the reservation" (O'Brien, 1989, p. 212; emphasis added). In addition, the ICWA states that if an Indian child does not reside on a reservation or resides in a state that has the authority to enforce its civil and criminal laws on reservations, the state court is required to transfer jurisdiction to the tribal court unless the parents object to the transfer (O'Brien, 1989). Thus, a therapist should not become involved in any court actions concerning American Indian families and issues of child abuse, foster care, or adoption unless he or she has extensive understanding of the applicability of the ICWA. The basic elements covered by the act are as follows (Goodluck, 1993):

- Child custody proceedings (e.g., procedures for defining a child as "Indian," tribal court jurisdiction, placement standards, and returning of the child to tribal jurisdiction)
- Indian child and family program development (procedures for providing information to tribes interested in developing service programs for Indian children)
- Record keeping and information (e.g., procedures for disclosure of information on Indians' rights and benefits)

Further information about the ICWA is available from all of the organizations listed in Box 6.1.

Familism

As is true for African Americans, Hispanics, and Asians, among American Indians the family has primacy; the individual is secondary. The individual is also secondary with respect to the role of the tribe (Richardson, 1981). Thus, the interests of both the family and the cultural group take precedence over those of the individual. In contrast with Hispanics and Asians, who generally emphasize the authority of the father, American Indians emphasize the "administration" of the family by the father and older relatives. Thus, mutual respect between wife and husband, between parents and children, between immediate family members and other relatives, and between family members and the tribe is highly valued (Ho, 1992; Matheson, 1986; Richardson, 1981).

Strong family relationships are emphasized in American Indian families, but individual family members' sense of independence is also rewarded, particularly among children and adolescents (Ho, 1992). For example, American Indian parents rarely tell their children directly what to do and often encourage them to make their own decisions. American Indians tend to believe that it is best to have few rules, and the rules that exist should be flexible and loosely written (Richardson, 1981). This cultural value applies to the "administration" of the family and children by parents, relatives, and tribal leaders. During the assessment and treatment of American Indian clients, then, is it particularly important that therapists avoid trying to determine who is the "head" of the family with the "authority" to make decisions regarding all family members. Unlike Asian and Hispanic families, American Indian families tend to view the father (or older adults) as only an "administrator" of the family; he does not control the family through absolute authority or *machismo*.

An important part of the American Indian cultural value of familism is the tradition of consulting tribal leaders, elders, and medicine men or women when marital conflicts emerge. Such consultation is particularly important when the husband and wife in conflict are from two different tribes (e.g., Cherokee and Hopi) and the main issue to be resolved involves the discipline of their children. If a therapist working with such a couple suspects that the conflict between them may be the result of the different values, norms, and beliefs held by the two tribes, the therapist should consult with an elder from one or both tribes to learn about the cultural differences between the tribes that may contribute to the conflict.

Sharing and the Concept of Time

American Indians tend to place great value on sharing; everything must be shared, including the solutions to problems, material goods, and time (Ho, 1992). American Indians treat time as a natural event, and they do not believe that time should control their natural way of living (Barcus, 2003; Ho, 1992; Sue & Sue, 2003). Time is not used as a measuring tool (i.e., to measure hours or minutes); rather, it is related holistically to whatever task is being performed (A. McDonald, personal communication, January 1994). That is, the event or task, rather than the clock, is what is important. (It has been suggested that many Hispanics hold a similar concept of time; see, e.g., Sue & Sue, 2003.) Many American Indians believe that in the same way material goods must be shared, time (to fulfill a given task) must also be shared with others. For example, an American Indian client may be late for a therapy session not because he or she wants to be late or is resistant to therapy, but because he or she met a friend on the way to the session and stopped to talk about family matters, business, or other issues. For this client, social contact with a friend (i.e., the task) is more important than arriving punctually for a therapy appointment (i.e., the clock). Therapists who work with American Indian clients should understand this cultural value and avoid questioning these clients about why they are sometimes late for therapy sessions.

Nonverbal Communication

Like Asians, American Indians place great emphasis on nonverbal forms of communication. Among American Indians, listening is more important than talking (Matheson, 1986; Richardson, 1981); the belief is that one can learn a great deal just by listening to what other people are saying. Thus, American Indians often communicate feelings and emotions nonverbally, through their bodies, eyes, and tone of voice (Barcus, 2003). The therapist should be aware that an American Indian client who is very quiet during a therapy session is listening intently and attending very carefully to what the therapist is saying, both verbally and nonverbally. Similarly, when an American Indian client speaks, he or she expects the therapist to listen and attend carefully to both verbal and nonverbal cues coming from the client. When the client perceives that the therapist is listening, this perception is translated into a recognition that the therapist understands the problem and that he or she may have good suggestions for the solution of that problem (Barcus, 2003; Sue & Sue, 2003).

Two special forms of nonverbal communication that are associated with American Indians are lack of eye contact and slight handshake. In Western culture, eye contact is generally interpreted as a sign of respect and attention to others. Among American Indians, however, eye contact is a sign of disrespect. Thus, an American Indian client is likely to feel very uncomfortable if the therapist insists that the client look him or her directly in the eye (Thompson et al., 1993). According to Johnson, Fenton, Kracht, Weiner, and Guggenheim (1988), American Indians generally clasp hands with a light touch in greeting, believing that a firm handshake is a sign of aggression (see Barcus, 2003, p. 25). Therapists' failure to appreciate American Indians' cultural values concerning eye contact and handshaking may lead to errors in the diagnoses of many American Indian clients. For example, a therapist might arrive at a diagnosis of depression for an American Indian client who avoids eye contact and firm handshakes and generally shows other nonverbal communication styles that Western culture might interpret as psychomotor retardation (Johnson et al., 1988).

Individualism and Collectivism

Like Hispanics and Asians, American Indians reject the mainstream American cultural concept of individualism, which they see as leading to unwanted competition among family members and between American Indians and other people (Richardson, 1981). Because of this attitude, American Indians are sometimes erroneously described as "unmotivated," "lazy," and "unproductive." Although American Indians value collectivism and the sense of "working together" as a group to achieve common goals, they also recognize the qualities of the individual and emphasize independence (O'Brien, 1989). Thus, therapists who work with American Indian clients need to understand the implicit harmony between the right of an individual to pursue self-actualization and the tribe's need for actualization and/or survival (A. McDonald, personal communication, January 1994). Therapists' failure to recognize the value that American Indians place on harmony between individualism and collectivism may fail to assess and treat members of this group effectively. For example, if an American Indian client believes that the therapist is recommending a procedure or technique that may cause discord among family and tribal members, the client is not likely to follow that recommendation (Sue & Sue, 2003).

The First Session

Making Introductory Statements

If the therapist is not an American Indian, he or she should begin the first session with an American Indian client by making a clear statement regarding his or her limited understanding of the cultural values, religions, and traditions among American Indians. The therapist should also state that he or she would like the client to alert him or her to any errors or offensive statements he or she might make as a result of that limited understanding (Richardson, 1981). In addition, during this session it is appropriate for the therapist to state that the history of American Indians shows that they are good people and that the client should feel proud of his or her heritage.

The therapist should avoid statements such as "Feel free to tell me . . ." or "You can rest assured I will not discuss your problems with . . . ." As several scholars have noted, Indians have heard statements like these many times in their history, from the "Great White Father" and federal bureaucrats, and each time they have been deceived (see, e.g., Richardson, 1981; Walker & LaDue, 1986). The therapist should also avoid asking questions that are not related to the client's core problem. For example, it may not be appropriate to ask an American Indian client in the first session, "What does your father think about the restriction on hunting?" or "Why don't Indians of various tribes share the same traditions concerning the management of children?" Most American Indians are likely to consider such questions offensive (Richardson, 1981).

Avoiding Any Discussion of Medication

It is particularly important in the first session that the therapist avoid making any statements concerning the use of medication to treat the client's problem. Many Indians believe that synthetic medications are not good for Indians' health (Thompson et al., 1993).

Accepting the Presence of Others

It is not unusual for an American Indian client to bring other people with him or her to a first therapy session. American Indians generally are very open about sharing their emotional problems with their relatives, friends, tribal leaders, and medicine men or women (Richardson, 1981).

Avoiding Taking Too Many Notes

An American Indian client expects the therapist to listen, and the therapist's taking notes may appear to such a client as a sign of "not listening" and "disrespect." Also, American Indians place a high value on simplicity and flexibility in their social contacts, and if the therapist takes notes, the client may see the process of the interview as uncomfortably formal and structured (Ho, 1987; Richardson, 1981). If the therapist must take notes, it is important that he or she ask the client's permission to do so first. Then, at the end of the session, the therapist should summarize the notes for the client to show that the therapist was listening while taking notes and *understood the client's main concern.* If the therapist senses (through nonverbal signals from the client) that the client does not want the therapist to take notes, the therapist should indicate to the client (nonverbally) that not taking notes is an acceptable option.

Listening Rather Than Talking

Generally, American Indian clients go to a therapist because they want the therapist to listen to what they have to say about the core clinical problem; these clients do not go to therapy to listen to the therapist. Thus, it is important that the therapist use his or her ears more than his or her mouth during the first session with an Indian client (Barcus, 2003).

Confidentiality and Resistance

During the first session, an American Indian client from a small Indian community may not want to answer questions about his or her personal or private life. A therapist who is unfamiliar with Indian clients may erroneously believe that this attitude indicates resistance and mistrust toward the therapist. It is more likely, however, that the client has a relative or friend who works in the same hospital or clinic as the therapist, and the client is afraid that his or her answers to these questions will be entered in the medical record and become public (Thompson et al., 1993). If that is the case, the therapist should first make an overall statement concerning confidentiality (as is always recommended with clients from all cultural groups), and then, if the client still refuses to answer such questions, the therapist should not label the client's behavior as "resistance" but rather consider it as an indication that issues of confidentiality have not been resolved to the client's satisfaction. Alternatively, the therapist might ask the client directly whether he or she has a relative or friend working in the hospital or clinic. If the answer is yes, the therapist should allow the client to make his or her own decision regarding the best way to handle the situation. It may be a bad tactic for the therapist to make a promise to such a client regarding the maintenance of confidentiality; only the client is likely to know whether his or her relative or friend can be trusted.

Exploring Important Potential Problems

During the first session with an American Indian client, the therapist should pay particular attention to screening for symptoms of alcoholism and depression. Alcoholism is not only the primary concern among American Indians, it is also a major cause of suicide and violence in this group (Choney, Berryhill-Paapke, & Robbins, 1995; O'Brien, 1989; Walker & LaDue, 1986). Screening Indian women for symptoms of alcoholism is also important for the prevention of fetal alcohol syndrome, which results in severe physical, social, and intellectual deficits in children. Feelings of inadequacy and low self-esteem are indications of depression in American Indians; these feelings have been associated with the negative impacts of reservation life and time spent at the Indian boarding schools (Walker & LaDue, 1986). In addition, stress and other emotional problems in American Indians are often associated with relocation (i.e., moving away from the reservations and relocating in urban areas). Thus, it is important for the therapist to determine whether or not the client has recently moved away from the reservation.

In subsequent sessions, an American Indian client who sees him- or herself as affected by the historical events experienced by earlier generations would benefit from discussing these events with a practitioner who has an understanding of the dramatic effects of these events on the lives of

American Indians, particularly during the Manifest Destiny and assimilation periods, as described above.

Conducting Psychotherapy

Traditional Healers and Mental Health Professionals

The use of traditional healers (e.g., medicine men and women) in the interpretation and solution of problems is increasing among American Indians, both those living in urban areas and those living on reservations (Choney et al., 1995; Matheson, 1986; Richardson, 1981; Walker & LaDue, 1986). Thus, many American Indian clients seeking professional help for mental health disorders expect therapists to be familiar with and ready to integrate traditional healing practices with Western healing practices.

Practitioners working with American Indians may greatly enhance these clients' perceptions of their credibility by having lists of legitimate healers available for them. Therapists can obtain such lists from local Indian boards or from specialized institutions such as Chief Dull Knife College (formerly Dull Knife Memorial College), a tribal college founded on the northern Cheyenne reservation in Montana in 1979 (see Box 6.1). In fact, some scholars recommend that clinicians (in particular non-Indian practitioners) encourage their American Indian clients to consult traditional healers in their Indian communities and to discuss with their therapists how they might integrate Western and traditional healing during the course of assessment and treatment (Thompson et al., 1993). (It is important to note here that although the practices of Indian healers are often aimed at controlling evil spirits, these healers do not generally practice black magic or witchcraft, i.e., the use of the healing process to harm others; see Thompson et al., 1993.)

Finally, Thompson et al. (1993) suggest that it is inappropriate for therapists to question their American Indian clients about the specific procedures used by Indian healers. According to these authors, many American Indians believe that if such procedures "are to be revealed at all to non-Indians, or even to someone from another tribe, it is only after a long and trusting relationship has been established" (p. 208).

Recommended Modalities of Therapy

The following guidelines apply to the use of all forms of psychotherapy conducted with American Indian clients (Ho, 1987, 1992; Thompson et al., 1993; Walker & LaDue, 1986):

1. For many Indians, the present is more important than the future. The practitioner should screen quickly for this perception of time to determine whether therapy should be present oriented.

2. Many American Indians believe that it is disrespectful to ask a lot of questions, thus therapists should be aware that when American Indian clients ask questions during the process of psychotherapy, the function of such questions is to clarify the therapist's instructions.

3. The therapist should use a nondirective approach to determine any basic survival issues and unmet needs in the particular American Indian family or client under treatment. For example, moving from the reservation to an urban area, unemployment, medical complications, and poverty are examples of survival issues that may lead to violence, heavy drinking, and marital problems.

4. Once the therapist has determined the potential impacts of the client's survival issues and unmet needs, he or she should use a directive problem-solving and social-skills training approach, suggesting a concrete and feasible solution to the client's problems. The therapist might combine the assistance of a medicine man or woman with the problem-solving and social-skills training approach.

5. Because many American Indian clients expect mental health professionals to provide them with some clarification concerning the causes of their problems and what exactly they can do to deal with those problems, therapists must be prepared to spend considerable time and display great flexibility with these clients.

6. If an American Indian client has to travel a great distance to see the therapist, it is important that the therapist be prepared to offer the client a plan that will encourage subsequent visits to the therapist and thus facilitate the effects of treatment. The therapist should consider the following in creating such a plan: the use of self-help groups close to the client's residence, the recruitment of the healthiest members of the client's family to serve as "cotherapists" (who can be instructed to assist in monitoring the client's compliance with the therapist's instructions at home), and the use of brief therapy with short-term objectives (Thompson et al., 1993).

Behavioral Approaches

Behavioral approaches are recommended with American Indian clients because such approaches emphasize the causes of behavior (including maladaptive behavior) as determined primarily by external events and avoid any attempt to explain behavior in terms of internal conflicts (Walker & LaDue, 1986). An important element of behavioral approaches that makes them appropriate for American Indian clients is their emphasis on how environmental events can lead to disruptions in the symbiotic relationship between the environment and the individual or the group. Similarly, many American Indians believe that problems in the individual and the group can result from a disruptive individual/group-environment relationship caused by the effects of negative events (e.g., epidemics, the creation of reservations, Indian boarding schools). In using behavioral approaches, therapists teach clients how to establish better relationships with the environment by making viable decisions in the presence of external (negative) events and by modifying external behavior-consequence relationships, leading to changes in behavior (Walker & LaDue, 1986).

Family Therapy

Many American Indian clients believe that they are experiencing family problems (e.g., marital problems, difficulties in handling their children, school problems) because their families are unable to meet the essential needs of all family members, including food, shelter, and health care (Ho, 1987). Thus, when conducting family therapy with American Indian clients, the therapist must deal initially with the family's basic needs, including the provision of concrete advice regarding the fulfillment of those needs. The therapist should keep on hand a list of local social agencies that specialize in assisting American Indian families and should discuss this list with the family. This approach shows that the therapist is sensitive to the fact that the family may have unmet needs and that he or she is able to provide immediate delivery of concrete services, which in turns enhances the development of a trusting therapeutic relationship.

The following additional guidelines apply during the family therapy process with American Indian clients (Ho, 1987):

1. The therapist should emphasize group decision making by involving all nuclear and extended family members (including the medicine man or woman and tribal leaders) in the process.

2. The therapist should present all suggestions he or she makes to the family in a concrete, slow, and calm mode to show the family that the therapist is sensitive to American Indians' task-oriented approach to time.

3. The therapist should determine the tribal identity of the family and whether all members involved in the family belong to the same tribe. As noted earlier, this is particularly important when the family's problems involve conflicts between husband and wife regarding the management of their children. For example, in the Hopi tribe, the wife is the one primarily responsible for the management of children, whereas in the Cherokee tribe, husband and wife are expected to share the discipline of children. Thus, a couple consisting of a Cherokee woman and a Hopi man might experience marital discord because of the wife's unhappiness that her husband shows no concern regarding the discipline of their children (see Ho, 1992, pp. 154–155).

4. The therapist should allow family members to decide exactly what they want to manage during the process of family therapy. For example, an American Indian family might enter family therapy to seek help in fulfilling some basic needs and then terminate therapy when this goal is accomplished

(Ho, 1987). If such a family returns for additional therapy sessions after having achieved the initial goal of fulfilling basic needs, this is a sign that the family members believe it is time for them to deal with relationship problems and whatever problems led to their initial contact with the therapist. These might include marital problems, school difficulties among the family's children and adolescents, and/or alcoholism (Ho, 1987).

Group Therapy

Despite the common belief that group therapy is not appropriate for American Indians, several scholars have argued that this is not necessarily the case. For example, Arthur McDonald (personal communication, January 1994); Barcus (2003); Manson, Walker, and Kivlahan (1987); and Thompson et al. (1993) recommend the use of group therapy with American Indian clients (particularly in the prevention and management of alcoholism), especially when it is programmed in combination with traditional Indian activities. In addition, Manson et al. (1987) point out that group therapy is appropriate for American Indian clients because this intervention "is an outgrowth of the natural emphasis on groups in the social ecology of most Indian and Native communities" (p. 170). Furthermore, Barcus (2003) suggests that group therapy, particularly when it is in accord with the "culture and values of Native people, may be the most effective treatment, specially for Native children, because of the interdependent nature of Native communities" (p. 27). Therapists who undertake group therapy with American Indian clients should follow these three specific guidelines (Sue & Sue, 2003; Thompson et al., 1993):

1. The therapist should obtain the support and/or permission of tribal officials before scheduling group therapy.

2. If the therapist is not an Indian, he or she should conduct group therapy with the assistance of Indian professionals (e.g., Indian social workers, teachers, school counselors, psychologists, psychiatrists).

3. The therapist should invite medicine men and women, tribal leaders, elders, and other respected tribal members to participate actively in some group therapy sessions. (The therapist should ask members of the group for help in selecting tribal members with appropriately high status in the tribe.)

Medication

The use of medication in the treatment of mental disorders among American Indians has not been systematically studied or reviewed. Thompson et al. (1993) state, however, that most classes of psychotropic medication are effective with this group. In any case, as noted above, the therapist should avoid any mention of the possibility of drug therapy during the first meeting with an American Indian client.

Psychodynamic Model

Many American Indians believe that mental problems are caused by external events rather than by internal conflicts or difficulties with the personality of the individual. Because, in general, psychodynamic therapy does not take into account environmental events and places heavy emphasis on internal conflicts, this approach is not recommended with American Indian clients (Walker & LaDue, 1986).

Treatment of Children

Regardless of the type of treatment used, if an American Indian child is the target client, the most important guideline for the therapist is to avoid giving recommendations to the child's parents that appear to indicate that they should force the child to behave in certain ways. A "rightness of choice" (Ho, 1987, p. 77) is expected among Indian children, and the main task of parents is to assist their children in making the right choices. Thus, a treatment plan that emphasizes parental orders, verbal reprimands, or threats is inappropriate for use with an Indian child.

Foster Care and Adoption

The therapist needs to be aware that under the Indian Child Welfare Act, Indian families have the right to make all decisions regarding foster care placement and adoption of Indian children. Thus, a clinician cannot make such a decision without consulting both the tribe and the child's parents (O'Brien, 1989; Thompson et al., 1993). Therapists should be particularly careful to follow this guideline when foster care and adoption decisions involve the placement of Indian children with non-Indian families.

Organizations Devoted to Assisting American Indians

Because many policies and regulations exist (some put in place by federal and state governments, others by the tribes) regarding American Indian communities, it is important that therapists consult regularly with organizations that specialize in assisting these communities (such as those listed in Box 6.1) to enhance the process of assessment and treatment of American Indian clients. A good quick reference source regarding the numerous policies and regulations across Indian tribes is O'Brien's book *American Indian Tribal Governments* (1989).

7

Guidelines for the Prevention of Attrition With African American, Hispanic, Asian, and American Indian Clients

Attrition is generally defined as the client's failure to return for continued therapy. It has been estimated that 50% of clients from the culturally diverse groups addressed in this volume terminate therapy after only one contact with a mental health professional (Boyd-Franklin, 1989; Maramba & Hall, 2002; Marin & Marin, 1991; Sue & Sue, 2003; Wilkinson & Spurlock, 1986; Yamamoto, 1986). The literature presents several strategies that therapists can use to prevent attrition, including making telephone calls and sending letters to clients to remind them about subsequent therapy sessions, sending greeting cards to clients (e.g., Christmas cards), reducing the cost of therapy, changing the schedule for therapy to accommodate the client's needs, and matching clients with therapists from the same race or ethnicity. These strategies, however, do not always seem to work with members of the culturally diverse groups discussed here. The best way to prevent attrition with such clients is probably to use an approach that emphasizes the cultural variables that can influence attrition.

In general, therapists' attention to the guidelines presented in Chapters 2 through 6 may dramatically reduce attrition among culturally diverse clients. The tables presented in this brief chapter summarize those guidelines for the therapist, emphasizing the importance of cultural sensitivity in the prevention of attrition among multicultural clients. Clinicians may find that they can generalize some of these guidelines across groups; that is, the guidelines recommended for clients from one group may also apply to therapy with clients from other cultural groups.

Table 7.1   General Guidelines for the Prevention of Attrition

1. Make sure that the client finds what he or she is looking for from a therapist (e.g., acceptance of the client's belief system).
2. Be aware that the client expects a quick solution to his or her problems.
3. Explore the client's expectations regarding therapy.
4. Involve the client's extended family members (including persons related to the client both biologically and nonbiologically) in the assessment and treatment process. Remember that with Asian clients, issues of shame and humiliation may preclude the inclusion of nonbiologically related extended family members (e.g., friends).
5. When the length and frequency of treatment sessions are reduced, explain the reasons to the client so that he or she does not perceive the changes as indicating lack of interest in working with members of the client's cultural group.
6. If paraprofessionals are used, avoid using them too frequently; the client may feel that he or she is being treated as a "second-class client" if he or she is not often seen by a professional.
7. Use a modality of therapy that is directive, active, and structured, and provide a tentative solution to the client's core problem (particularly during the first session).
8. Ensure that all mental health professionals (e.g., psychologists, psychiatrists, social workers) and support staff (e.g., secretaries, receptionists) who come in contact with multicultural clients have had cross-cultural training.

Table 7.2   Guidelines for the Prevention of Attrition With African American Clients

1. Discuss racial differences with the client.
2. Avoid linking the client's mental problems with his or her parents' behaviors; the client probably holds the belief that such problems result from environmental conflicts in society.
3. Do not try to gather information about the client's family secrets by questioning the client directly regarding those secrets.
4. Assure the client that members of his or her church can be included in the client's assessment and treatment.
5. Do not recommend medication as the first treatment choice; this is an *impersonal* treatment, and the client may get the impression that you do not want to work with him or her.
6. Avoid giving the impression that you consider yourself to be a "protector of the race" when discussing racial issues.
7. Be aware that the client may view referrals made by the schools or social welfare agencies as a threat to his or her autonomy and an indication of the possibility that family secrets will be made public. Discuss this feeling with the client.

Table 7.3   Guidelines for the Prevention of Attrition With Hispanic Clients

1. Use *formalismo* (formalism) during first contact with the client, but gradually move to *personalismo* (personalism) in subsequent contacts.
2. Assure the client that members of his or her church can be included in the client's assessment and treatment.
3. Conduct a brief separate interview with the father to recognize his authority in the family.
4. Talk about spiritual events that the client believes can lead to emotional problems (e.g., *mal puesto,* or hex; *mal de ojo,* or evil eye).
5. Do not suggest that the client take actions that may compete with the cultural ideals of *machismo* and *marianismo* (e.g., husband controls the family; wife is submissive and passive).
6. Ensure that when the client leaves the first session, you have provided him or her with concrete recommendations regarding how to handle the problem; avoid giving the client the impression that you need to gather more information in subsequent sessions before providing recommendations.
7. Because the client is likely to expect medication, discuss the possibility of prescribing medication during the first and subsequent sessions.
8. Be aware that time is not a fundamental variable in Hispanic cultures; do not ask the client why he or she is late for therapy.

Table 7.4   Guidelines for the Prevention of Attrition With Asian Clients

All Asian Clients

1. Avoid personalism; maintain an emphasis on formalism during the entire process of therapy.
2. Ensure your credibility with the client and the client's confidence in your competence by disclosing your educational background.
3. Do not force or encourage the client to reveal his or her problems; wait until the client is ready to discuss these problems. Be aware that many Asians suppress the public admission of problems because they fear bringing shame and humiliation on themselves and their families.
4. Do not recommend that children exercise independence from the family (particularly their parents).
5. Avoid discussing hospitalization of the client without first considering other alternatives (e.g., home treatment).

Southeast Asian Refugee Clients

6. Assist the client in obtaining concrete social services (e.g., housing, school).
7. Avoid discussing traumatic events the client has experienced (e.g., deaths in the family during wartime) too early in the process of psychotherapy. Premature discussion of such events can lead the client to suffer additional stress, which may increase the probability of attrition.

Table 7.5 Guidelines for the Prevention of Attrition With American Indian Clients

---

1. Emphasize listening to the client rather than talking to him or her.
2. Be aware that time is not a fundamental variable in American Indian culture; do not ask the client why he or she is late for therapy.
3. Recommend therapies that lead to a sense of "working together" to achieve a common goal; competition is not encouraged in Indian culture.
4. Avoid making promises of secrecy; the client is likely to view such promises skeptically.
5. Be aware that the client does not expect to receive synthetic medication, particularly during the first session.
6. Avoid therapies that emphasize order and authority (e.g., "*I want* you to do . . ."; "*You should* learn how to *control* . . .").
7. Talk about "administration" of the problem rather than "control" of the problem.
8. Avoid personalism.

8

Guidelines for Evaluating
and Using the Epidemiological
Mental Health Literature With
Culturally Diverse Clients

A central issue in the assessment and treatment of clients from multicultural groups is the therapist's ability to evaluate and use the data on the epidemiology of psychiatric disorders or mental problems reported in the literature regarding these groups. In general, the methodology used in collecting epidemiological data is as follows: Researchers take a sample from a given population (e.g., the total population of African Americans), screen the individuals in that sample in relation to the particular variable or event under study (e.g., schizophrenia, depression, phobias), and then calculate a score for that sample. The researchers then use that score to estimate the *prevalence* (i.e., the frequency in the sample of the event or variable at the moment the sample was screened) and *incidence* (i.e., number of new cases) of the event or variable. Finally, the researchers use the resulting prevalence and incidence data to make generalizations about the manifestation of that particular variable or event (e.g., the prevalence and incidence of depression) in the population from which the sample was drawn.

When practitioners read the epidemiological mental health literature concerning the four cultural groups discussed in this volume, the first conclusion they often encounter is that both the prevalence and the incidence of mental disorders are higher among African Americans, Hispanics, Asians, and American Indians than among Whites in general or among other ethnic groups (e.g., Greek, Italian, Irish, and Polish Americans). The same literature suggests that, of the four groups that are the focus of this text, African Americans have the highest prevalence and incidence of mental disorders (Escobar, 1993).

The main guideline for practitioners in regard to the epidemiological literature is that they should avoid making generalizations based on such literature as they go about assessing and treating culturally diverse clients in their daily clinical practice. This guideline is offered because much of the epidemiological research to date has had four weaknesses: (a) a lack of uniformity in how mental problems or psychiatric disorders are defined across studies, (b) a lack of cultural validity, (c) a failure to examine the perception of racial discrimination as a stressful event leading to mental disorders or emotional problems, and (d) bias in the reporting of findings concerning the epidemiology of mental health problems in members of culturally diverse groups.

Lack of Uniformity in Definitions of Mental Disorders

Investigators have not yet agreed on the use of one particular instrument to measure the dependent variable (i.e., mental disorder) in psychiatric epidemiology. This means that no uniform definitions of mental disorders exist across studies investigating the prevalence and incidence of such disorders (Neighbors & Lumpkin, 1990). For example, Koslow and Rehm (1991) list 21 instruments that investigators can use to assess the prevalence and incidence of depression in children and adolescents (e.g., the Children's Depression Inventory, the Children's Depression Scale, the Schedule for Affective Disorders and Schizophrenia for Children, and the Depression Scale Modified for Children). The same problem exists in the assessment of depression in adults, as well as with respect to other mental disorders (e.g., conduct disorder, attention-deficit/hyperactivity disorder, schizophrenia, personality disorders) in both younger and older populations (for a list of instruments, see Murphy, 2002, p. 280). The use of different instruments to measure the prevalence and incidence of such disorders may yield different results across studies, particularly when such instruments do not share the same items, the same number of items, or the same cutoff scores (e.g., the scores considered to indicate the presence of "depression" versus "nondepression").

Thus, practitioners should keep in mind that statements such as "Black children have been found to exhibit the highest rates of childhood psychopathology and psychiatric impairment" (Ho, 1992, p. 80) and "Prevalence of schizophrenia was found to be highest among African Americans, intermediate among [Whites], and lowest among Hispanics" (Escobar, 1993, p. 55), and similar statements about different cultural groups (Robins & Regier, 1991), are linked with the results obtained with particular instruments. When different instruments are used to measure the same events, similar results may not be found.

It should be noted here that, given that no one instrument has been shown to be best for measuring any particular mental disorder, researchers have no choice but to use available instruments that are at least reliable and valid in methodological terms (not necessarily in cultural terms; see the discussion of cultural validity below). Researchers are expected to report on the limitations of their studies (e.g., the uniformity of definition of mental disorders), however, when they discuss the applications of their results for clinical practice.

Lack of Cultural Validity

To determine whether a researcher has considered the impact of culture in interpreting his or her data on the epidemiology of mental health, a practitioner should read the research report with the following question in mind: Does the report include information about the potential effects on the data of language, folk beliefs, acculturation, and the perception of racial discrimination? If the answer is no, the study is probably culturally invalid.

Effects of Language

Some data suggest that practitioners may perceive more psychopathology in bilingual multicultural clients when the clients are interviewed in English than when they are interviewed in their native languages. For example, Marcos, Alpert, Urcuyo, and Kesselman (1973) asked mental health professionals to view videotapes of Hispanic clients communicating in either Spanish or English and rate the clients on psychopathology. The researchers found that the professionals detected more psychopathology in the clients during their interviews in English. Marcos et al. suggest that when bilingual clients whose first language is not English are instructed to speak in English (rather than their native languages), they might appear tense, uncooperative, and emotionally withdrawn.

As Martinez (1986) notes, during verbal exchanges in therapy, many Hispanic clients who speak minimal or no English first think in Spanish, then translate from Spanish to English in their minds, and finally respond to the therapist. During this process, the therapist may interpret the client's verbal and nonverbal behaviors as psychopathological. For example, a Hispanic client with little command of English might answer a question or remark from the therapist with a simple and restricted verbal output, and the therapist might interpret this as a case of "impoverishment of thought." In addition, looking for the right word or sentences in English can create anxiety in such a client, leading to "thought derailment" or "loosening of association" (Martinez, 1986, p. 71).

Similar observations have been made about the potential effects of clients' use of nonstandard English on the evaluation of psychopathology. For example, Russell (1988) cites a study conducted by D. S. Guy in which White and African American therapists observed a "client" (played by an actor) describing his mental problems in either Black English or Standard English. Guy found that the African American therapists detected less psychopathology in the client when he spoke in Black English and more psychopathology when he spoke in Standard English; the reverse was true of the White therapists. In a similar study, Arroyo (1996) had non-Hispanic White psychologists view two videotapes: one in which the client appeared with light skin color and spoke Standard English, and one in which the same client appeared with dark skin color and spoke English with a Hispanic accent. In general, Arroyo found that the psychologists reported inability to empathize with the client, poor prognosis with treatment, and blunted affect significantly more often for the Hispanic client than for the non-Hispanic client.

Another element that practitioners should consider in evaluating epidemiological research findings is whether code switching was allowed during the process of the interview. Code switching is "a total or partial language shift within a given situation or conversation" (Russell, 1988, p. 35). Scholars have noted that this phenomenon may allow a client to be more or less (depending on the nature of the interview) emotionally distant from important issues in the understanding of the psychiatric problem under consideration (Pitta, Marcos, & Alpert, 1978; Yamamoto, Silva, Justice, Chang, & Leong, 1993). It should be noted that although code switching is generally associated with bilingual clients in psychotherapy, the same phenomenon has been observed in African American clients, who may switch from Standard English to Black English several minutes into an interview, perhaps because they can provide more information in Black English or as a way of divorcing themselves emotionally from the topic under consideration (Russell, 1988).

Practitioners can determine whether a particular epidemiological study took the potential effects of language into consideration by examining the research report for the following information:

1. Was the interview conducted in the interviewee's first language (e.g., Spanish), or did the researcher consider the potential effect of conducting the interview in the interviewee's second language in the interpretation of the results?

2. Was the interviewee allowed to use nonstandard English to facilitate both process and content during the interview (e.g., African Americans interviewed in Black English; see Russell, 1988; Yamamoto et al., 1993, p. 113)?

3. Was code switching allowed during the process of the interview with bilingual interviewees or interviewees who speak nonstandard English?

Effects of Folk Beliefs

Beliefs in the power of spirits and other unseen entities are culturally accepted among some members of the four groups discussed in this text. If a therapist does not take such beliefs into account when formulating a clinical diagnosis for a client from one of these groups, he or she may erroneously diagnose the client with a psychiatric disorder. For example, if a Hispanic client reports, "An evil eye coming from people I know must be responsible for my bad behavior," a clinician who is unfamiliar with the place of "evil eye" (*mal de ojo*) in the client's belief system would erroneously conclude that this client is demonstrating a "delusion," which may lead to a diagnosis of schizophrenia (Martinez, 1986). Similarly, if the clinician does not view certain items on the Minnesota Multiphasic Personality Inventory (MMPI), such as "Evil spirits possess me at times," in the context of the client's cultural beliefs, the outcome of assessment using this instrument would be that the client is mentally ill, when the reality is that the client simply shares a culturally accepted belief with his or her peers of the same cultural background (Malgady, Rogler, & Constantino, 1987). Thus, in evaluating the findings reported in the mental health epidemiological literature, practitioners should examine studies to determine whether the researchers took into account the potential impacts of folk beliefs on results indicating the prevalence and incidence of psychiatric disorders in various cultural groups, particularly Hispanics.

Effects of Acculturation

As Dana (1993a, 1995) notes, acculturation is one of the fundamental moderator variables in the interpretation of clinical interview and psychological test data. In evaluating and interpreting psychiatric epidemiological data, practitioners should examine whether the researchers took the potential effects of acculturation into account. If a given study did not include a measure of acculturation and the researchers failed to report the potential impacts of this variable on the epidemiological data, the study is probably culturally invalid. For example, results obtained using the Developmental Inventory of Black Consciousness and the Racial Identity Attitude Scale, which are recommended for measuring acculturation among African Americans, have been related to elevations on MMPI subscales, particularly the F (higher scores suggesting greater psychopathology or deviant response sets), 4 (Antisocial Characteristics), 6 (Paranoia), 8 (Schizophrenia), and 9 (Hypomania) scales (Dana, 1993b; Whatley, Allen, & Dana, 2003). Similarly, Hispanics tend to receive higher MMPI profiles when researchers do not take acculturation into consideration (Dana, 1993b, 1995; Montgomery & Orozco, 1985). Findings of this nature have been reported with the MMPI and the MMPI-2 (for a review of the literature, see Whatley et al., 2003, pp. 345–347). The same results have been reported with the Rosebud Personal Opinion Survey (Hoffmann, Dana, & Bolton, 1985), which is recommended for measuring acculturation among American Plains Indians (for information on the Plains culture, see Brandon, 1989, pp. 320–349; Force & Force, 1991, pp. 50–53).

An example of lack of cultural validity in a major psychiatric epidemiology study is the Epidemiologic Catchment Area (ECA) Study. In a major report on this study (described below), the researchers did not consider the potential impacts of acculturation on the interpretation of ECA data involving African American and Hispanics (mainly Mexican Americans) (Robins & Regier, 1991). In addition, it appears that only the Los Angeles ECA site (among five such sites) included a measure of acculturation, but only for the Mexican American group (Burnam, Hough, Karno, Escobar, & Telles, 1987). Burnam et al. (1987) selected items from the Acculturation Rating Scale for Mexican Americans (Cuéllar, Harris, & Jasso, 1980) and the Behavioral Acculturation Scale (Szapocznik, Scopetta, Arnalde, & Kurtines, 1978) and found that, "consistent with the acculturation findings, native-born Mexican Americans, who tended to have high levels of acculturation, had higher lifetime prevalence of disorders (phobias, alcohol abuse or dependence, drug abuse or dependence, as well as major depression and dysthymia) than immigrant Mexican Americans [i.e., the least acculturated group]" (p. 89).

Table 8.1 lists many of the acculturation scales currently available for use with clients from the four cultural groups discussed in this book. Scales such as these should be used in epidemiological studies to determine the impacts of acculturation on the data collected on members of these groups.

Failure to Examine the Perception of Racial Discrimination as a Cause of Emotional Problems

An important area of multicultural research is the assessment of the perception of racial discrimination as a stressful event leading to the manifestation of emotional problems among members of the culturally diverse groups discussed in this book. Therefore, studies examining the epidemiology of mental health problems among members of these groups would be expected to consider this particular stressor (i.e., perceived racial discrimination) in the interpretation of their data. The fundamental question that therapists should ask when reading the epidemiological literature in this context is this: Are emotional or mental disorders reported with the particular sample (e.g., African Americans, Hispanics) the result of generic stressors (e.g., marital separation, divorce, moving to a different city, losing a job) experienced by members of the general population, or are they the result of perceptions of racial discrimination among members of that particular sample?

Table 8.1   Acculturation Scales

Name of Scale	Group	Reference
Abbreviated Multidimensional Acculturation Scale	Central/South Americans, Caribbeans, Mexicans, Spanish	Zea, Asner-Self, Birman, and Buki (2003)
Acculturation Questionnaire	Vietnamese, Nicaraguan refugees	Smither and Rodriguez-Giegling (1982)
Acculturation Rating Scale for Mexican Americans	Mexican Americans	Cuéllar, Harris, and Jasso (1980)
		Cuéllar, Arnold, and Maldonado (1995)
Acculturation Balance Scale	Mexican Americans, Japanese	Pierce, Clark, and Kiefer (1972)
Asian American Multidimensional Acculturation Scale	Asian Americans	Chung, Kim, and Abreu (2004)
Behavioral Acculturation Scale	Cubans	Szapocznik, Scopetta, Arnalde, and Kurtines (1978)
Brief Acculturation Scale for Hispanics	Mexican Americans, Puerto Ricans	Norris, Ford, and Bova (1996)
Children's Acculturation Scale	Mexican Americans	Franco (1983)
Cuban Behavioral Identity Questionnaire	Cubans	Garcia and Lega (1979)
Cultural Life Style Inventory	Mexican Americans	Mendoza (1989)
Developmental Inventory of Black Consciousness	African Americans	Milliones (1980)
Ethnic Identity Questionnaire	Japanese Americans	Masuda, Matsumoto, and Meredith (1970)
Multicultural Acculturation Scale	Southeast Asians, Hispanics, Anglo-Americans	Wong-Rieger and Quintana (1987)
Multicultural Experience Inventory	Mexican Americans	Ramirez (1984)
Racial Identity Attitude Scale	African Americans	Helms (1986)
Rosebud Personal Opinion Survey	American Indians	Hoffmann, Dana, and Bolton (1985)
Suinn-Lew Asian Self-Identity Acculturation Scale	Chinese, Japanese, Koreans	Suinn, Rickard-Figueroa, Lew, and Vigil (1987); Suinn, Ahuna, and Khoo (1992)

The multicultural literature suggests that clients from these groups may display low self-esteem and satisfaction, as well as such psychiatric symptoms as anxiety, depression, paranoia, obsessive-compulsive behaviors, and somatization, as a result of experiencing racial discrimination in particular contexts (Klonoff, Landrine, & Ullman, 1999; Utsey, Chae, Brown, & Kelly, 2002). For example, Klonoff et al. (1999) asked 520 African Americans ranging in age from 18 to 79 years (mean age = 28.2 years, $SD = 10.1$ years) to complete the Schedule of Racist Events (SRE; Landrine & Klonoff, 1996), the Psychiatric Epidemiological Research Interview Life Events Scale (PERI-LES; Dohrenwend, Krasnoff, Askenasy, & Dohrenwend, 1978), and the Symptom Checklist-58 (Derogatis, Lipman, Rickels, Uhlenhuth, & Covi, 1974). The SRE measures perception of racial discrimination resulting from "culturally specific stressful events" (Klonoff et al., 1999, p. 331), including, for example, perception of racial discrimination in salary or housing, unfair treatment in the general working environment, and unfair treatment by individuals in service jobs (e.g., store clerks, waiters, bank tellers). The PERI-LES, by contrast, measures stressful events that are considered to be "generic"—that is, that may affect any member of the population regardless of racial/ethnicity status (see Klonoff et al., 1999, p. 331), such as getting arrested, getting married, getting divorced or separated, changing jobs, losing a job, and moving to a different city. The Symptom Checklist-58 measures psychological symptoms, producing a total symptoms score and scores for five subscales (Somatization, Obsessive-Compulsive, Interpersonal Sensitivity, Depression, and Anxiety). In addition, Klonoff et al. gathered data from participants on four demographic variables: age, gender, income, and education. The researchers used multiple regressions to answer the following question: "Which of the variables [i.e., demographic, culturally specific stressful events, or generic stressful events] was the best predictor of Blacks' symptoms?" (p. 332).

In general, Klonoff et al. (1999) found that the perception of overall racial discrimination was the best predictor of anxiety, somatization, and total symptom scores; generic stressful events were the best predictors of depression, interpersonal sensitivity, and obsessive-compulsive disorder. The researchers further analyzed the predictive role of overall racial discrimination in terms of three variants: recent racist events, lifetime racist events, and appraised racist events (whether the individual perceived the event as stressful versus nonstressful) and found that all variants of racist events "contributed significantly to all regressions . . . and in some cases accounted for a large percentage of the variance" (p. 333). Two additional significant findings were (a) that among all demographic variables, only gender contributed significantly to the predictive model of symptoms, and (b) being an African American woman, experiencing significant generic stressful events (e.g., divorce, separation), *and* experiencing racial discrimination "predicted increased psychiatric symptoms" (p. 336). These results suggest that the perception of racial discrimination may play a critical role in the development of psychiatric disorders, particularly among African Americans. Similar results have been reported with members of other non-Anglo-American cultural groups (e.g., Szalacha et al., 2003).

Bias in Reporting on the Epidemiology of Mental Disorders

The preceding discussion emphasizes two issues that may affect the nature of psychiatric epidemiological data: lack of a uniform definition of mental disorders and lack of cultural validity. Once the collection of data has been completed, the next steps for the researcher are to translate the data into prevalence and incidence scores and then report those scores. Practitioners should be aware that bias may be introduced in the ways in which the scores are reported. The task for practitioners is to determine how the reporting of psychiatric epidemiological data on culturally diverse groups may be biased (regardless of the nature of the data). This may seem very difficult to some practitioners who are extremely busy with clients and have little time to devote to careful reading of the literature, but it is possible for practitioners to screen quickly for bias in the reporting of epidemiological data collected with culturally diverse groups by taking the following three steps:

1. Identify the sample (e.g., African Americans, Hispanics) from which the data were collected.

2. Determine the larger population from which the sample was selected to reach conclusions regarding the representativeness of the sample (e.g., Is the study's sample of African Americans representative of the entire population of African Americans in the United States?).

3. Read the conclusions of the study (i.e., the researcher's summary of major findings expressed in words rather than in complex statistics) carefully.

If the sample is too small or is not representative of the particular group under study, the reporting on the data is probably biased. That is, bias is introduced by the researcher's assumption that the data can be generalized to the entire population (from which the sample was selected), when in fact this may not be true.

The National Institute of Mental Health's Epidemiologic Catchment Area Study, which has been considered "a landmark in psychiatric epidemiology" (Escobar, 1993, p. 51), serves to illustrate this point. In this study, 19,182 people age 18 and older were interviewed across five major U.S. cities (Baltimore, Maryland; Durham, North Carolina; New Haven, Connecticut; Los Angeles, California; and St. Louis, Missouri) from 1978 through 1986 (see Leaf, Myers, & McEvoy, 1991; Murphy, 2002). Escobar (1993) has summarized several important results from this study, including that lifetime prevalence of schizophrenia, manic disorders, and phobias was higher among African Americans than among Whites and Hispanics; that the prevalence of alcoholism among younger males was highest among Hispanics and Whites, and lowest among African Americans, but that among older males (age 45 and older), African Americans had the highest lifetime prevalence rate (i.e., having the symptoms anytime during the lifetime of the individual) for alcoholism; and that the lifetime prevalence rate for major depression was higher among Whites than among Hispanics and African Americans. In one of the key published reports that came out of the ECA Study, Robins et al. (1984) conclude that "we might be tempted to infer from these . . . results in the Northeast, mid-Atlantic, and Midwestern areas that *there is* little regional variation in the lifetime prevalence of these disorders *in the United States*" (p. 957; emphasis added). In a paper summarizing ECA data on schizophrenic disorders, Keith, Regier, and Rae (1991) conclude that they "found a somewhat higher rate of schizophrenia in the U.S. population than rates found in community studies in Europe. . . . We can have considerable confidence in these rates *because of the large sample*" (p. 52; emphasis added). Another example of generalization in the reporting of ECA data is the statement that "lifetime, one-year, and one-month prevalence rates for Hispanic men are higher than for the other two groups [i.e., Whites and African Americans]" (Helzer, Burnam, & McEvoy, 1991, p. 86). Similar statements regarding ECA results can be found in Robins and Regier's (1991) summaries concerning other psychiatric disorders.

Can the results of the ECA Study be generalized to the entire population of African Americans and Hispanics in the United States? Probably not. First, in this study, lifetime prevalence rates were based on small numbers of cases across subsamples. The numbers of African Americans across ECA sites ranged from 157 to 1,497, and the total (all sites) was 4,638 (10.4% of the total sample). The numbers of Hispanics ranged from 17 to 1,458 across sites, and the total was 1,600, or 5.5% of the total sample (Leaf et al., 1991, Table 2-5). In 1980 (when most ECA data were collected), the total number of African Americans in the United States between the ages of 15 and 65 was approximately 18.4 million (U.S. Bureau of the Census, 1992; U.S. Department of Health and Human Services, 1991), and the total number of Hispanics in the same age range was approximately 15 million. Thus, the ECA Study included 0.02% of all African Americans and 0.01% of all Hispanics in the United States. These percentages did not represent the proportions of the entire U.S. population accounted for by African Americans and Hispanics in 1980. Thus, reports on the prevalence of psychiatric disorders in African Americans and Hispanics based on the ECA data set (e.g., Robins et al., 1984) may be considered to be biased *if* they fail to inform readers that the results should be interpreted with caution because of the small numbers of cases in both groups.

In addition, Leaf et al. (1991) report that a total of 1,600 "Hispanics" were included in the ECA data set, but according to Escobar (1993), most of the Hispanics in the ECA sample were Mexican Americans. In fact, in the Los Angeles ECA site, 93% of the respondents were Mexican Americans (Escobar, 1993). Thus, extrapolations of the ECA conclusions to other Hispanics in the United States (e.g., Cubans, Dominicans, Puerto Ricans) could also be interpreted as cases of bias in the reporting of the data (Escobar, 1993). For example, the conclusion that "lifetime . . . prevalence rates [of alcoholism] for Hispanic men are higher than for the other two groups" (Helzer et al., 1991, p. 86) in reality applies only to Mexican Americans.

It should be noted that some researchers who took part in the ECA Study have acknowledged that many of the reported results were not statistically significant because of small subsample sizes (e.g., Karno & Golding, 1991, p. 211; Robins et al., 1984, p. 955). In addition, some have pointed out that a major limitation in the study was that the sample of Hispanics was made up mainly of Mexican Americans, with two other major Hispanic groups (Cubans and Puerto Ricans) underrepresented (Leaf et al., 1991). Most of the published reports that have summarized the ECA data, however, have not included explicit discussion of these limitations to avoid discouraging researchers (as well as others, e.g., practitioners, administrators of mental health services) from using the data to generalize to populations beyond the ECA sample.

Thompson, Walker, and Silk-Walker (1993) provide an example of bias in reporting concerning mental health epidemiological data on American Indians. Thompson et al. note that data from the Indian Health Service (IHS; created in 1955 as part of the U.S. Public Health Service to provide health care for Indians) "are widely quoted as being representative of all Indians" (p. 199), but a major bias in the reporting of such data comes from the fact that the IHS recognizes only the persons living on 32 reservations as "Indians"; Indians who live on other reservations (of which there are approximately 246) and those living in urban areas are not included in IHS statistics. Thompson et al. also point out that "some tribes are *not recognized* by the federal government and, therefore, are not included in most statistics" (p. 199). Thus, given that the IHS sample is not representative of the majority of Indians in the United States, the obvious conclusion is that any reporting on IHS data has a certain degree of bias.

In summary, a practitioner should read the mental health epidemiological literature with the following guidelines in mind. First, granted that the absence of any uniform definitions of mental disorders is an inherent problem in current research, studies should at least use reliable and valid instruments; the practitioner should look for evidence that reliable and valid instruments were used in a study, and also should check to see whether the researcher acknowledges that definitional problems limit the generalizability of the data to clinical practice. Second, the practitioner should examine the study to determine whether it is culturally valid (e.g., does the research report include discussion of the impacts of language on the data?). Third, the practitioner should evaluate whether the study included any assessment of acculturation. Fourth, the practitioner should look at the larger population from which the study sample was selected and determine whether the sample is representative of that population. Finally, the practitioner should read the conclusions offered in the study report to identify potential biases regarding the generalizability of results from the sample to the entire population.

9

Using Culturally Biased Instruments

Inaccuracies in the assessment and diagnosis of mental disorders can have three consequences: overdiagnosis, underdiagnosis, and misdiagnosis. Biases in testing are generally considered to be determining factors in such inaccuracies. Many scholars have attempted to eliminate or control biases in the assessment and diagnosis of members of multicultural groups, including by translating assessment instruments into the languages of the groups being tested and by developing culturally appropriate norms (Dana, 2000; Turner, DeMers, Fox, & Reed, 2001; Westermeyer, 1993; Yamamoto, 1986). Despite these attempts, the overall sense among researchers and clinicians is that biases in cross-cultural testing are still a reality (Anastasi, 1988; Dana, 1993b).

As Flaherty et al. (1988) point out, a culture-free test (i.e., a test that is not biased against any cultural groups) must fulfill five validity criteria:

1. Content equivalence (Are the items relevant for the cultures being tested?)

2. Semantic equivalence (Is the meaning of each item the same in all cultures being tested?)

3. Technical equivalence (Is the method of assessment comparable across cultures?)

4. Criterion equivalence (Would the interpretation of variables remain the same when compared with the norms for all cultures studied?)

5. Conceptual equivalence (Does the test measure the same theoretical construct across cultures?)

Currently, researchers and clinicians lack a test or assessment instrument of any kind that can fulfill these five criteria (Escobar, 1993). This suggests that culture-free tests are not yet available for use in the assessment of clients from the multicultural groups discussed in this book.

Researchers and clinicians agree, however, that despite the reality of bias in most tests, it is important that they use the tests that are available, in part because the tests provide clinicians with a common language in their assessment and diagnosis of psychiatric disorders (Yamamoto, 1986). In addition, many therapists are required to use existing tests in their clinical practice for reimbursement and institutional purposes. Therefore, it would be a bad strategy for practitioners simply to stop using these tests because they are biased (Dana, 1993b, 2000). A better strategy is for practitioners to recognize that they do not need to throw out every assessment instrument that contains bias against their clients from multicultural groups (P. B. Pedersen, personal communication, April 19, 1993); rather, they need to determine "how best to utilize [these tests] with patients from a different cultural background" (Yamamoto, 1986, p. 116). The literature suggests the following 10 guidelines that practitioners may use to minimize bias during the assessment and diagnosis of clients from multicultural groups using the instruments currently available (Bulhan, 1985; Jenkins & Ramsey, 1991; Wilkinson & Spurlock, 1986):

1. The practitioner should examine his or her own biases and prejudices before engaging in the evaluation of clients who do not share the practitioner's race and ethnicity (see Chapter 1 for discussion of the distinction between race and ethnicity).

2. The practitioner should be aware of the potential effects of racism.

3. The practitioner should include an evaluation of socioeconomic variables.

4. The practitioner should try to reduce the sociocultural gap between the client and the person conducting the assessment.

5. The practitioner should include an evaluation of culture-related syndromes and distinguish them from cultural variations.

6. The practitioner should ask culturally appropriate questions.

7. The practitioner should consult with paraprofessionals and folk healers within the client's particular cultural group.

8. The practitioner should use the mental status examination in a cultural context.

9. The practitioner should try to use the least biased assessment strategies first, then consider using more biased strategies under special circumstances.

10. The practitioner should use Dana's (1993a, 1993b) assessment model as an overall approach to minimizing bias.

Examining Practitioner Biases and Prejudices

Biases that influence the assessment and diagnosis of clients from culturally diverse groups may not necessarily be related to the particular strategies of assessment; rather, they may come from the biases and prejudices of the practitioner conducting the assessment (see Dana, 2002, pp. 7–8; Jenkins & Ramsey, 1991). Thus, before practitioners attempt to use any of the other guidelines for dealing with biased assessment strategies, it is important that they examine the possibility of bias and prejudice in themselves. D. K. Cheek (cited in Jenkins & Ramsey, 1991) has proposed a set of questions that practitioners might ask themselves to assess their level of bias and prejudice against African American clients. Examples include "Are you comfortable with African-American language?"; "Are you familiar with the current literature, journals, and periodicals in which African-Americans express their professional views?"; and "As a parent, would you approve your son or daughter dating an average (whatever you consider average) African-American youth?" (quoted in Jenkins & Ramsey, 1991, p. 735). Cheek suggests that clinicians answer these questions using a three-point scale on which the responses are "very much," "somewhat," and "not at all." According to Cheek, a "not at all" response "to any of these questions means that the therapist is not yet ready to counsel African-Americans effectively" (Jenkins & Ramsey, 1991, p. 735).

Although Cheek's questions deal specifically with clinicians' attitudes toward African American clients, similar questions may be appropriate for practitioners working with clients from other cultural groups. In the first edition of this book, I elaborated on Cheek's questions to adapt them to clients from the Asian, American Indian, and White communities and added several questions to those that Cheek developed to construct the Self-Evaluation of Biases and Prejudices Scale (SEBPS; see Paniagua, 1994), which appears here as Table 9.1. As my colleagues and I have noted, "The goal of the [SEBPS is not] to assess actual biases and prejudices against [the culturally diverse groups discussed in this book]. The main objective is to assist mental health professionals serving clients from these groups to self-evaluate the possibility of *unintended* biases and prejudices in their responses across items in the scale" (Paniagua, O'Boyle, Tan, & Lew, 2000, p. 828; emphasis added). For example, a clinician's lack of cultural knowledge about any of the groups discussed in this book (see item 2 on the SEBPS) may lead to unintentional bias and prejudice; a clinician who is unaware of the critical role of the extended family in the lives of many clients from these groups, for instance, may be unintentionally biased in trying to assess a client's family relationships.

The SEBPS consists of 10 items that are designed to measure the potential for (unintended) biases and prejudices in clinicians toward African American, American Indian, Asian, Hispanic, and White clients. The rating

Table 9.1 Self-Evaluation of Biases and Prejudices Scale

Question	*1* *(Very Much)*	*2* *(Somewhat)*	*3* *(Not at All)*
1. Have you had formal training with?			
African Americans	1	2	3
American Indians	1	2	3
Asians	1	2	3
Hispanics	1	2	3
Whites	1	2	3
2. Do you have cultural knowledge about?			
African Americans	1	2	3
American Indians	1	2	3
Asians	1	2	3
Hispanics	1	2	3
Whites	1	2	3
3. As a parent, would you approve your son or daughter dating?			
African Americans	1	2	3
American Indians	1	2	3
Asians	1	2	3
Hispanics	1	2	3
Whites	1	2	3
4. Would you date or marry a member of the following group?			
African Americans	1	2	3
American Indians	1	2	3
Asians	1	2	3
Hispanics	1	2	3
Whites	1	2	3
5. Would you feel comfortable providing clinical services to?			
African Americans	1	2	3
American Indians	1	2	3
Asians	1	2	3
Hispanics	1	2	3
Whites	1	2	3
6. Have you been exposed to professional views of?			
African Americans	1	2	3
American Indians	1	2	3
Asians	1	2	3
Hispanics	1	2	3
Whites	1	2	3

(Continued)

Table 9.1 (Continued)

Question	1 (Very Much)	2 (Somewhat)	3 (Not at All)
7. Are you familiar with the current literature (journals and other periodicals, books) on?			
African Americans	1	2	3
American Indians	1	2	3
Asians	1	2	3
Hispanics	1	2	3
Whites	1	2	3
8. Would you feel comfortable if you have problems understanding?			
African Americans	1	2	3
American Indians	1	2	3
Asians	1	2	3
Hispanics	1	2	3
Whites	1	2	3
9. Would you expect favorable therapy outcomes with?			
African Americans	1	2	3
American Indians	1	2	3
Asians	1	2	3
Hispanics	1	2	3
Whites	1	2	3
10. Would you expect favorable therapeutic relationships with?			
African Americans	1	2	3
American Indians	1	2	3
Asians	1	2	3
Hispanics	1	2	3
Whites	1	2	3
Total score (ratio)[a]			
African Americans _____ ( )			
American Indians _____ ( )			
Asians _____ ( )			
Hispanics _____ ( )			
Whites _____ ( )			

a. For example, if response 1 is marked for all questions involving African Americans, the total score for African Americans is 10 and the ratio is 1.0 (10 divided by 10). The maximum bias and prejudice ratio, 3.0, suggests a high degree of bias and prejudice toward a given group.

scale is numbered from 1 (*Very Much*) to 3 (*Not at All*). Adding the response numbers a clinician has chosen for all items concerning a given cultural group and dividing that total by the total number of questions answered about that group produces a bias and prejudice ratio for that group. For example, if the practitioner answers all questions dealing with African American clients by marking 1 (*Very Much*), his or her total score for African Americans is 10 and his or her bias and prejudice ratio is 1.0 (10/10 = 1.0). This score suggests that the practitioner is probably free of bias and prejudice toward African Americans and so is ready to conduct assessment, diagnosis, and treatment with African American clients. As the score increases, the potential for bias and prejudice increases. A score of 3.0 suggests a high level of bias and prejudice, and a practitioner receiving this score for a given group should refer clients from that group to another clinician; consult with other professionals, paraprofessionals, or folk healers within the particular group; and/or seek additional training with emphasis on cross-cultural issues associated with that particular racial/ethnic group.

In addition to serving as a self-assessment tool for individual clinicians, the SEBPS may be used to assess unintended bias and prejudice among groups of mental health professionals, paraprofessionals, and clerical staff in settings that serve culturally diverse clients. When the scale is employed in the assessment of a group, an overall score (derived from the participants' individual scores) rather than individual scores is used to determine the need for cross-cultural training in that particular setting. In order to enhance the confidentiality and validity of the process during group administration of the SEBPS, identifying information (e.g., names) should not be required from individuals completing the scale. In addition, the integrity of the results will be enhanced if the analysis of individuals' responses on the scale (from which the overall score is derived) is conducted by an independent observer (someone not associated with the clinical setting, such as a representative of a company that conducts surveys). Participants should be informed about this procedure to enhance their interest in completing the scale.

In previous work, my colleagues and I reported preliminary results from a study of an earlier version of the SEBPS (Paniagua et al., 2000). In addition to the 10 items listed in Table 9.1, that version included items inquiring about participants' demographic information (e.g., gender) and professional activities (e.g., profession, years of experience, working environment, race/ethnicity of clients, prior cross-cultural training). We distributed the SEBPS prior to the presentation of a cross-cultural workshop scheduled with participants, and the return of the SEBPS was considered to indicate the respondent's consent to participate in that study. The sample included 22 women (56.4%) and 12 men (43.6%) representing different professions (e.g., counselors, psychologists, teachers, and social workers) and ranging in age from 20 to over 50. Most respondents were White (56.4%), followed by African Americans (30.8%) and Hispanic (12.8%). Most participants reported a master's degree as the highest level of education achieved (43.6%), followed by high school diploma (25.6%), bachelor's degree (23.1%), doctorate (5.1%), and other degrees (2.6%).

The coefficient alpha was .87, suggesting an acceptable internal consistency across items. Approximately 35.9% of the respondents reported having between 11 and 20 years of experience in their particular professions, and 25.6% reported more than 20 years. This level of experience occurred primarily in government agencies (69.2%; e.g., child protective services, probation offices); school settings (28.9%); and the private sector (2.6%). The majority of participants served clients from the African American (41.7%) and Mexican American (24.4%) communities. The proportions of participants serving clients from other racial/ethnic groups (e.g., American Indian, Asian, and White) ranged from 6.9% to 18.2%. Most participants (82.1%) reported that they had received multicultural training in their working environments and through formal university courses, continuing education programs, and professional meetings.

Table 9.2 shows the means for participants' responses to the 10 items by race/ethnicity. In general, the findings displayed in this table suggest that participants' levels of *unintended* bias and prejudice across items were generally lower toward clients from their own racial/ethnic groups. For example, Hispanic ($M = 1.6$, $SD = 1.3$) and White participants ($M = 1.6$, $SD = 2.8$) tended to be more likely to display biased attitudes against African Americans than were African American participants ($M = 1.2$, $SD = 1.9$; $p < .002$, $F = 11.32$, $df = 2$, $df = 30$). White participants' scores indicated lower levels of unintended bias in the case of White clients ($M = 1.3$, $SD = 2.1$) than did the scores of African American ($M = 1.7$, $SD = 2.4$) and Hispanic ($M = 1.5$, $SD = 2.7$) participants ($p < .007$, $F = 9.54$, $df = 2$, $df = 28$). In general, participants' levels of unintended bias and prejudice against American Indian and Asian clients tended to be higher than those they showed toward African American, Hispanic, and White clients.

Being Aware of the Potential Effects of Racism

When differences in the prevalence and incidence of psychiatric disorders and in intelligence test results are asserted to be the results of differences among races, this explanation is termed *racism*. An emphasis on race as "explanation" in this context is considered to be a fundamental bias, because it prevents practitioners from exploring more plausible explanations for the same phenomena (De La Cancela, 1993; Good, James, Good, & Becker, 2003).

Table 9.2 Means and Standard Deviations for Participants' Scores by Race/Ethnicity

| | Race/Ethnicity of Client | | | | | | | | | |
| | African American | | American Indian* | | Asian | | Hispanic | | White* | |
Race/Ethnicity of Participant	M	SD	M	SD	M	SD	M	SD	M	SD
African American	1.2	1.9	2.1	4.1	2.1	3.6	1.6	2.8	1.7	2.4
Hispanic	1.6	1.3	1.7	2.7	1.9	2.6	1.4	2.5	1.5	2.7
White	1.6	2.8	1.8	3.2	1.8	2.8	1.5	2.9	1.3	2.1

SOURCE: Reprinted with permission from Paniagua, F. A., O'Boyle, M., Tan, V. L., & Lew, A. S. (2000). Self-evaluation of unintended biases and prejudices. *Psychological Reports, 87,* 823–829, Table 2.

*$p < .002$.

Intelligence test results are generally lower among African American, American Indian, Asian, and Hispanic test subjects than they are among White subjects (Jenkins & Ramsey, 1991). African Americans and Hispanics receive diagnoses of schizophrenia in higher proportions than do Whites (Good et al., 2003; Kilkus, Pumariega, & Cuffe, 1995; Wilkinson & Spurlock, 1986). Good et al. (2003) recently conducted a review of the literature on health disparities (i.e., sharp differences in prevalence and inci-dence of diseases, provision of clinical care, utilization of services, and so on) among distinctive racial/ethnic groups, with an emphasis on the over-diagnosis and misdiagnosis of mental disorders among African Americans and Hispanics, and found that African Americans are "diagnosed with schiz-ophrenia at almost twice the rate of white Americans, and . . . Hispanics are diagnosed with schizophrenia at one and a half times the rate of non-Hispanic whites" (p. 613). In addition, Good et al. found that when clini-cians are not aware of a client's racial/ethnic identity, they tend to arrive at the correct diagnosis, whereas when they know the racial/ethnic identity of a non-Anglo-American client, their diagnoses tend to be more severe (e.g., paranoid-type schizophrenia versus a less severe diagnosis of brief psy-chosis disorder; see American Psychiatric Association, 2000, pp. 313, 329).

Another important finding in this context is that the race/ethnicity of the clinician making the diagnosis might not be a critical variable in whether a given client is overdiagnosed or misdiagnosed. For example, in their review of the literature, Good et al. (2003) found that African American psychiatrists also tend to arrive at more severe psychiatric diag-noses for African American clients and less severe diagnoses for White clients when they know the racial/ethnic identity of the clients (participants in the relevant study viewed a series of case vignettes illustrating several *DSM-IV-TR* psychiatric disorders displayed by either White clients or African American clients). Good et al. suggest that mistaken diagnoses of culturally diverse clients (particularly African American and Hispanic clients) might result from clinicians' failure to differentiate "between majority norms and normative ways of experiencing and communicating symptoms among [culturally diverse] persons" (p. 614). Examples of such culturally normative ways of experiencing and communicating symptoms that may suggest psychiatric disorders but are actually unrelated to psy-chosis include the auditory and visual hallucinations that some Hispanic clients report experiencing in the culture-bound syndrome known as *ataque de nervios* and symptoms of the "ghost sickness" culture-bound syndrome experienced by some American Indian clients (described below; see also American Psychiatric Association, 2000, p. 900; Paniagua, 2001a, p. 21).

The assumption that underlies the racist explanation for findings such as those noted above is that race is the fundamental cause of differences in intelligence test results and in the prevalence and incidence of mental disor-ders. Research has shown, however, that when other factors (e.g., social background, income, education level, culturally normative ways of experiencing and communicating symptoms) are considered, significant differences between Whites and members of other cultural groups are not apparent (Escobar, 1993; Good et al., 2003; Jenkins & Ramsey, 1991). If a practitioner makes the mistake of accepting the racist explanation for differences between groups, another negative consequence is the increased probability that he or she will make another error: overdiagnosing clients from culturally diverse groups (e.g., seeing "schizophrenia" in an African American client simply because the client is African American).

Racism can also lead to underdiagnosis and misdiagnosis of major depressive disorder among members of culturally diverse groups. For example, depression has been reported more frequently in White clients in comparison with African American clients (Wilkinson & Spurlock, 1986). In this case, African American clients who are actually depressed may be underdiagnosed simply because the literature indicates that depression is not as common in this group as it is in the White population, or because of the "myth that African Americans could not . . . become depressed" (Griffith & Baker, 1993, p. 161). For example, many diagnostic instruments, including the *DSM-IV-TR,* do not include complaints of headaches, backaches, and pains in the extremities to be symptoms of depression, but these symptoms may suggest depression in an African American client (Wilkinson & Spurlock, 1986, p. 23).

Similarly, clinicians may underdiagnose depression among Asians because of the tendency of members of this group to display only somatic symptoms of depression (e.g., weight loss) and not because of their race per se (Yamamoto, Silva, Justice, Chang, & Leong, 1993). Asians also tend to show the lowest prevalence and incidence of psychiatric disorders among the culturally diverse groups addressed in the epidemiological literature (Jenkins & Ramsey, 1991). It has been suggested that this is probably related to the high value that Asian cultures place on avoiding the "shame" associated with making personal problems public and not to race itself (Sue & Sue, 2003).

Autism is diagnosed in African American children far less often than in White children. Wilkinson and Spurlock (1986) suggest that "there is a strong probability that instead of [autism's] being rare [among African Americans], it frequently may be diagnosed erroneously as mental retardation" (p. 22).

As the above examples show, race seems to play a major role in clinicians' interpretations of the manifestations of mental disorders. If the client is White, clinicians tend to expect to find mental problems A, B, and C, according to mental health epidemiological data, whereas if the client is African American, clinicians expect to see mental problems D, E, and F. As Wilkinson and Spurlock (1986) argue, such conclusions may "reflect biases in the assignment of diagnosis according to race" (p. 17; see also Good et al., 2003, pp. 612–618).

Evaluating Socioeconomic Variables

During the first session with an African American, Hispanic, Asian, or American Indian client, practitioners often collect socioeconomic data on the client and his or her family (e.g., income level; area of residence, e.g., urban versus rural; parents' education level; contacts with welfare agencies). During the process of clinical assessment and diagnosis, however, many practitioners rarely consider socioeconomic variables, even though the research shows that the prevalence and incidence of mental health problems are higher among families of lower socioeconomic status (Jenkins & Ramsey, 1991; Wilkinson & Spurlock, 1986, p. 22; Yamamoto, 1986, p. 108). Many members of the four cultural groups discussed in this book live in families with low socioeconomic status. When clinicians attempt to assess members of these groups without taking into consideration the impact of socioeconomic variables, the result can be bias in the assignment of diagnoses.

For example, studies assessing the mental health status of Vietnamese refugees found that symptoms of depression were present when the head of the family did not have a job (Yamamoto, 1986, p. 108). Similar observations have been made regarding members of other cultural groups. For example, the Hispanic Health and Nutrition Examination Study found that Puerto Ricans, the most socioeconomically disadvantaged subgroup among Hispanics, had a significantly higher prevalence of major depressive disorders than did the members of other Hispanic subgroups (e.g., Mexican Americans; Escobar, 1993).

Minimizing the Sociocultural Gap

Some research suggests that inaccuracies in the assessment and diagnosis of mental disorders may be the result of differences in sociocultural background between therapist and client, and that the greater the differences in sociocultural variables, the less accurate the assessment and diagnosis (Jackson, Berkowitz, & Farley, 1974). For example, African Americans score lower on intelligence tests when the tests are administered by White clinicians than they do when African American clinicians administer the tests (Jenkins & Ramsey, 1991). Studies have also shown that African Americans tend to alter their responses on self-report measures when the race of the examiner changes (Lineberger & Calhoun, 1983). In addition, Marcos (1976) suggests that when bilingual Hispanic clients are interviewed in English rather than in their native language (i.e., Spanish), the probability of errors in assessment and diagnosis of psychiatric disorders may increase. Thus, to minimize bias in the assessment and diagnosis of members of culturally diverse groups using standard instruments, clinicians should minimize the sociocultural gap between examiner and client.

Sue (1988) suggests that *ethnic match* seems more important than *racial match* in minimizing bias. That is, in terms of minimizing potential bias in assessment and diagnosis, it is more important for the examiner and client to share similar cultural values and lifestyles than it is for them to be members of the same race. Sue also suggests that if the examiner and client are from the same racial group (e.g., Asian examiner and Asian client) but do not share similar cultural values (e.g., an acculturated Asian examiner may hold values that are different from those held by a recent Asian immigrant), bias in the assessment and diagnosis of the client may increase. Thus, clinicians should emphasize ethnic match between examiner and client to minimize bias in the assessment process.

Distinguishing Culture-Related Syndromes From Cultural Variations

In the literature, disorders that are specific to particular cultures are often referred to as *culture-bound syndromes* (Paniagua, 2000). Because many such syndromes have been noted across different cultures, Simons and Hughes (1993) have proposed the term *culture-related syndromes*. The following are some of the culture-related syndromes that practitioners are likely to encounter while working with clients from the four cultural groups discussed in this book (American Psychiatric Association, 2000; Griffith & Baker, 1993; Rubel, O'Nell, & Collado-Ardón, 1991; Simons & Hughes, 1993):

- *Ataque de nervios* among Hispanics (i.e., an out-of-consciousness state resulting from evil spirits)
- *Amok, mal de pelea* among clients from Malaysia, Laos, the Philippines, Polynesia, Papua New Guinea, and Puerto Rico (a dissociative disorder involving outbursts of violent and aggressive or homicidal behavior directed at people and objects)
- *Dhat* among clients from India, China, and Sri Lanka (extreme anxiety associated with a sense of weakness, exhaustion, and the discharge of semen)
- *Falling out* among African Americans (seizurelike symptoms resulting from traumatic experiences, such as being robbed)
- *Ghost sickness* among American Indians (weakness, dizziness, hallucinations, and confusion resulting from the actions of witches and evil forces)
- *Hwa-byung* among Asians (pain in the upper abdomen, fear of death, tiredness resulting from imbalance between reality and anger)
- *Koro* among Asians (a man's desire to grasp his penis resulting from the fear that it will retract into his body and cause death)
- *Pibloktoq* among clients from the Arctic and Subarctic Eskimo communities (excitement, coma, and convulsive seizures resembling an abrupt dissociative episode, often associated with amnesia, withdrawal, irritability,

and irrational behaviors such as breaking furniture, eating feces, and
verbalization of obscenities)

- *Taijin kyofusho* among Asians (guilt about embarrassing others, timidity
  resulting from the feeling that one's appearance, odor, or facial expressions
  are offensive to other people)
- *Mal puesto,* hex, root-work, and voodoo death among African Americans
  and Hispanics (unnatural diseases and death resulting from the powers of
  people who use evil spirits)
- *Susto, espanto, pasmo,* and *miedo* among Hispanics (tiredness and weakness resulting from frightening and startling experiences)
- *Wacinko* among American Indians (anger, withdrawal, mutism, suicide
  resulting from reaction to disappointment and interpersonal problems)
- *Wind/cold illness* among Hispanics and Asians (fear of the cold and the
  wind; feeling weakness and susceptibility to illness resulting from the
  belief that natural and supernatural elements are not balanced)

Given the importance of the impacts of culture-related syndromes on
the assessment of clients from the cultural groups discussed in this book, a
crucial question is, Why do more clinicians not consider such syndromes in
their clinical practice? At least two answers to this question may be proposed. First, current standard clinical ratings and diagnostic instruments do
not include criteria for the assessment of such syndromes. For example,
clinical rating instruments such as the MMPI, the Child Behavior Checklist,
and the Zung Depression Scale as well as diagnostic instruments such as
the *DSM-IV-TR* and the Schedule for Affective Disorders and Schizophrenia (Rutter, Tuma, & Lann, 1988) do not require and/or do not include
any assessment tools designed to distinguish between these syndromes
and "true" psychopathology. Thus, clinicians may not be concerned about
screening clients for culture-related syndromes when making diagnoses of
mental disorders. The *DSM-IV-TR* includes an outline of cultural formulations and a summary of major culture-bound syndromes in response to recommendations from experts concerning the impacts of cultural variables on
the diagnosis of psychiatric disorders (Cervantes & Arroyo, 1994; Rogler,
1993; see Chapter 10). Practitioners using the *DSM-IV-TR,* however, are not
explicitly required to consider the presence of these variables in their
multiaxial evaluations; they are simply encouraged to consider these variables when making psychiatric diagnoses. As noted in Chapter 10, however,
two major contributions in the *DSM-IV-TR* are the "specific culture" features included in the descriptions of several psychiatric disorders and a
summary of culture-bound syndromes.

The second reason more clinicians do not routinely consider culture-
related syndromes is that reimbursement for assessment and treatment of
such syndromes is not a practice among major private insurance companies,
Medicaid, and Medicare. For example, a practitioner cannot expect to
receive payment for the assessment and treatment of *susto,* ghost sickness,

mal puesto, koro, or *ataque de nervios.* A clinician in private practice is not likely to spend time screening clients for such syndromes when his or her efforts will not lead to reimbursement.

A distinction should be made between clinicians' assessing clients for such syndromes only when they can expect reimbursement for doing so and their assessing for these syndromes to ensure that their culturally diverse clients are having mental problems rather than manifestations of culture-related syndromes. The first motivation is a matter of money, whereas the second is a matter of clinicians' adhering to ethical standards regarding cultural competence in the assessment of clients from multicultural groups. An important guideline to prevent clinicians from participating in discriminatory practices and unethical behaviors in the assessment of African American, American Indian, Asian, and Hispanic clients is that they should be familiar with the culture-related syndromes likely to be displayed by members of these groups. In addition, a clinician should formulate a list of any symptoms a client displays that suggest the presence of culture-related syndromes and consider the possibility of the presence of such syndromes before applying a psychiatric diagnosis to the client (American Psychological Association, 1992). The clinician should also consult with the client's family members and with peers of the client within his or her particular cultural group.

For example, an American Indian client might tell a therapist, "I believe that my weakness, loss of appetite, and fainting are the results of the actions of witches and evil supernatural forces." If the therapist is unfamiliar with the effects of "ghost sickness" among American Indians, he or she may interpret this statement as an indication of schizophrenia. By consulting with the client's family members and peers, the therapist can find out whether the client's symptoms are part of a culture-related syndrome; if other members of the client's culture do not share the client's beliefs, the beliefs are probably not culturally supported (Westermeyer, 1993). Because current clinical ratings and diagnostic instruments do not include criteria for the assessment of culture-related syndromes in clinical practice, practitioners need to develop their own systems for assessing clients for the presence of such syndromes.

Despite the importance of considering culture-related syndromes in clinical practice, too much emphasis on such syndromes may prevent practitioners from considering the possible presence of severe psychiatric disorders in multicultural clients. This could lead therapists not only to misdiagnose real psychiatric disorders but also to turn clients over to folk healers for treatment under the assumption that the clients have culture-related syndromes that mental health professionals cannot treat. As Westermeyer (1993) notes, a therapist may commit a major error in sending a client to a folk healer too quickly because the client's presenting symptoms resemble a culture-related condition. Thus, a practitioner should always assume that a client who displays symptoms associated with a culture-related syndrome may potentially have a severe psychiatric disorder until further cross-cultural assessment reveals that culture *is* the major element in the manifestation of the client's symptoms. If culture is the major element, the client does not require psychiatric treatment (Paniagua, 2000).

It is also important for practitioners to distinguish between culture-bound syndromes and cultural variations when diagnosing culturally diverse clients (Paniagua, 2000). Briefly, culture-bound syndromes are "locally specific troubling experiences that are limited to certain societies or cultural areas" (Smart & Smart, 1997, p. 394; see also American Psychiatric Association, 2000, p. 898). As noted above, such experiences have specific names within particular cultures (e.g., *ataque de nervios, koro, mal puesto, susto*). Therapists need to be aware that the symptoms associated with a given mental disorder may be related to a particular cultural context without being part of a culture-bound syndrome per se. A clinician should conduct an assessment of the cultural variations that may be contributing to the client's symptoms rather than search for the culture-bound syndrome that may or may not apply to the particular case. Although neither the fourth edition (*DSM-IV*) nor the later revision of that edition of the *Diagnostic and Statistical Manual of Mental Disorders (DSM-IV-TR)* explicitly distinguishes culture-bound syndromes from cultural variations leading to symptoms of given mental disorders, the fact that both discuss cultural variations across many mental disorders suggests the validity of such a distinction (see American Psychiatric Association, 1994, 2000).

For example, one of the key recommendations made by the Task Force on Culture and *DSM-IV* was the inclusion of dissociative identity disorder and anorexia nervosa as examples of culture-bound syndromes in the glossary of the *DSM-IV* (Lewis-Fernandez & Kleinman, 1995). This change was not introduced in the *DSM-IV* or the *DSM-IV-TR,* however, probably because the individuals who made the final decisions regarding what to include or exclude and where to insert suggested clinical materials across the multiaxial system in the main sections of the manual (i.e., Axes I-V), as well as in the appendices, did not consider those mental disorders to be examples of "locally specific troubling experiences" associated with given societies or cultures. As I have noted previously, "In the *DSM-IV* [and also in the *DSM-IV-TR*], however, cultural variations were considered as potential factors contributing to Dissociative Identity Disorder and Anorexia Nervosa" (Paniagua, 2000, p. 142). For example, in both the *DSM-IV* and the *DSM-IV-TR,* dissociative identity disorder was considered as particularly specific to the American culture because of the relatively high rates of the disorder in the United States. Similarly, the high prevalence of anorexia nervosa in the United States and other industrialized countries (e.g., Canada and Japan) is generally perceived to be the result of the "abundance of food and the linkage of attractiveness with being thin" (Paniagua, 2000, p. 147; see also

American Psychiatric Association, 1994, pp. 542–543; Castillo, 1997). Chapter 10 is devoted to an extensive summary of examples of cultural variations that might result in symptoms associated with mental disorders.

Asking Culturally Appropriate Questions

During the interviewing process with culturally diverse clients, practitioners should use culturally appropriate lines of questioning to avoid misunderstanding these clients and thus possibly making errors in diagnosis. For example, it is not always appropriate for a therapist to ask an Asian client questions such as "What is your opinion of yourself compared with other people?" and "Do you feel better, or not as good, or about the same as most?" (Yamamoto, 1986, p. 112). Asians, in general, do not like to compare themselves with other people. An Asian client may not answer the question, "Are you angry with your parents?" because of the high value Asian cultures place on always showing respect toward parents (particularly elderly parents), even if the relationship between the client and his or her parents is not good. A practitioner who is unfamiliar with Asian cultural values is likely to misunderstand why the client does not answer such questions, which may lead to an incorrect diagnosis. More appropriate questions for an Asian client than the first two mentioned above would be "Do you like yourself?" and "Do you feel okay about yourself as a person?" (Yamamoto, 1986, p. 112). Instead of asking, "Are you angry with your parents?" Gaw (1993b) suggests that the therapist might ask, "How is the relationship between you and your [parents]?" (p. 274).

Consulting Paraprofessionals and Folk Healers

Clinicians can minimize bias in the process of assessment and diagnosis with clients from culturally diverse groups by consulting with individuals who are members of those groups during the process. The ideal strategy is for the clinician to consult with mental health professionals within the client's own cultural group. This may be difficult to do, however, given the shortage of African American (1.2%), American Indian (0.2%), Asian (1.0%), and Hispanic (0.7%) mental health professionals in the United States (Russo, Olmedo, Stapp, & Fulcher, 1981). A more practical and realistic course of action for the therapist is to consult with paraprofessionals and folk healers within the client's cultural group.

For example, Southeast Asian refugees sometimes feel insecure and threatened in unfamiliar settings (e.g., the office of a White therapist), and this may lead them to display suspiciousness or mistrust that resembles "paranoid symptoms" (Westermeyer, 1993). By consulting with a paraprofessional who is also a Southeast Asian refugee, a therapist can quickly learn that such "symptoms" are to be expected in refugees who have experienced repressive regimes and survived concentration camps.

Therapists working with African American and Hispanic clients might consult with folk healers or *espiritistas* and *curanderos/as* when they evaluate these clients with the MMPI and the clients give responses of "true" on items such as "Evil spirits possess me at times," "I believe I am being plotted against," and "I believe I am a condemned person." According to the profiles of the MMPI, answers of "true" on these items indicate the presence of symptoms of paranoia or schizophrenia. As noted previously, however, some African Americans and Hispanics hold cultural beliefs in the power of evil spirits, the actions of witches, and malevolent supernatural entities (Martinez, 1986); by consulting with healers in these cultures, therapists can better understand these clients' responses on the MMPI.

Because medicine men and women play a central role in American Indian culture, clinicians working with Indian clients should always consult such healers before reaching conclusions regarding the diagnosis and treatment of these clients (Walker & LaDue, 1986, pp. 176–177).

Using the Mental Status Examination in Cultural Context

In prior editions of this book, I recommended that practitioners *avoid* conducting the mental status exam with clients from the culturally diverse groups discussed here because that exam could be biased against these clients (see Paniagua, 1994, p. 117; 1998, p. 118). My intention at the time was to emphasize the potential for cultural bias in the interpretation of results of the mental status exam. Several readers have pointed out, however, that my advice to *avoid* the exam was probably not clinically appropriate, and I want to clarify this issue in this edition. As Sadock and Sadock (2003) note, the mental status exam is a critical clinical tool that all clinicians are expected to use at least during the first diagnostic evaluation, particularly when symptoms suggest a *DSM-IV-TR* diagnosis of major depressive disorder and during emergency clinical situations (e.g., screening clients brought to hospital emergency rooms for suicidal ideation and/or suicide attempts). Therefore, clinicians should not avoid administering the exam, but they should be careful to be aware of *cultural contexts* when using the exam with clients from the culturally diverse communities discussed in this book.

Clinicians generally use the mental status exam to reinforce clinical data obtained with standard clinical rating and diagnostic instruments. This exam makes the assumption that a series of "normal" behaviors and cognitive processes are shared by "normal" people, regardless of cultural background. This assumption, however, could dramatically multiply the impact of existing bias in current clinical ratings and diagnostic instruments (Hughes, 1993) if the clinician does not take the client's cultural context into account. The main components of the mental status exam are summarized below, followed by some examples of how clinicians can apply this exam in cultural context (Hughes, 1993; Mueller, Kiernan, & Langston, 1992; Westermeyer, 1993).

Components of the Mental Status Exam

Case vignette: The director of a hospital emergency room is informed that a Mexican American man seen in the ER the previous night killed himself the following morning at home. The director reviews the client's medical record and finds that the man was interviewed for approximately an hour in the ER. The client's medical chart states, "Patient reported a history of suicidal ideation without attempts about 6 months ago, but during this emergency assessment of symptoms patient denied suicidal ideation and/ or attempts." A diagnosis of major depression with psychotic features (American Psychiatric Association, 2000, pp. 347–356) is also noted in the client's medical record. But it appears that several critical elements of the mental status exam were not assessed. The ER director asks the individual who administered the exam why the exam was only "partially conducted," and the answer is that "the patient denied suicidal ideation and/or attempts and it was not feasible to conduct most elements of the mental status exam because the patient had difficulty speaking and understanding English."

In the above vignette, the fact that the client reported he was not suicidal during an emergency situation tells us nothing about the client's general mental status, and that is why the mental status exam should have been performed before any decision was made concerning whether or not to admit the client to the hospital for further assessment and inpatient treatment.

During the mental status exam, the clinician observes the client as he or she answers questions, paying particular attention to the following (Hughes, 1993; Sadock & Sadock, 2003):

- *Appearance/behavior:* The clinician checks the client's overall appearance, including grooming (e.g., does the client exhibit peculiarities in dressing, dirty fingernails, uncombed hair?).
- *State of consciousness:* The clinician observes whether the client is alert (aware of both internal and external stimuli), hyperalert, or lethargic (e.g., do the client's thoughts "wander"?).
- *Speech:* The clinician observes whether the client speaks softly or loudly, and checks for delay in answering questions (due to fear, suspicion, intellectual deficiency); blocking (suddenly stopping talking due to delusion, hallucination, changes in affect/mood); and mutism (no response at all).
- *Mood/affect:* The clinician checks the client for the presence of tears, sweating, tremors, and dissociation between affect and thought content

(e.g., appearing happy when the attitude should be of sadness, anxiety, or concern).

- *Thought content:* The clinician checks the client for preoccupation (particularly concerning suicidal ideation, suicide attempts, and homicide); phobias; perceptual disturbances (e.g., hallucinations); and delusions (e.g., somatic delusions, delusions of persecution, and delusions of self-deprecation, such as feelings of ugliness or sinfulness).

- *Thought process:* The clinician checks the client for coherence of speech. Does the client get off the track of the conversation; stick to a single thought, phrase, or word; take forever to make a point; jump from idea to idea (i.e., "flight of ideas" phenomenon); or display "thought blocking"?

- *General knowledge:* The clinician checks the client for practical judgment (i.e., real-life problem-solving skills); abstract thinking (similarity and proverb interpretation); recent memory (e.g., repetition of four words 10 minutes later); remote memory (e.g., names of past presidents, dates of wars); calculations (e.g., can the client calculate the cost of three apples if a dozen apples costs $3.00?); and fund knowledge (e.g., can the client tell the distance from Houston to Chicago or list the five largest cities in the United States?).

- *Concentration and vigilance/attention:* The clinician checks the client for impaired concentration and vigilance/attention by asking him or her to perform some tasks that require these cognitive abilities (e.g., to subtract serial 7s from 100, to spell a word backward, to name four objects that start with the letter *T*).

- *Orientation/awareness:* The clinician observes the client's responses to questions about person (name? age? when born?), place (Where are you right now? What is your home address?), time (today's date? day of the week? time? season?), and situation (Why are you here?).

- *Insight:* The clinician checks to see if the client is able to understand the significance and severity of his or her symptoms. Also, is the client able to understand that treatment cannot be delayed?

- *Reliability:* The clinician checks the client's reports about symptoms and past history of the presenting problem for consistency.

- *Assets:* The clinician concludes his or her report on the exam with an assessment of the client's assets, such as individual resources (e.g., education, work experience) and social, emotional, and psychological support from nuclear and extended family members.

Following the exam, as Sadock and Sadock (2003) note, "the mental status part of the [clinical report] concludes with the [clinician's] impressions of the patient's reliability and capacity to report his or her situation accurately" (p. 242).

Examples of Using the Mental Status Exam in Cultural Context

Assuming that the mental status exam was conducted with the Mexican American client in the above vignette, which specific components of the exam would a clinician have to view in cultural context to prevent a biased clinical assessment of this client? In general, results on the following six areas of the mental status exam are strongly influenced by client culture, education level, and socioeconomic status: appearance/behavior, speech, thought process, general knowledge, concentration and vigilance/attention, and orientation/awareness.

Observation of the client's general *appearance/behavior* is the first element of the mental status exam, performed as soon as the clinician comes into contact with the client. Among the kinds of appearance and behavior issues that a clinician might interpret as signs of psychiatric disorders in a client are failure to maintain eye contact and careless or bizarre dressing and grooming (Hughes, 1993). Clinicians should be aware that many clients from the four cultural groups described in this book avoid making eye contact during social interactions (Hughes, 1993; Sue & Sue, 2003) because in their cultures, it is considered impolite to look directly into the eyes of another person. In addition, clinicians might not share clients' views concerning what constitutes "normal" or appropriate dress and grooming. For example, a client who goes to see the therapist directly after finishing a long working day as a garage mechanic will probably have a soiled face and dirty fingernails, which the therapist might interpret as carelessness about appearance. In addition to being familiar with culturally accepted standards of appearance and behavior across cultures, the clinician should also ask the client questions during the exam to help determine whether the client's appearance and behavior are within expected norms in his or her community. Sadock and Sadock (2003) suggest three questions for this portion of the mental status exam that may be useful for exploring the potential impact of cultural variables on the client's appearance and behavior: "Has anyone ever commented on how you look?"; "How would you describe your look?"; and "Can you help me understand some of the choices you make in how you look?" (p. 238).

When assessment of the client's *speech* is not conducted in the client's first language, the client may speak very softly and exhibit delays in answering questions or suddenly stop talking, not because he or she is experiencing fear, intellectual deficiency, changes in affect/mood, or hallucinations, but because of a language barrier. In addition, the client may not feel comfortable communicating with a clinician whose racial or ethnic background is different from the client's (Sue & Sue, 2003), and this may lead to "speech problems" during the exam. Awareness of these cultural variables can prevent the clinician conducting the mental status exam from inferring mental problems from the client's speech difficulties.

The assessment of *thought process* is a crucial component of the mental status exam. Clinicians should be aware that clients who are not fluent in English might exhibit thought blocking (a sudden cessation of thought or speech that may be suggestive of schizophrenia, depression, and anxiety;

Mueller et al., 1992) during the exam. Clients with little command of Standard English may spend a great deal of time looking for the correct word, phrase, or sentence before answering a question, and this could create anxiety that results in thought blocking (Martinez, 1986). African Americans who use Black English in most conversational contexts may also spend time silently constructing phrases or sentences in Standard English before they speak in situations where they feel they are expected to use Standard English (Dillard, 1973; Yamamoto et al., 1993).

The assessment of *general knowledge* can reveal poor educational background, severe deterioration in intellectual functioning, and the ability to access remote memory. In conducting this part of the mental status exam, a clinician asks questions such as the following: "What are the colors of the American flag?" "How far is it from Houston to Chicago?" "What are the names of three countries in Central America?" "Who is the president of the United States?" "Who was the U.S. president before the current president?" "What is the total population of the United States?" As Hughes (1993) notes, the ability to answer such questions implies that an individual has a certain level of general knowledge about the world and about the United States in particular. However, many members of the four cultural groups discussed in this volume do not have this kind of knowledge for two reasons: They are too poor to travel (which is one way individuals can gain the knowledge needed to answer some of these questions), and many are illiterate (Westermeyer, 1993). In addition, clients with non-American cultural backgrounds are likely to perform poorly when asked questions that focus on the United States. The following are some examples of questions that clinicians might use to assess general knowledge in such clients: "What are the colors of your native country's flag?" "Who is the president of your native country?" and "What is the approximate distance from your house to your church?"

During the assessment of *concentration and vigilance/attention,* the clinician typically asks the client to subtract 7 from 100 and then continue subtracting 7 from each answer. If the client has a problem performing this task, the clinician may assume this to be a sign of possible anxiety, depression, or schizophrenia. If this assumption is "confirmed" by the client's scores on a clinical rating scale, the practitioner is likely to think that he or she is on the right track concerning the client's diagnosis. Aside from the fact that many researchers have questioned the validity of this test (see Hughes, 1993, pp. 27–28), many members of the cultural groups addressed in this book would fail this task because they are not versed in the skill of counting, whether forward or backward. A culturally sensitive alternative to this task would be for the clinician to determine the client's arithmetic skill level and then ask the client to select two numbers and subtract the smaller number from the larger several times.

Assessment of the client's *orientation/awareness* is concerned with revealing any negativism, confusion, distraction, hearing impairment, and receptive language disorders that may be present. This test emphasizes the client's orientation to the self (the person), place, and time. The therapist typically asks questions such as the following: "What is your last name?" "What is the name of this month?" "Where are you right now?" In response to the first of these questions, a Hispanic client may look confused and distracted because he or she has to decide which of two last names to report, as Hispanics often use the last names of both their parents (e.g., a man whose father's surname is Rodriguez and whose mother's surname is Arias may be known as Federico Antonio Rodriguez Arias). If the client is asked the name of the current month and he or she does not know the name in Standard English, or is asked where he or she is at that moment but is not familiar with the name of the hospital or clinic, the practitioner might mistakenly assume that the client is exhibiting negativism, hearing impairment, or receptive language disorder. To assess the client's orientation/awareness in a way that takes cultural context into account, the clinician might ask, "People from your country often use two last names, one for the father and one for the mother. Could you tell me the two last names you generally use?"

To appreciate why members of the cultural groups discussed in this book may have difficulty with many components of the mental status examination, try to imagine how well you would deal with this exam. Would you pass all the tests? For example, subtract 7 from 100 and continue subtracting 7 from each answer until you get to the lowest number you can; how well and quickly can you do this? Studies suggest that normal subjects typically make between 3 and 12 errors on this test (Hughes, 1993). Now try the orientation test: Imagine that you have experienced a panic attack in an unfamiliar city; do you think you could easily answer when someone asks you the name of the hospital to which you've been taken? What about the general knowledge test? Can you name the capitals of three countries in the Middle East? Estimate the distance from New York to Los Angeles, the distance from the sun to the earth, or the distance from your house to your parents' house? Name the colors in your state flag and describe the main difference between the American flag and the flag of Malaysia? For the assessment of your thought process, pretend that you are not fluent in Spanish and you visit Mexico City: Would you need to take time to think about what you want to say before you open your mouth and say it? Would you look up and down as you search your mind for the right Spanish phrase, word, or sentence before you order lunch? Concerning your appearance: Pretend that you are a taxi driver in New York City, and at 3:00 P.M. on a hot summer day, you realize that you are due at your first appointment with a therapist. You go straight from work to your appointment and later learn that the therapist made a note on meeting you that you were probably depressed or psychotic because you dressed carelessly and had dirty hands and a soiled face. Would you return for a second appointment?

Using the Least Biased Assessment Strategies First

A review of the literature suggests that there are different degrees of bias in assessment strategies (see, e.g., Dana, 1993b; Jenkins & Ramsey, 1991), with the degree of bias increasing across types of strategies in the following order:

1. Physiological assessment (e.g., the use of electrodermal activity in the assessment of psychopathology; Boucsein, 1992)

2. Direct behavioral observations (e.g., the percentage of intervals during which African American and White children display attention to task materials; Anderson, 1988; Paniagua, 2001b; Paniagua & Black, 1990)

3. Self-monitoring (e.g., clients' recording of their own overt and covert behaviors, such as obsessive thoughts and number of tasks completed)

4. Behavioral self-report rating scales (e.g., Fear Survey Schedule; Wolpe & Lang, 1964)

5. Clinical interview (which includes the mental status examination)

6. Trait measures (e.g., California Psychological Inventory; Dana, 1993b)

7. Self-report of psychopathology measures (e.g., MMPI, Beck Depression Inventory; Dana, 1993b, 1995)

8. Projective tests with structured stimuli (e.g., Tell-Me-a-Story Test, or TEMAS; Constantino, Malgady, & Rogler, 1988; Malgady, Constantino, & Rogler, 1984)

9. Projective tests with ambiguous stimuli (e.g., Rorschach test; Dana, 1993b)

All of the assessment strategies listed above have some degree of bias (Dana, 1993b; Jenkins & Ramsey, 1991), but those with the least bias are those in which clinician interpretation and speculation are minimized. For example, the level of clinician interpretation and speculation is much greater with projective tests than it is with direct behavioral observation. Thus, the use of direct behavioral observation (or behavioral assessment strategies) to measure particular events (e.g., number of times a depressed client refuses to eat or does not participate in social activities) may result in less bias in assessment than the use of projective tests.

Some practitioners use only behavioral assessment strategies in evaluating their clients (e.g., behavior analysts; Paniagua, 2001b). The majority of practitioners, however, use a combination of trait measures, intelligence measures, self-report of psychopathology measures, and projective measures. If a practitioner uses these kinds of measures, he or she should make an effort to select only those that have been shown to have cross-cultural validity. Table 9.3 lists some of the tests that are recommended for use with

Table 9.3 Tests Recommended for Clients From Culturally Diverse Groups

Name	Area	Reference
Center for Epidemiologic Studies Depression Scale (CES-D)	Depression	Radloff (1977)
Culture-Fair Intelligence Test (CFIT)	Intelligence	Anastasi (1988)
Draw-a-Person Test (DAP)	Projective	French (1993)
Eysenck Personality Questionnaire (EPQ)	Personality	Eysenck and Eysenck (1975)
Holtzman Inkblot Technique (HIT)	Projective	Holtzman (1988)
Kaufman Assessment Battery for Children (K-ABC)	Intelligence	Kaufman, Kamphaus, and Kaufman (1985)
Leiter International Performance Scale	Intelligence	Anastasi (1988)
Progressive Matrices	Intelligence	Anastasi (1988)
Schedule for Affective Disorders and Schizophrenia (SADS)	Most disorders	Spitzer and Endicott (1978)
System of Multicultural Pluralistic Assessment (SOMPA)	Intelligence	Mercer and Lewis (1978)
Tell-Me-a-Story Test (TEMAS)	Personality/ cognition	Constantino, Malgady, and Rogler (1988)

clients from culturally diverse groups. The tests included in the table may minimize bias, but they cannot totally eliminate it (Dana, 1993b; French, 1993; Lopez & Nunez, 1987). (For a review of these tests, see Dana, 1993b.)

Using Dana's Assessment Model

Dana (1993a, 1993b) has developed an assessment model that clinicians can use in combination with the above guidelines to minimize bias in the assessment of multicultural clients. Dana recommends that clinicians take the five steps outlined below in applying this model.

Conduct an assessment of acculturation. Dana (1993a) emphasizes that this assessment "should be administered and interpreted prior to application of any assessment procedures whatsoever" (p. 10). See Table 8.1 in Chapter 8 for examples of acculturation scales designed for use with clients from the four cultural groups discussed in this text.

Provide a culture-specific service delivery style. This step emphasizes the need for the therapist to observe culturally appropriate etiquette in interacting with the client, to facilitate both the task-oriented approach and the trusting client-therapist relationship necessary to initiate and complete the testing procedures. For example, addressing a Hispanic client by title of courtesy and last name (e.g., *Señor* Garcia, *Señorita* Martinez) in an environment that includes features (e.g., pictures, furniture) associated with the client's Hispanic culture could greatly enhance the testing process.

Use the client's native language (or preferred language). For example, the therapist might say to a Hispanic or Asian client, "Perhaps you would feel more comfortable if we do this test in your native language, or we can do the test in English. What is your preference?" (See Table 2.3 in Chapter 2 for information on English-language abilities among Hispanics and Asians in the United States.)

Select assessment measures that are appropriate for the client's cultural orientation and preferences. Dana (1993a, 1993b) recommends that clinicians use culture-specific instruments and an assessment process tailored for less acculturated clients. This guideline represents the *emic perspective* in the assessment of clients from multicultural groups, which emphasizes understanding these clients in their cultural context. For example, it is recommended that the clinician conduct behavioral observation (either in the clinic or at the client's home) to understand how the members of a Hispanic family interact verbally and nonverbally. The use of *life history* reports may provide Asian, Hispanic, and American Indian clients with opportunities to talk about their problems using culture-specific modes of communication (e.g., language, gestures). The tests listed in Table 9.3 are also recommended (see also Dana, 1993b, pp. 141–167).

Use a culture-specific strategy when informing the client about the findings derived from the assessment process. Examples from assessments using the MMPI scales (Graham, 1990) and subscales of the Wechsler Adult Intelligence Scale (WAIS; e.g., Golden, 1990) serve to illustrate this recommendation. After administering the MMPI to a Hispanic adolescent client, the clinician might say to the client's parents, "I understand that in the Hispanic culture, many people believe that they can be affected by evil spirits. Perhaps the findings from this test [i.e., the MMPI] suggest that your son is expressing this cultural belief rather than that he is really mentally ill." (The clinician should keep in mind the distinction in the minds of many Hispanics between having a mental disorder, or *enfermedad mental,* and being *loco,* or crazy, which is a much more severe condition; see Chapter 4.) A therapist might explain test results to an American Indian client this way: "This finding suggests that you have low self-esteem, are reserved and timid, and lack interest in activities, and that you are a shy person. My understanding, however, is that among American Indians, these behaviors are generally culturally accepted. So we probably need to talk more about these behaviors so that I can be sure that they are not part of the clinical diagnosis of the mental problem you reported to me earlier."

The K-scale is one of the validity scales used to detect instances of test bias during the interpretation of results derived from the clinical scales of the MMPI profiles. An extremely low score on the K-scale suggests, among other things, that the client is skeptical and tends to be suspicious about the motivations of other people. The phenomenon of healthy cultural paranoia could explain why an African American client has a low score on the K-scale. In the case of Asian clients, the expression of psychological problems in terms of somatic complaints is a culturally accepted phenomenon, and therapists should take that into account in interpreting high scores on the Hypochondriasis Scale among Asians.

Cuéllar (personal communication, January 1994) notes that some clients may not admit that they are actually suffering from mental problems if they are given the option (e.g., in the presence of MMPI scores) of interpreting their problems in terms of cultural variables. Cuéllar suggests that a clinician might use the alternative approach of sitting down with the client and/or the client's family members and discussing possible culture-related explanations for test findings. On the basis of this informal discussion, the clinician decides whether or not cultural variables explain the test findings. In this process, the clinician may give minimal weight to the opinions of the client and/or the client's family members regarding the interpretation of test data in terms of cultural variables.

In the case of the WAIS (and the same test for children), Golden (1990) points out that this test "remains heavily influenced by cultural and language concepts that reflect the life of the average American, but not that of most [members of multicultural] groups" (p. 46). This is particularly true in the case of the WAIS Information, Comprehension, Vocabulary, Picture Completion, and Picture Arrangement subtests, which are associated with Anglo-American cultural background. For example, a Hispanic client may receive a very low score on the Information subtest (e.g., below 5, where a mean is 10 and the standard deviation is 3) not because the client is not intelligent, but because he or she lacks information about the total U.S. population, the average height of women, the number of U.S. senators, and other "general knowledge" that the average American may be expected to have. Similar problems exist for many culturally diverse clients with the Comprehension subtest (the client may not understand because of unfamiliarity with basic U.S. customs and situations), the Vocabulary subtest (the client may not be able to define words using Standard English), the Picture Completion subtest (the client may not be able to complete various pictures because he or she is not familiar with the objects depicted), and the Picture Arrangement subtest (the client may not be able to arrange the pictures to tell a logical and coherent story because the concept of linear storytelling is not part of the client's cultural background). Whichever measure is involved, the task for the therapist is to explain the potential impacts of cultural variables on the client's scores. For example, to a Hispanic client who has scored poorly on the Vocabulary subtest, the therapist could say, "Your score on this test is very low. Perhaps you have problems communicating in English. I will repeat the same test using words from your own language" (translations of the WAIS are available in Spanish and other languages).

As both Golden (1990) and Sue and Sue (2003) note, many mental health professionals (particularly within the African American and Hispanic communities) have suggested that all Wechsler tests (and other individual intelligence tests, such as the Stanford-Binet) are biased against multicultural groups (particularly African Americans and Hispanics). As noted at the beginning of this chapter, however, it would be a bad tactic for clinicians simply to exclude these tests from their practice. Instead, practitioners need to learn how to use cross-cultural skills to interpret the results that such biased tests (e.g., the WAIS) produce. For example, if a Hispanic client has a low score on the WAIS Information subtest, this could be interpreted as an indication of brain damage (Golden, 1990); however, a clinician with cross-cultural skills in this area would understand that the client probably scored low because of a lack of familiarity with American culture.

10

Using Cultural Variables in the *Diagnostic and Statistical Manual of Mental Disorders*

A major contribution in the latest edition of the *Diagnostic and Statistical Manual of Mental Disorders* (*DSM-IV-TR;* American Psychiatric Association, 2000) is an emphasis on the therapist's need to consider the potential impacts of cultural variables on the assessment and diagnosis of psychiatric disorders. Clinicians should be aware, however, that the *DSM-IV-TR* does not provide criteria or guidelines regarding the use of cultural variables with specific cultural groups, particularly the groups discussed in this book. Because the *DSM-IV-TR* discusses cultural variables in general terms, clinicians must rely on the literature on culturally diverse groups for information on how to apply such variables across specific communities (e.g., Barcus, 2003; Cuéllar & Paniagua, 2000; Gibbs, Huang, & Associates, 2003; Iwamasa, 2003; Paniagua, 2001a; Sue & Sue, 2003). Practitioners who are unfamiliar with the potential impacts of these variables on the assessment and diagnosis of psychiatric disorders in culturally diverse clients "may incorrectly judge as psychopathology those normal variations in behavior, belief, or experience that are particular to the individual's culture. For example, certain religious practices or beliefs (e.g., hearing or seeing a deceased relative during bereavement) may be misdiagnosed as manifestations of a Psychotic Disorder" (American Psychiatric Association, 2000, p. xxiv).

Practitioners are not required to include these variables when making *DSM-IV-TR* multiaxial classifications. This would require a new axis that deals specifically with culture-bound syndromes and the beliefs and behaviors associated with these syndromes. As noted in Chapter 9, clinicians who use these syndromes to diagnosis clients are not reimbursed for doing so by insurance companies, Medicaid, or Medicare because these entities have no provisions for covering such syndromes. Despite these limitations, practitioners who are concerned about the underrepresentation of cultural considerations in the assessment and diagnosis of multicultural groups generally agree that the *DSM-IV-TR* has made a tremendous contribution in terms of encouraging clinicians to consider cultural variables seriously when they are diagnosing mental disorders in clients from the four cultural groups described in this book (Moffic & Kinzie, 1996; Paniagua, 2000).

The *DSM-IV-TR* includes three recommendations regarding how clinicians should deal with cultural/ethnic variations when assessing and diagnosing psychiatric disorders in culturally diverse clients. Two of these recommendations are included in Appendix I of the manual, which consists of a summary of culture-bound syndromes and guidelines regarding cultural formulations that clinicians should consider in exploring the impacts of client culture on diagnosis. The third recommendation is found in a "discussion . . . of cultural variations in the clinical presentations of those disorders . . . included in the *DSM-IV-TR* Classification" (American Psychiatric Association, 2000, p. xxiv). Cultural variations are not described across the entire *DSM-IV-TR* classification of mental disorders, however. In addition, whereas the descriptions of some disorders include discussion of cultural variations and provide specific examples, other descriptions of disorders describe cultural variations but do not include any examples. Given that busy clinicians may not have time to examine the *DSM-IV-TR* for all the recommendations it offers concerning cultural variations, this chapter is intended to assist practitioners by providing an overview of those variations. Table 10.1 lists the psychiatric disorders for which the *DSM-IV-TR* describes cultural variations and provides examples, Table 10.2 lists the disorders for which the manual describes cultural variations but does not give examples, and Table 10.3 summarizes those disorders for which the manual does not include discussion of cultural variations. This chapter also addresses the potential impacts of cultural variations on the conditions that the *DSM-IV-TR* classifies as "other conditions that may be a focus of clinical attention" (American Psychiatric Association, 2000, pp. 731–742).

As Tables 10.1 and 10.2 show, the *DSM-IV-TR* sometimes includes information about cultural variations (under the heading "Specific Culture, Age, and Gender Features") for a set of disorders (e.g., mental retardation) but not for the subtypes within the set (e.g., mild, moderate, severe, and profound mental retardation). For example, the *DSM-IV-TR* recommends that "care should be taken to ensure that intellectual testing procedures reflect adequate attention to the individual's ethnic or cultural background" (American Psychiatric Association, 2000, p. 46) during the diagnosis of all subtypes of mental retardation. In other instances, the *DSM-IV-TR* makes

(text continues on p. 168)

Table 10.1   *DSM-IV-TR* Disorders for Which Cultural Variations Are
                        Described and Examples Are Provided

Disorder	*Subtype*
Attention-Deficit and Disruptive Behavior Disorders	*Conduct Disorder* May be misapplied to individuals residing in settings (e.g., threatening, high-crime, impoverished areas) where undesirable behaviors could be considered as protective. Immigrant youth with histories of aggressive behaviors resulting from their home countries' long histories of wars would not warrant the diagnosis of conduct disorder. If the behavior is the result of reaction to the immediate social context, it would not be diagnosed as conduct disorder.
Delirium and Dementia	*All Subtypes* Clients from certain cultures may be unfamiliar with the information included in tests used to measure general knowledge, memory, and orientation.
Alcohol-Related Disorders	*All Subtypes* Alcohol use patterns could be the result of cultural traditions in which the consumption of alcohol is expected in family, religious, and social settings, particularly during childhood. Among Asians, the prevalence of alcohol consumption is generally lower than in other groups. Low level of education, unemployment, and low socioeconomic status are often associated with alcohol consumption. In the United States, the prevalence of alcohol-related disorders is often higher among Hispanic males than among White and African American males.
Caffeine-Related Disorders	*All Subtypes* Caffeine use varies widely across cultures. For example, in most developing countries, caffeine use is less than 50 mg/day, in comparison with 400 mg/day or more in Sweden, the United States, and some European countries.

(Continued)

Table 10.1 (Continued)

Disorder	Subtype
Schizophrenia and Other Psychotic Disorders	*All Subtypes* If clinicians and clients do not share same race/ethnicity, cultural differences between them should be considered. Delusional ideas (e.g., witchcraft) and auditory hallucinations (e.g., seeing the Virgin Mary or hearing God's voice) may be abnormal in one culture and normal in other cultures. Variability in language, style of emotional expressions, body language, and eye contact across cultures should be considered in the assessment of symptoms of schizophrenia. Catatonic behavior is more common in non-Western countries. *Schizophreniform Disorder* In addition to the above cultural variations and examples, in developing countries, recovery from psychotic disorders is often more rapid, which may result in higher rates of schizophreniform disorder than of schizophrenia. *Schizoaffective Disorder* Same cultural variations and examples as described for schizophrenia. *Brief Psychotic Disorder* This disorder should be distinguished from culturally sanctioned response patterns. For example, in certain religious ceremonies, a person may report hearing voices, which is not considered abnormal by members of that religion and generally does not persist beyond the termination of such ceremonies.
Mood Disorders	*Major Depressive Disorder* Symptoms of depression can be influenced by cultural/ethnic variables. For example, in certain cultures, symptoms of depression might be presented in somatic terms rather than as sadness or guilt. Among Hispanic and Mediterranean cultures, depressive experiences might be manifested in terms of complaints of "nerves" and headaches; Asians may show similar experiences in terms of

Table 10.1 (Continued)

Disorder	*Subtype*
	weakness, tiredness, or "imbalance," whereas among in people from the Middle East and American Indian tribes, these experiences might be shown in terms of difficulties with the "heart" or being "heartbroken," respectively. The severity of the depression might also be evaluated differently across cultures (e.g., sadness may lead to less concern than irritability in some cultures). Actual hallucinations and delusions that are sometimes part of a major depressive disorder should be differentiated from cultural hallucinations and delusions (e.g., fear of being hexed, feeling of being visited by those who have died).
Anxiety Disorders	*Social Phobia*
	In some cultures, social demands may lead to symptoms of social phobia. In certain cultures (e.g., Japan and Korea), an individual may develop persistent and excessive fears of giving offense to others in social situations, instead of being embarrassed. These fears may be expressed in terms of extreme anxiety resulting from the belief that one's body odor, facial expression, or eye contact will be offensive to others (a culture-bound syndrome known as *taijin kyofusho;* see American Psychiatric Association, 2000, p. 903; see also Chapter 9, this volume).
	Posttraumatic Stress Disorder
	Immigrants from countries with high frequency of social unrest, wars, and civil conflicts may show high rates of PTSD. These immigrants may be particularly reluctant to divulge experiences of torture and trauma because of their political immigrant status.
Somatoform Disorders	*Somaticization Disorder*
	Frequency and types of somatic symptoms may vary across cultures. For example, people from African and South Asian countries tend to show more symptoms of burning hands and feet as well as nondelusional experiences of worms in the head or ants crawling under the skin in comparison with individuals from North America. In cultures where semen loss is of great concern, symptoms associated with male reproductive function tend to be more prevalent.

(Continued)

Table 10.1 (Continued)

Disorder	Subtype
	In India, Sri Lanka, and China, severe anxiety associated with that concern is known as *dhat* (see American Psychiatric Association, 2000, p. 900; see also Chapter 9, this volume).
Dissociative Disorders	*Dissociative Fugue*
	Some culture-bound syndromes may have symptoms resembling this disorder. For example, *pibloktoq,* a dissociative episode involving extreme excitement, convulsive seizures, and coma, is observed primarily in Arctic and Subarctic Eskimo communities (see American Psychiatric Association, 2000, p. 901; see also Chapter 9, this volume).
	Dissociative Identity Disorder
	This may be a culture-specific syndrome, given that especially high rates of the disorder are found in the United States.
Eating Disorders	*All Subtypes*
	Most prevalent in industrialized countries, including the United States, Canada, and Japan. In the case of anorexia nervosa, abundance of food and the link between attractiveness and being thin may explain the high prevalence rates of this disorder in such countries.
Impulse-Control Disorders Not Elsewhere Classified	*Intermittent Explosive Disorder*
	This disorder should be differentiated from the culture-bound syndrome known as *amok* (American Psychiatric Association, 2000, p. 899; see also Chapter 9, this volume), which is characterized by an episode of acute, unrestrained violent behavior for which the individual claims amnesia. *Amok* is often reported in Southeast Asian countries, but cases have been reported in Canada and the United States. *Amok* often occurs as a single episode rather than as a pattern of aggressive behavior (more often seen in cases of intermittent explosive disorder) and is generally associated with prominent dissociative features.

Table 10.1 (Continued)

Disorder	Subtype
	Pathological Gambling
	Cultural variations have been reported in the prevalence and types of gambling activities, including cockfighting and horse racing.
Personality Disorders	*Paranoid Personality Disorder*
	Behaviors influenced by sociocultural contexts or specific life circumstances may be erroneously labeled paranoid. For example, immigrants, political and economic refugees, and members of non-Anglo-American groups may show guarded or defensive behaviors because of unfamiliarity with English, unfamiliarity with the rules and regulations of the United States, or their perceptions of the neglect or indifference of the dominant society.
	Schizoid Personality Disorder
	Defensive behaviors and interpersonal styles displayed by individuals from different cultural backgrounds may be erroneously interpreted as schizoid. For example, individuals who have moved from rural to metropolitan areas may show "emotional freezing" as manifested by solitary activities and constricted affect. Immigrants may also be mistakenly perceived as cold, hostile, and indifferent (additional suggested symptoms for this disorder).
	Schizotypal Personality Disorder
	Cognitive and perceptual distortions may be associated with religious beliefs and rituals, which may appear to be schizotypal to clinicians who are uninformed about these cultural variations. Examples of these distortions include voodoo ceremonies, speaking in tongues, belief in life beyond death, mind reading, evil eye, and magical beliefs associated with health and illness.
	Antisocial Personality Disorder
	Clinicians should consider the social and economic contexts in which the behaviors occur. Many behaviors associated with this disorder appear to be associated with low socioeconomic status, urban settings, and social contexts in which seemingly antisocial behaviors may be part of a protective survival strategy.

Table 10.2   *DSM-IV-TR* Disorders for Which Cultural Variations Are Described and No Examples Are Provided

Disorder	Subtype
Mental Retardation	*All Subtypes* The individual's ethnic or cultural background should be taken into consideration during intellectual testing procedures. The clinician should use tests in which the client's relevant characteristics are represented in the standardization sample of the test or should employ an examiner familiar with aspects of the individual's ethnic or cultural background.
Learning Disorders	*All Subtypes* Same cultural variations as described for mental retardation.
Communication Disorders	*Expressive Language Disorder* The individual's cultural and language contexts must be taken into consideration during the assessment of the development of communication abilities, particularly for persons growing up in bilingual settings. The standardized measures of language development and of nonverbal intellectual capacity must be relevant for the individual's cultural and linguistic group. *Mixed Receptive-Expressive Language Disorder* Same as above. *Phonological Disorder* Same as above.
Attention-Deficit and Disruptive Behavior Disorders	*Attention-Deficit/Hyperactivity Disorder* Symptoms of this disorder are known to occur in various cultures, with variations in reported prevalence among Western countries as a result of different diagnostic practices rather than clinical presentation.

Table 10.2 (Continued)

Disorder	*Subtype*
Feeding and Eating Disorders of Infancy or Early Childhood	*Pica* The eating of dirt or other seemingly nonnutritive substances is considered of value in some cultures.
Tic Disorders	*Tourette's Disorder* Symptoms of this disorder are widely reported in diverse racial and ethnic groups.
Other Disorders of Infancy, Childhood, or Adolescence	*Separation Anxiety Disorder* Clinicians should differentiate separation anxiety disorder from the high value some cultures place on strong interdependence among family members. Cultural variations exist in the degree to which separation is tolerated. *Selective Mutism* When immigrant children refuse to talk to strangers in a new environment because they are unfamiliar or uncomfortable with the new language, the diagnosis of selective mutism should not be used.
Amnestic Disorder	*All Subtypes* Educational and cultural variables should be considered in the assessment of memory. Persons from certain backgrounds might not be familiar with materials used in tests to assess memory.
Amphetamine-Related Disorders	*All Subtypes* Dependence and abuse have been reported across all levels of society; intravenous use is more common among individuals from lower socioeconomic groups.
Cannabis-Related Disorders	*All Subtypes* Cannabis is among the first drugs of experimentation for all cultural groups in the United States.

(Continued)

Table 10.2 (Continued)

Disorder	Subtype
Cocaine-Related Disorders	*All Subtypes*
	All race groups are affected by cocaine use. Use by the most affluent has shifted to persons of low socioeconomic status living in metropolitan areas. Individuals from rural areas may also be affected.
Hallucinogen-Related Disorders	*All Subtypes*
	Hallucinogens may be used as part of some cultures' religious practices. Regional differences in their use have been reported in the United States. Individuals living in economically depressed areas are particularly affected.
Nicotine-Related Disorders	*All Subtypes*
	Nicotine use is decreasing in most industrialized countries and increasing in developing countries.
Opioid-Related Disorders	*All Subtypes*
	Opioid dependency, found primarily among White, middle-class Americans in the earlier 1900s, appears to have shifted toward use primarily by non-Anglo groups living in economically depressed areas.
Phencyclidine-Related Disorders	*All Subtypes*
	Prevalence of these disorders appears to be about twice as high among non-Anglo ethnic groups as it is among Anglos.
Sedative-, Hypnotic-, or Anxiolytic-Related Disorders	*All Subtypes*
	Marked variations in prescription patterns for (and availability of) this class of substances are reported in different countries.
Schizophrenia and Other Psychotic Disorders	*Delusional Disorder*
	The clinician should consider the individual's cultural and religious background in determining the possible presence of delusional disorder. The content of delusions varies across cultures.

Table 10.2 (Continued)

Disorder	Subtype
Mood Disorders	*Bipolar I Disorder*
	Differences in the prevalence of this disorder among various racial/ethnic groups have not been reported. Some evidence suggests that clinicians may overdiagnose schizophrenia rather than bipolar disorder in some ethnic groups.
Anxiety Disorders	*Panic Disorder With or Without Agoraphobia*
	Panic attacks might include intense fear of magic or witchcraft in some cultures. Panic disorder as described in the *DSM-IV-TR* has been reported in epidemiological studies across the world. In addition, several culture-bound syndromes described in the *DSM-IV-TR* might be associated with panic disorder. The participation of women in public life is restricted in some ethnic and cultural groups, and this situation should be differentiated from agoraphobia.
	Specific Phobia
	Both the content and the prevalence of this disorder vary with culture and ethnicity. Fears of magic or spirits are present in many cultures. These fears should be considered a specific phobia when the fears are excessive in the context of the individual's culture and cause significant impairment and distress.
	Obsessive-Compulsive Disorder
	Behaviors that are culturally prescribed should be differentiated from obsessive-compulsive disorder unless these behaviors exceed cultural norms, occur at times and places judged inappropriate by other members of the individual's culture, and interfere with social role functioning.
	Acute Stress Disorder
	The severity of this disorder may be determined by cultural differences in the implications of loss. Coping behaviors may also be culturally determined. For example, dissociative symptoms may be more common in cultures where these symptoms are commonly accepted.

(Continued)

Table 10.2 (Continued)

Disorder	Subtype
	Generalized Anxiety Disorder
	Considerable cultural variations exist in the expression of anxiety. In some cultures, anxiety is expressed predominantly through somatic symptoms, in others through cognitive symptoms. The clinician should consider cultural context when evaluating a client's worries about certain situations.
Somatoform Disorders	*Undifferentiated Somatoform Disorder*
	Unexplained symptoms and worry about physical illness may be the result of culturally shaped "idioms of distress" used to express concerns about personal and social problems, without evidence of psychopathology.
	Conversion Disorder
	This disorder is reported to be most common in rural areas and among persons of low socioeconomic status. Higher rates are reported in developing countries. Symptoms may reflect local cultural ideas about accepted and credible ways to express distress. Symptoms are common aspects of certain culturally sanctioned religious and healing rituals.
	Pain Disorder
	Differences exist across cultural and ethnic groups in terms of expected reactions to pain and responses to painful stimuli.
	Hypochondriasis
	Symptoms of hypochondriasis should be evaluated relative to the individual's cultural background and explanatory models. The clinician should determine whether the individual's ideas about disease have been reinforced by traditional healers, who may disagree with the reassurances given by medical evaluations.
	Body Dysmorphic Disorder
	Preoccupation with an imagined physical deformity may be determined by cultural concerns about physical appearance and the importance of physical self-presentation.

Table 10.2 (Continued)

Disorder	Subtype
Dissociative Disorders	*Depersonalization Disorder*
	Induced experiences of depersonalization have been reported in many religions and cultures. These experiences should not be confused with depersonalization disorder.
Sexual Dysfunctions	*All Subtypes*
	The individual's ethnic, cultural, and religious background should be considered during the assessment of sexual dysfunction. Cultural variations may affect sexual desire, expectations, and attitudes about performance. In some societies, the sexual desire of females is not considered very relevant, particularly when fertility is the primary concern.
Paraphilia	*All Subtypes*
	What is considered appropriate in one culture may be seen as inappropriate in other cultures; this makes the diagnosis of paraphilia across cultures and religions a complicated task for the clinician.
	Parasomnias Nightmare Disorder
	The importance assigned to nightmares varies by culture. In some cultures, nightmares are associated with spiritual or supernatural phenomena; in others, they may be viewed as indicators of mental or physical disturbances.
	Sleep Terror Disorder
	This disorder may differ across cultures, but clear evidence regarding culture-related differences in the presentation of this disorder is lacking.
	Sleepwalking Disorder
	Same as above.
Sleep Disorders Related to Another Mental Disorder	*All Subtypes*
	Sleep complaints may be viewed as less stigmatizing than mental disorders in some cultures. For this reason, individuals from some cultures may be more likely to complain of

(Continued)

Table 10.2 (Continued)

Disorder	Subtype
	insomnia or hypersomnia than to complain of symptoms of mental disorders such as depression and anxiety.
Impulse-Control Disorder Not Elsewhere Classified	*Trichotillomania* The fact that this disorder is more common in females than in males might indicate the effect of cultural attitudes with respect to appearance (e.g., males' acceptance of normative hair loss).
Adjustment Disorders	*All Subtypes* The clinician should consider the client's cultural setting in determining whether the individual's response to stressors is inappropriate or in excess of what would be expected in his or her culture. Variability exists across cultures with respect to the nature and meaning of stressors, how stressors are experienced, and the evaluation of responses to stressors.
Personality Disorders	*Borderline Personality Disorder* Behaviors associated with this disorder have been seen in many settings around the world. *Histrionic Personality Disorder* Norms for personal appearance, emotional expressiveness, and interpersonal behavior vary widely across cultures. Symptoms associated with this disorder (e.g., emotionality, seductiveness, impressionability) may be culturally accepted by the individual's community. It is important for the clinician to determine whether these symptoms cause clinically significant impairment or distress to the individual in comparison with what is culturally expected. *Avoidant Personality Disorder* Variations exist in the degrees to which different cultures and ethnic groups regard diffidence and avoidance as appropriate. Symptoms of this

Table 10.2 (Continued)

Disorder	Subtype
	disorder may also result from acculturation problems associated with immigration.
	Dependent Personality Disorder
	The appropriateness of dependent behaviors varies across sociocultural groups. Behaviors associated with this disorder (e.g., passivity, difficulty in making everyday decisions) should be considered characteristic of this disorder only when they are clearly in excess of the individual's cultural norms or reflect unrealistic concerns. In addition, some cultures may differentially foster and discourage dependent behavior in males and females.
	Obsessive-Compulsive Personality Disorder
	Habits, customs, and interpersonal styles that are culturally sanctioned by the individual's reference groups should not be considered as indicative of this disorder. The individual may place heavy emphasis on work and productivity, for example, because these behaviors are reinforced by his or her reference group.

Table 10.3 *DSM-IV-TR* Disorders for Which No Cultural Variations Are Described

Disorder	Subtype
Motor skills disorders	Developmental coordination disorder,
Communication disorders	stuttering
Pervasive developmental disorders	Autistic disorder, Rett's disorder
	Childhood disintegrative disorder
	Asperger's disorder
Attention-deficit and disruptive behavior disorders	Oppositional defiant disorder
Feeding and eating disorders of infancy or early childhood	Rumination disorder
	Feeding disorder of infancy or early childhood
Tic disorders	Chronic motor or vocal tic disorder
	Transient tic disorder
Elimination disorders	Encopresis, enuresis

(Continued)

Table 10.3 (Continued)

Disorder	Subtype
Other disorders of infancy, childhood, or adolescence	Reactive attachment disorder of infancy or early childhood Stereotypic movement disorder
Mental disorders due to general medical condition	Catatonic disorder due to a general medical condition, personality change due to a general medical condition
Polysubstance-related disorders	All subtypes
Other (or unknown) substance-related disorders	All subtypes
Schizophrenia and other psychotic disorders	Shared psychotic disorder
Psychotic disorders due to general medical condition	Substance-induced psychotic disorder
Mood disorders	Dysthymic disorder, bipolar II disorder, cyclothymic disorder, other mood disorders
Mood disorders due to a general medical condition	Substance-induced mood disorder
Anxiety disorders	Anxiety disorder due to a general medical condition, substance-induced anxiety disorder
Factitious disorders	No subtype listed in DSM-IV
Dissociative disorders	Dissociative amnesia
Gender identity disorders	No subtype listed in DSM-IV
Sleep disorders	Primary insomnia, primary hypersomnia, narcolepsy, breathing-related sleep disorder, circadian rhythm sleep disorder
Other sleep disorders	Sleep disorder due to a general medical condition, substance-induced sleep disorder
Impulse-control disorders not elsewhere classified	Kleptomania, pyromania
Personality disorders	Narcissistic personality disorder

a general statement regarding cultural variations for a set of disorders (e.g., mood disorders, personality disorders) and mentions cultural variations in the descriptions of only some of the subtypes of the set. For example, the manual provides a description of cultural variations for all mood disorders, but within the subtypes of depressive disorders, such variations are described only in regard to major depressive disorder (see Table 10.1); no specific cultural variations are mentioned in the description of dysthymic disorder. In still other cases, the *DSM-IV-TR* provides no general statement about cultural variations in a given set of disorders but mentions specific cultural considerations in the descriptions of subtypes within that set of disorders. For example, in the case of attention-deficit and disruptive behavior disorders, no cultural variations are described for the set of disorders as a whole, but variations are described for the subtypes attention-deficit/hyperactivity disorder and conduct disorder; no variations are described for another subtype, oppositional defiant disorder.

Thus, the names of some mental disorders (e.g., attention-deficit and disruptive behavior disorders, or ADDBD) are repeated across these three tables. For example, conduct disorder is listed in Table 10.1 because the *DSM-IV-TR* includes a description of cultural variations with examples for this subtype of ADDBD. Attention-deficit/hyperactivity disorder is listed in Table 10.2 because the manual includes a description of cultural variations for this subtype of ADDBD but does not give any specific examples to illustrate the applicability of these variations. Oppositional defiant disorder is included in Table 10.3 because the manual does not mention any cultural variations in regard to this subtype of ADDBD.

Cultural Considerations With Other Conditions That May Be a Focus of Clinical Attention

In the *DSM-IV-TR,* only three V Codes are explicitly considered to be culturally relevant for Axis IV (Psychosocial and Environmental Problems): Religious or Spiritual Problem, Acculturation Problem, and Noncompliance With Treatment. Box 10.1 shows three additional V Codes that clinicians might also consider culturally relevant for Axis IV when using the cultural variations suggested in the *DSM-IV-TR.*

Box 10.1   Culturally Relevant V Codes in the *DSM-IV-TR*

Explicitly Recommended V Codes

1. Religious or Spiritual Problem (V62.89, p. 741)

2. Acculturation Problem (V62.4, p. 741)

3. Noncompliance With Treatment (V15.85, p. 739)

Additional V Codes With Cultural Relevance

4. Partner Relational Problem (V61.1, p. 737)

5. Parent-Child Relational Problem (V61.20, p. 737)

6. Identity Problem (V313.82, p. 741)

Religious or Spiritual Problem

The *DSM-IV-TR* suggests that a client's religious and spiritual beliefs may be the "focus of clinical attention" when those beliefs lead to "distressing experiences that involve loss or questioning of faith, problems associated with conversion to a new faith, or questioning of spiritual values" (American Psychiatric Association, 2000, p. 741). Religious or spiritual problems, however, may also be the focus of clinical attention when a clinician believes that such problems interfere with the overall assessment and treatment of the particular disorder. For example, many Hispanic clients believe that mental problems are caused by evil spirits, and so the church, not the mental health professional, has the power to treat these problems. Hispanics often believe that prayers will cure physical and mental problems, and they seek help from clinicians only after they have exhausted all religious and folk resources to handle such problems. This is one way in which clients' religious and spiritual beliefs may interfere with their assessment and treatment by professionals.

Acculturation Problem

The *DSM-IV-TR* recommends that a clinician should emphasize the process of acculturation as the "focus of clinical attention" when the client's problems involve "adjustment to a different culture (e.g., following migration)" (American Psychiatric Association, 2000, p. 741). Discrepancies in levels or degrees of acculturation among family members may also be the focus of clinical attention (Flores, Tschann, Marin, & Pantoja, 2004). For example, a Hispanic family may experience conflict when a highly acculturated adolescent girl clashes with her less acculturated parents over the issue of dating. As noted in Chapter 4, in Hispanic cultures, young women are expected to include immediate family members in the process of dating (e.g., as chaperones). The adolescent in such a case may develop a psychiatric disorder (e.g., depression) because of her parents' insistence that she abide by their cultural expectations concerning dating.

Acculturation may also be the focus of clinical attention when marital conflicts result from different levels of acculturation in a husband and wife (see Flores et al., 2004). In addition, some immigrants (particularly Mexican immigrants; see Hovey, 2000) may experience high levels of acculturation as stressful, and such stress can lead to emotional problems (e.g., depression, suicidal ideation). Grieger and Ponterotto (1995, pp. 366–369) present additional examples of instances in which the client's and family's levels of acculturation may be the focus of clinical attention. In clinical practice, clinicians should seriously consider both discrepancies in levels of acculturation among family members and clients' perceptions of "elevated levels of acculturative stress" (Hovey, 2000, p. 134) as the focus of clinical attention during assessment, diagnosis, and treatment.

Practitioners can use one of the acculturation scales listed in Table 8.1 (Chapter 8) to determine whether an acculturation problem should be a focus of clinical attention during the management of a given disorder in Axis I and Axis II of the *DSM-IV-TR*. Clinicians may also use the Brief Acculturation Scale presented in Chapter 2 (Figure 2.1).

Noncompliance With Treatment

As the *DSM-IV-TR* notes, a client might show noncompliance with medical treatment because of his or her "personal values judgment or religious or cultural beliefs about the advantages and disadvantages of the proposed treatment" (American Psychiatric Association, 2000, p. 739). For example, an American Indian client may not follow through with treatment that involves managing his or her psychiatric disorder with drug therapy because of the belief (held by many American Indians) that synthetic medications are not good for Indians' health. As Thompson, Walker, and Silk-Walker (1993) note, however, most classes of psychotropic medication are effective with American Indian clients. The clinician's task is to accept the client's beliefs and values while gradually (through the psychotherapy process) introducing information about the effectiveness of drug therapy (citing empirical data) in the treatment of the client's disorder.

Another example of a culture-related reason for noncompliance with treatment is the belief among many Asians that herbal remedies can be used in combination with psychotropic medications in the treatment of physical and mental disorders (see Chien, 1993, pp. 416–417). Because such combinations may result in negative side effects (Chien, 1993), the clinician should evaluate the likelihood of such effects carefully and inform the client about them. In doing so, the clinician should keep in mind that abruptly instructing an Asian client to stop using herbal remedies may lead to noncompliance with treatment.

Partner Relational Problem

As noted above, differences in levels of acculturation between partners can lead to partner relational problems. For example, a Hispanic couple may experience negative communications if the two spouses have differing expectations regarding the role the wife should play at home (e.g., if the wife does not share the husband's values concerning *machismo* and *marianismo,* cultural ideals reinforced by many members of the Hispanic community). Similarly, a highly acculturated individual may have problems in relating to a less acculturated partner who recently immigrated to the United States from a country where the cultural values, beliefs, and lifestyles are very different from those of mainstream American society. As noted in Chapter 6, American Indians may experience partner relational problems related to intertribal marriage, for example, when the two spouses' tribes differ in their beliefs about how children should be disciplined.

Parent-Child Relational Problem

According to the *DSM-IV-TR,* parent-child relational problems may include "impaired communication, overprotection, [and] inadequate discipline" (American Psychiatric Association, 2000, p. 737). Differences in levels of acculturation may lead to parent-child relational problems in the form of impaired communication. For example, more acculturated Asian and Hispanic adolescents may disagree with their less acculturated parents on certain issues involving customs and lifestyles (e.g., dressing, dating; see Chapter 4). The Hispanic cultural phenomenon of *machismo* may lead Hispanic fathers to be overprotective of their children. Inadequate discipline of children and adolescents among American Indian parents may be the result of the parents' belonging to different tribes (see Chapter 6). Practitioners should be aware that cultural variables such as those noted here can easily explain why some parent-child relational problems exist in clients from various cultural groups, and they should take such variables into account during the assessment and treatment of clients from these groups.

Identity Problem

The *DSM-IV-TR* encourages clinicians to include in Axis IV the category "Identity Problem" when the "focus of clinical attention is uncertainty about multiple issues" (American Psychiatric Association, 2000, p. 741), including, for example, the client's difficulty in determining a career choice and long-term goals, difficulty in deciding about sexual orientation, and problems with moral values and loyalties toward a given group. The client may also experience an identity problem of a racial and/or ethnic nature, however. In this particular instance, the focus of clinical attention should be on the exploration of the client's difficulty in dealing with his or her own cultural identity.

Marsella and Yamada (2000) define *cultural identity* (or *ethnocultural identity*) in terms of the "extent to which an individual endorses and manifests the cultural traditions and practices of the particular group" (p. 13). A cultural identity conflict arises when the individual struggles to identify with his or her own culture at the same time he or she displays a strong sense of cultural identification with a different cultural group. It is particularly important for clinicians to assess this kind of conflict in biracial children and adolescents, as well as in children and adolescents who have been adopted by parents who do not share their racial and/or ethnic backgrounds (Dana, 1997; Gibbs, 2003; Koss-Chioino & Vargas, 1999). Research has shown that conflicts associated with an individual's acceptance or rejection of his or her cultural identity may be risk factors for severe mental disorders (Paniagua, 2001a; Scholl, Upshaw, Rashid, Jackson, & Bethea, 2004).

Although the *DSM-IV-TR* does not explicitly recommend an exploration of the cultural identity of the client as the focus of clinical attention in the assessment of the client's identity problem (see American Psychiatric Association, 2000, p. 741), it is important to note that in the "Outline for Cultural Formulation" (Appendix I, pp. 897–898), the manual includes a section titled "Cultural Identity of the Individual" and encourages the clinician to "note the individual's ethnic or cultural reference groups" (p. 897). In the particular case of an immigrant client, the clinician is particularly encouraged to note the client's "degree of involvement with both the culture of origin and the host culture . . . language abilities, use, and preference" (p. 897).

The present discussion suggests that it may be extremely important for future editions of the *DSM* to include the cultural identity of the client among the "other conditions that may be a focus of clinical attention." This could be achieved either through the inclusion of examples of cultural identity conflicts in the "Identity Problem" section (i.e., V Code 313.82) or through the insertion of a new V Code titled "Cultural Identity of the Client." In any case, the clinician should be encouraged to include an assessment of the cultural identity of the individual when conducting the cultural formulation of a case involving a client from any of the culturally diverse groups discussed in this book. Examples of assessment tools a clinician might use to conduct an assessment of the cultural identity of the client include the Multigroup Ethnic Identity Measure (Phinney, 1992; Utsey, Chae, Brown, & Kelly, 2002), the Multiethnic Climate Inventory (Johnson & Johnson, 1996; Negy, Shreve, Jensen, & Uddin, 2003), the Self-Identity Inventory (Sevig, Highlen, & Adams, 2000), and the Racial Identity Attitude Scale (Helms & Parham, 1996; Whatley, Allen, & Dana, 2003).

References

Allen, A. (1988). West Indians. In L. Comas-Diaz & E. E. H. Griffith (Eds.), *Clinical guidelines in cross-cultural mental health* (pp. 305–333). New York: John Wiley.

American Psychiatric Association. (1994). *Diagnostic and statistical manual of mental disorders* (4th ed.). Washington, DC: Author.

American Psychiatric Association. (2000). *Diagnostic and statistical manual of mental disorders* (4th ed., text rev.). Washington, DC: Author.

American Psychological Association. (1992). *Ethical principles of psychologists and code of conduct.* Washington, DC: Author.

American Psychological Association. (2003). Guidelines on multicultural education, training, research, practice, and organizational change for psychologists. *American Psychologist, 58,* 377–402.

Anastasi, A. (1988). *Psychological testing* (6th ed.). New York: Macmillan.

Ancis, J. R. (Ed.). (2003). *Culturally responsive interventions: Innovative approaches to working with diverse populations.* New York: Brunner-Routledge.

Anderson, L. P., Eaddy, C. L., & Williams, E. A. (1990). Psychosocial competence: Toward a theory of understanding positive mental health among Black Americans. In D. S. Ruiz (Ed.), *Handbook of mental health and mental disorder among Black Americans* (pp. 255–271). Westport, CT: Greenwood.

Anderson, W. H. (1988). The behavioral assessment of conduct disorder in Black children. In R. L. Jones (Ed.), *Psychoeducational assessment of minority group children: A case book* (pp. 103–123). Berkeley, CA: Cobb & Henry.

Arroyo, J. A. (1996). Psychotherapist bias with Hispanics: An analog study. *Hispanic Journal of Behavioral Sciences, 18,* 21–28.

Atkinson, D. R., & Wampold, B. E. (1993). Mexican Americans' initial preferences for counselors: Simple choice can be misleading—Comments on Lopez, Lopez, and Fong (1991). *Journal of Consulting Psychology, 40,* 245–248.

Baker, F. M. (1988). Afro-Americans. In L. Comas-Diaz & E. E. H. Griffith (Eds.), *Clinical guidelines in cross-cultural mental health* (pp. 151–181). New York: John Wiley.

Baker, F. M., & Lightfoot, O. B. (1993). Psychiatric care of ethnic elders. In A. C. Gaw (Ed.), *Culture, ethnicity, and mental illness* (pp. 517–552). Washington, DC: American Psychiatric Press.

Bamford, K. W. (1991). Bilingual issues in mental health assessment and treatment. *Hispanic Journal of Behavioral Sciences, 13,* 377–390.

Barcus, C. (2003). Recommendations for the treatment of American Indian populations. Council of National Psychological Associations for the Advancement of Ethnic Minority Interests (Ed.), *Psychological treatment of ethnic minority populations* (pp. 24–28). Washington, DC: Association of Black Psychologists.

Berg, I. K., & Jaya, A. (1993). Different and same: Family therapy with Asian-American families. *Journal of Marital and Family Therapy, 19,* 31–38.

Bernal, G., & Gutierrez, M. (1988). Cubans. In L. Comas-Diaz & E. E. H. Griffith (Eds.), *Clinical guidelines in cross-cultural mental health* (pp. 233–261). New York: John Wiley.

Berry, J. W. (1990). Psychology of acculturation: Understanding individuals moving between cultures. In R. W. Brislin (Ed.), *Applied cross-cultural psychology* (pp. 232–253). Newbury Park, CA: Sage.

Berry, J. W., Poortinga, Y. H., Segall, M. H., & Darsen, P. R. (1992). *Cross-cultural psychology: Research and applications*. Cambridge UK: Cambridge University Press.

Berry, J. W., Trimble, J. E., & Olmedo, E. (1986). Assessment of acculturation. In W. J. Lonner & J. W. Berry (Eds.), *Field methods in cross-cultural research* (pp. 291–324). Beverly Hills, CA: Sage.

Betancourt, H., & Lopez, S. R. (1993). The study of culture, ethnicity, and race in American psychology. *American Psychologist, 48,* 629–637.

Bishaw, A., & Iceland, J. (2003). *Poverty: 1999* (Census 2000 Brief C2KBR-19). Washington, DC: U.S. Department of Commerce, Economic and Statistics Administration, Bureau of the Census.

Borak, J., Fiellin, M., & Chemerynski, S. (2004). Who is Hispanic? Implications for epidemiologic research in the United States. *Epidemiology, 15,* 240–244.

Boucsein, W. (1992). *Electrodermal activity.* New York: Plenum.

Boyd-Franklin, N. (1989). *Black families in therapy: A multisystem approach.* New York: Guilford.

Brandon, W. (1989). *Indians.* Boston: Houghton Mifflin.

Buki, L. P., Ma, T.-C., Strom, R. D., & Strom, S. K. (2003). Chinese immigrant mothers of adolescents: Self-perceptions of acculturation effects on parenting. *Cultural Diversity and Ethnic Minority Psychology, 9,* 127–140.

Bulhan, A. H. (1985). Black Americans and psychopathology: An overview of research and theory. *Psychotherapy, 22,* 370–378.

Burnam, M. A., Hough, R. L., Karno, M., Escobar, J. I., & Telles, C. A. (1987). Acculturation and lifetime prevalence of psychiatric disorders among Mexican Americans in Los Angeles. *Journal of Health and Social Behavior, 28,* 89–102.

Canino, I. A., & Canino, G. J. (1993). Psychiatric care of Puerto Ricans. In A. C. Gaw (Ed.), *Culture, ethnicity, and mental illness* (pp. 467–499). Washington, DC: American Psychiatric Press.

Casas, J. M., & Pytluk, S. D. (1995). Hispanic identity development: Implications for research and practice. In J. G. Ponterotto, J. M. Casas, L. A. Suzuki, & C. M. Alexander (Eds.), *Handbook of multicultural counseling* (pp. 155–180). Thousand Oaks, CA: Sage.

Castillo, R. J. (1997). *Culture and mental illness.* Pacific Grove, CA: Brooks/Cole.

Central Intelligence Agency. (2003). *The world factbook.* Washington, DC: Author.

Cervantes, R. C., & Arroyo, W. (1994). *DSM-IV:* Implications for Hispanic children and adolescents. *Hispanic Journal of Behavioral Sciences, 16,* 8–27.

Chien, C. P. (1993). Ethnopsychopharmacology. In A. C. Gaw (Ed.), *Culture, ethnicity, and mental illness* (pp. 413–430). Washington, DC: American Psychiatric Press.

Choney, S. K., Berryhill-Paapke, E., & Robbins, R. R. (1995). The acculturation of American Indians: Developing frameworks for research and practice. In J. G. Ponterotto, J. M. Casas, L. A. Suzuki, & C. M. Alexander (Eds.), *Handbook of multicultural counseling* (pp. 73–92). Thousand Oaks, CA: Sage.

Chung, D. K. (1992). Asian cultural commonalities: A comparison with mainstream American culture. In A. M. Furuto, R. Biswas, D. K. Chung, K. Murase, & F. Ross-Sheriff (Eds.), *Social work practice with Asian Americans* (pp. 27–44). Newbury Park, CA: Sage.

Chung, R. H., Kim, B. S. K., & Abreu, J. M. (2004). Asian American Multidimensional Acculturation Scale: Development, factor analysis, reliability, and validity. *Cultural Diversity and Ethnic Minority Psychology, 10,* 66–80.

Comas-Diaz, L. (1988). Cross-cultural mental health treatment. In L. Comas-Diaz & E. E. H. Griffith (Eds.), *Clinical guidelines in cross-cultural mental health* (pp. 337–361). New York: John Wiley.

Comas-Diaz, L. (2001). Hispanics, Latinos, or Americanos: The evolution of identity. *Cultural Diversity and Ethnic Minority Psychology, 7,* 115–120.

Comas-Diaz, L., & Duncan, J. W. (1985). The cultural context: A factor in assertiveness training with mainland Puerto Rican women. *Psychology of Women Quarterly, 9,* 463–476.

Comas-Diaz, L., & Griffith, E. E. H. (Eds.). (1988). *Clinical guidelines in cross-cultural mental health.* New York: John Wiley.

Constantino, G., Malgady, R. G., & Rogler, L. H. (1988). *Technical manual: The TEMAS Thematic Apperception Test.* Los Angeles: Western Psychological Services.

Cook, K. O., & Timberlake, E. M. (1989). Cross-cultural counseling with Vietnamese refugees. In D. R. Koslow & E. P. Salett (Eds.), *Crossing cultures in mental health* (pp. 84–100). Washington, DC: International Counseling Center.

Costello, R. M., & Hays, J. R. (1988). *Texas law and the practice of psychology: A source book.* Austin: Texas Psychological Association.

Cuéllar, I. (2000). Acculturation and mental health: Ecological transactional relations of adjustment. In I. Cuéllar & F. A. Paniagua (Eds.), *Handbook of multicultural mental health: Assessment and treatment of diverse populations* (pp. 45–62). New York: Academic Press.

Cuéllar, I., Arnold, B., & Maldonado, R. (1995). Acculturation Rating Scale for Mexicans–II: A revision of the original ARSMA scale. *Hispanic Journal of Behavioral Sciences, 17,* 275–304.

Cuéllar, I., Harris, L. C., & Jasso, R. (1980). An acculturation scale for Mexican American normal and clinical populations. *Hispanic Journal of Behavioral Sciences, 2,* 199–217.

Cuéllar, I., & Paniagua, F. A. (Eds.). (2000). *Handbook of multicultural mental health: Assessment and treatment of diverse populations.* New York: Academic Press.

Dana, R. H. (1993a, November 5). *Can "corrections" for culture using moderator variables contribute to cultural competence in assessment?* Paper presented at the annual meeting of the Texas Psychological Association, Austin.

Dana, R. H. (1993b). *Multicultural assessment perspectives for professional psychology.* Boston: Allyn & Bacon.

Dana, R. H. (1995). Culturally competent MMPI assessment of Hispanic populations. *Hispanic Journal of Behavioral Sciences, 17,* 305–319.

Dana, R. H. (1997). *Understanding cultural identity in intervention and assessment.* Thousand Oaks, CA: Sage.

Dana, R. H. (2000). Culture and methodology in personality assessment. In I. Cuéllar & F. A. Paniagua (Eds.), *Handbook of multicultural mental health: Assessment and treatment of diverse populations* (pp. 97–136). New York: Academic Press.

Dana, R. H. (2002). Mental health services for African Americans: A cultural/racial perspective. *Cultural Diversity and Ethnic Minority Psychology, 8,* 3–18.

De La Cancela, V. (1993). Rainbow warriors: Reducing institutional racism in mental health. *Journal of Mental Health Counseling, 15,* 55–71.

Derogatis, L. R., Lipman, R. S., Rickels, K., Uhlenhuth, E. H., & Covi, L. (1974). The Hopkins Symptom Checklist (HSCL): A self-report symptom inventory. *Behavioral Science, 19,* 1–15.

Dillard, D. A., & Manson, S. M. (2000). Assessing and treating American Indians and Alaska Natives. In I. Cuéllar & F. A. Paniagua (Eds.), *Handbook of multicultural mental health: Assessment and treatment of diverse populations* (pp. 225–248). New York: Academic Press.

Dillard, J. L. (1973). *Black English: Its history and use in the United States.* New York: Vintage.

Dohrenwend, B. S., Krasnoff, L., Askenasy, A. R., & Dohrenwend, B. P. (1978). Exemplification of a method for scaling life events: The PERI Life Events Scale. *Journal of Health and Social Behavior, 19,* 205–229.

Endicott, J., Spitzer, R. L., Fleiss, J. L., & Cohen, J. (1976). The Global Assessment Scale: A procedure for measuring overall severity of psychiatric disturbance. *Archives of General Psychiatry, 33,* 766–771.

Escobar, J. E. (1993). Psychiatric epidemiology. In A. C. Gaw (Ed.), *Culture, ethnicity, and mental illness* (pp. 43–73). Washington, DC: American Psychiatric Press.

Eysenck, H. J., & Eysenck, S. B. S. (1975). *Manual for the Eysenck Personality Questionnaire.* San Diego, CA: Educational and Industrial Testing Service.

Fairchild, H. H. (1985). Black, Negro, or African American? The differences are crucial. *Journal of Black Studies, 16,* 47–55.

Flaherty, J. H., Gaviria, F. M., Pathak, D., Mitchell, T., Wintrob, R., Richman, J. A., et al. (1988). Developing instruments for cross-cultural psychiatric research. *Journal of Nervous and Mental Disease, 176,* 257–263.

Flaskerud, J. H., & Anh, N. T. (1988). Mental health needs of Vietnamese refugees. *Hospital and Community Psychiatry, 39,* 435–436.

Fleming, C. M. (1992). American Indians and Alaska Natives: Changing societies past and present. In M. Orlandi & R. Weston (Eds.), *Cultural competence for evaluators* (pp. 147–171). Rockville, MD: U.S. Department of Health and Human Services.

Flores, E., Tschann, J. M., Marin, B. V., & Pantoja, P. (2004). Marital conflict and acculturation among Mexican American husbands and wives. *Cultural Diversity and Ethnic Minority Psychology, 10,* 39–52.

Force, R. W., & Force, M. T. (1991). *The American Indians.* New York: Chelsea House.

Foreman, J. (1993, June 6). Navajos refuse to panic over perplexing disease. *Houston Chronicle,* pp. A1, A18.

Franco, J. N. (1983). An acculturation scale for Mexican American children. *Journal of General Psychology, 108,* 175–181.

French, L. A. (1993). Adapting projective tests for minority children. *Psychological Reports, 72,* 15–18.

Fuertes, J. N., & Brobst, K. (2002). Clients' ratings of counselor multicultural competency. *Cultural Diversity and Ethnic Minority Psychology, 8,* 214–223.

Fujii, J. S., Fukushima, S. N., & Yamamoto, J. (1993). Psychiatric care of Japanese Americans. In A. C. Gaw (Ed.), *Culture, ethnicity, and mental illness* (pp. 305–345). Washington, DC: American Psychiatric Press.

Garcia, M., & Lega, L. I. (1979). Development of a Cuban ethnic identity questionnaire. *Hispanic Journal of Behavioral Sciences, 1,* 247–261.

Garza-Trevino, E. S., Ruiz, P., & Venegas-Samuels, K. (1997). A psychiatric curriculum directed to the care of the Hispanic patient. *Academic Psychiatry, 21,* 1–10.

Gaw, A. C. (Ed.). (1993a). *Culture, ethnicity, and mental illness.* Washington, DC: American Psychiatric Press.

Gaw, A. C. (1993b). Psychiatric care of Chinese Americans. In A. C. Gaw (Ed.), *Culture, ethnicity, and mental illness* (pp. 245–280). Washington, DC: American Psychiatric Press.

Gibbs, J. T. (2003). Biracial and bicultural children and adolescents. In J. T. Gibbs, L. N. Huang, & Associates, *Children of color: Psychological interventions with culturally diverse youth* (pp. 145–182). San Francisco: Jossey-Bass.

Gibbs, J. T., Huang, L. N., & Associates. (2003). *Children of color: Psychological interventions with culturally diverse youth.* San Francisco: Jossey-Bass.

Golden, C. J. (1990). *Clinical interpretation of objective psychological tests* (2nd ed.). Needham, MA: Allyn & Bacon.

Good, M.-J. D., James, C., Good, B. J., & Becker, A. E. (2003). The culture of medicine and racial, ethnic, and class disparities in health care. In B. D. Smedley, A. Y. Stith, &

A. R. Nelson (Eds.), *Unequal treatment: Confronting racial and ethnic disparities in health care* (pp. 594–625). Washington, DC: National Academies Press.

Goodluck, C. T. (1993). Social services with Native Americans: Current status of the Indian Child Welfare Act. In H. P. McAdoo (Ed.), *Family ethnicity: Strength and diversity* (pp. 217–226). Newbury Park, CA: Sage.

Graham, J. R. (1990). *MMPI-2: Assessing personality and psychopathology.* New York: Oxford University Press.

Gregory, S. (1996). "We've been down this road already." In S. Gregory & R. Sanjek (Eds.), *Race* (pp. 18–38). New Brunswick, NJ: Rutgers University Press.

Grieco, E. M., & Cassidy, R. C. (2001). *Overview of race and Hispanic origin: 2000* (Census 2000 Brief C2KBR/01-1). Washington, DC: U.S. Department of Commerce, Economics and Statistics Administration, Bureau of the Census.

Grieger, I., & Ponterotto, J. G. (1995). A framework for assessment in multicultural counseling. In J. G. Ponterotto, J. M. Casas, L. A. Suzuki, & C. M. Alexander (Eds.), *Handbook of multicultural counseling* (pp. 357–374). Thousand Oaks, CA: Sage.

Griffith, E. E. H., & Baker, F. M. (1993). Psychiatric care of African Americans. In A. C. Gaw (Ed.), *Culture, ethnicity, and mental illness* (pp. 147–173). Washington, DC: American Psychiatric Press.

Griffith, E. E. H., English, T., & Mayfield, V. (1980). Possession, prayer, and testimony: Therapeutic aspects of the Wednesday night meeting in a Black church. *Psychiatry, 43,* 120–128.

Gurung, R. A. R., & Mehta, V. (2001). Relating ethnic identity, acculturation, and attitudes toward treating minority clients. *Cultural Diversity and Ethnic Minority Psychology, 7,* 139–151.

Harjo, S. S. (1993). The American Indian experience. In H. P. McAdoo (Ed.), *Family ethnicity: Strength in diversity* (pp. 199–216). Newbury Park, CA: Sage.

Helms, J. E. (1986). Expanding racial identity theory to cover the counseling process. *Journal of Counseling Psychology, 33,* 62–64.

Helms, J. E., & Parham, T. A. (1996). The Racial Identity Attitude Scale. In R. L. Jones (Ed.), *Handbook of tests and measurements for Black populations* (pp. 167–174). Hampton, VA: Cobb & Henry.

Helzer, J. E., Burnam, A., & McEvoy, L. T. (1991). Alcohol abuse and dependence. In L. N. Robins & D. A. Regier (Eds.), *Psychiatric disorders in America: The Epidemiologic Catchment Area Study* (pp. 81–115). New York: Free Press.

Ho, M. K. (1987). *Family therapy with ethnic minorities.* Newbury Park, CA: Sage.

Ho, M. K. (1992). *Minority children and adolescents in therapy.* Newbury Park, CA: Sage.

Hoffmann, T., Dana, R. H., & Bolton, B. (1985). Measured acculturation and MMPI-168 performance of Native American adults. *Journal of Cross-Cultural Psychology, 16,* 243–256.

Holtzman, W. H. (1988). Beyond the Rorschach. *Journal of Personality Assessment, 52,* 578–609.

Hovey, J. D. (2000). Acculturative stress, depression, and suicidal ideation in Mexican immigrants. *Cultural Diversity and Ethnic Minority Psychology, 6,* 134–151.

Hughes, C. C. (1993). Culture in clinical psychiatry. In A. C. Gaw (Ed.), *Culture, ethnicity, and mental illness* (pp. 3–41). Washington, DC: American Psychiatric Press.

Ivey, A. E., Ivey, M. B., & Simek-Morgan, L. (Eds.). (1996). *Counseling and psychotherapy: A multicultural perspective.* Boston: Allyn & Bacon.

Iwamasa, G. Y. (2003). Recommendations for the treatment of Asian American/Pacific Islander populations. Council of National Psychological Associations for the Advancement of Ethnic Minority Interests (Ed.), *Psychological treatment of ethnic minority populations* (pp. 8–12). Washington, DC: Association of Black Psychologists.

Jackson, A., Berkowitz, H., & Farley, G. (1974). Race as a variable affecting the treatment involvement of children. *Journal of the American Academy of Child Psychiatry, 13,* 20–31.

Jackson, E. L., & Westmoreland, G. (1992). Therapeutic issues for Black children in foster care. In L. A. Vargas & J. D. Koss-Chioino (Eds.), *Working with culture: Psychotherapeutic interventions with ethnic minority children and adolescents* (pp. 43–62). San Francisco: Jossey-Bass.

Jaimes, M. A. (1996). American racism: The impact on American-Indian identity and survival. In S. Gregory & R. Sanjek (Eds.), *Race* (pp. 41–61). New Brunswick, NJ: Rutgers University Press.

Jalali, B. (1988). Ethnicity, cultural adjustment, and behavior: Implications for family therapy. In L. Comas-Diaz & E. E. H. Griffith (Eds.), *Clinical guidelines in cross-cultural mental health* (pp. 9–32). New York: John Wiley.

Jenkins, J. O., & Ramsey, G. A. (1991). Minorities. In M. Hersen, A. E. Kazdin, & A. S. Bellack (Eds.), *The clinical psychology handbook* (pp. 724–740). New York: Pergamon.

Johnson, P. E., & Johnson, R. E. (1996). The role of concrete-abstract thinking levels in teachers' multiethnic beliefs. *Journal of Research and Development in Education, 29,* 134–140.

Johnson, T. M., Fenton, B. J., Kracht, B. R., Weiner, M. F., & Guggenheim, F. G. (1988). Providing culturally sensitive care: Intervention by a consultation-liaison team. *Hospital and Community Psychiatry, 39,* 200–202.

Jones, A. C. (1992). Self-esteem and identity in psychotherapy with adolescents from upwardly mobile middle-class African American families. In L. A. Vargas & J. D. Koss-Chioino (Eds.), *Working with culture: Psychotherapeutic interventions with ethnic minority children and adolescents* (pp. 25–42). San Francisco: Jossey-Bass.

Joyce, P. R., & Paykel, E. S. (1989). Predictors of drug response in depression. *Archives of General Psychiatry, 46,* 89–99.

Karkabi, B. (1993, July 21). More than semantics: Heritage, image influence Blacks' self-perception. *Houston Chronicle,* pp. 1D, 5D.

Karno, M., & Golding, J. M. (1991). Obsessive compulsive disorder. In L. N. Robins & D. A. Regier (Eds.), *Psychiatric disorders in America: The Epidemiologic Catchment Area Study* (pp. 204–219). New York: Free Press.

Kaufman, S., Kamphaus, R. W., & Kaufman, N. L. (1985). New directions in intelligence testing: The Kaufman Assessment Battery for Children (K-ABC). In B. B. Wolman (Ed.), *Handbook of intelligence: Theories, measurements, and applications* (pp. 663–698). New York: John Wiley.

Keith, S. J., Regier, D. A., & Rae, D. S. (1991). Schizophrenic disorders. In L. N. Robins & D. A. Regier (Eds.), *Psychiatric disorders in America: The Epidemiologic Catchment Area Study* (pp. 33–52). New York: Free Press.

Kilkus, M. D., Pumariega, A. J., & Cuffe, S. P. (1995). Influence of race on diagnosis in adolescent psychiatric inpatients. *Journal of the American Academy of Child and Adolescent Psychiatry, 34,* 67–72.

Kim, B. S. K., Brenner, B. R., Liang, C. T. H., & Asay, P. A. (2003). A qualitative study of adaptation experiences of 1.5-generation Asian Americans. *Cultural Diversity and Ethnic Minority Psychology, 9,* 156–170.

Kim, L. I. C. (1993). Psychiatric care of Korean Americans. In A. C. Gaw (Ed.), *Culture, ethnicity, and mental illness* (pp. 347–375). Washington, DC: American Psychiatric Press.

Kim, S., McLeod, J. H., & Shantzis, C. (1992). Cultural competence for evaluators working with Asian-American communities: Some practical considerations. In M. Orlandi & R. Weston (Eds.), *Cultural competence for evaluators* (pp. 203–260). Rockville, MD: U.S. Department of Health and Human Services.

Kim, S. C. (1985). Family therapy for Asian Americans: Strategic-structural framework. *Psychotherapy, 22,* 342–348.

Kim-ju, G. M., & Liem, R. (2003). Ethnic self-awareness as a function of ethnic group status, group composition, and ethnic identity orientation. *Cultural Diversity and Ethnic Minority Psychology, 9,* 289–302.

Kinzie, J. D., & Leung, P. K. (1993). Psychiatric care of Indochinese Americans. In A. C. Gaw (Ed.), *Culture, ethnicity, and mental illness* (pp. 281–304). Washington, DC: American Psychiatric Press.

Klonoff, E. A., Landrine, H., & Ullman, J. B. (1999). Racial discrimination and psychiatric symptoms among Blacks. *Cultural Diversity and Ethnic Minority Psychology, 5,* 329–339.

Kolko, D. J. (1987). Simplified inpatient treatment of nocturnal enuresis in psychiatrically disturbed children. *Behavior Therapy, 18,* 99–112.

Koslow, D. R., & Salett, E. P. (Eds.). (1989). *Crossing cultures in mental health.* Washington, DC: International Counseling Center.

Koslow, N. J., & Rehm, L. P. (1991). Childhood depression. In T. R. Kratochwill & R. J. Morris (Eds.), *The practice of child therapy* (2nd ed., pp. 43–75). New York: Pergamon.

Koss-Chioino, J., & Vargas, L. A. (1999). *Working with Latino youth.* San Francisco: Jossey-Bass.

Kratochwill, T. R., & Bergan, J. R. (1990). *Behavioral consultation in applied settings: An individual guide.* New York: Plenum.

LaFromboise, T. D., & Dizon, M. R. (2003). American Indian children and adolescents. In J. T. Gibbs, L. N. Huang, & Associates, *Children of color: Psychological interventions with culturally diverse youth* (pp. 45–90). San Francisco: Jossey-Bass.

LaFromboise, T. D., Foster, S., & James, A. (1996). Ethics in multicultural counseling. In P. B. Pedersen, J. G. Draguns, W. J. Lonner, & J. E. Trimble (Eds.), *Counseling across cultures* (4th ed., pp. 47–72). Thousand Oaks, CA: Sage.

Landrine, H., & Klonoff, E. A. (1996). The Schedule of Racist Events: A measure of racial discrimination and a study of its negative physical and mental health consequences. *Journal of Black Psychology, 22,* 144–168.

Lange, A. J., & Jakubowski, P. (1976). *Responsible assertive behavior.* Champaign, IL: Research Press.

Leaf, P. J., Myers, J. K., & McEvoy, L. T. (1991). Procedures used in the Epidemiologic Catchment Area Study. In L. N. Robins & D. A. Regier (Eds.), *Psychiatric disorders in America: The Epidemiologic Catchment Area Study* (pp. 11–30). New York: Free Press.

Lefley, H. P., & Pedersen, P. B. (Eds.). (1986). *Cross-cultural training for mental health professionals.* Springfield, IL: Charles C Thomas.

Levin, J. S., & Taylor, R. J. (1993). Gender and age differences in religiosity among Black Americans. *Gerontologist, 33,* 16–23.

Lewis-Fernandez, R., & Kleinman, A. (1995). Cultural psychiatry: Theoretical, clinical, and research issues. *Psychiatric Clinics of North America, 18,* 433–448.

Lineberger, M. H., & Calhoun, K. S. (1983). Assertive behavior in Black and White American undergraduates. *Journal of Psychology, 13,* 139–148.

Lonner, W. J., & Ibrahim, F. A. (1996). Appraisal and assessment in cross-cultural counseling. In P. B. Pedersen, J. G. Draguns, W. J. Lonner, & J. E. Trimble (Eds.), *Counseling across cultures* (4th ed., pp. 293–322). Thousand Oaks, CA: Sage.

Lopez, S., & Nunez, J. A. (1987). Cultural factors considered in selected diagnostic criteria and interview schedule. *Journal of Abnormal Psychology, 96,* 270–272.

Lopez, S. R., Lopez, A. A., & Fong, K. T. (1991). Mexican Americans' initial preferences for counselors: The role of ethnic factors. *Journal of Counseling Psychology, 38,* 487–496.

Malgady, R. G., Constantino, G., & Rogler, L. H. (1984). Development of a thematic apperception test (TEMAS) for urban Hispanic children. *Journal of Consulting and Clinical Psychology, 52,* 986–996.

Malgady, R. G., Rogler, L. H., & Constantino, G. (1987). Ethnocultural and linguistic bias in mental health evaluation of Hispanics. *American Psychologist, 42,* 228–234.

Manson, S. M., Walker, R. D., & Kivlahan, D. R. (1987). Psychiatric assessment and treatment of American Indians and Alaska Natives. *Hospital Community Psychiatry, 38,* 165–173.

Maramba, G. G., & Hall, G. C. N. (2002). Meta-analyses of ethnic match as a predictor of dropout, utilization, and level of functioning. *Cultural Diversity and Ethnic Minority Psychology, 8,* 290–297.

Marcos, L. R. (1976). Bilinguals in psychotherapy: Language as an emotional barrier. *American Journal of Psychotherapy, 30,* 552–560.

Marcos, L. R., Alpert, M., Urcuyo, L., & Kesselman, M. (1973). The effect of interview language on the evaluation of psychopathology in Spanish-American schizophrenic patients. *American Journal of Psychiatry, 130,* 549–553.

Marin, G., & Marin, B. V. (1991). *Research with Hispanic populations.* Newbury Park, CA: Sage.

Marsella, A. J., & Yamada, A. M. (2000). Culture and mental health: An introduction and overview of foundations, concepts, and issues. In I. Cuéllar & F. A. Paniagua (Eds.), *Handbook of multicultural mental health: Assessment and treatment of diverse populations* (pp. 3–24). New York: Academic Press.

Martinez, C. (1986). Hispanic psychiatric issues. In C. B. Wilkinson (Ed.), *Ethnic psychiatry* (pp. 61–87). New York: Plenum Medical.

Martinez, C. (1988). Mexican-Americans. In L. Comas-Diaz & E. E. H. Griffith (Eds.), *Clinical guidelines in cross-cultural mental health* (pp. 182–203). New York: John Wiley.

Martinez, C. (1993). Psychiatric care of Mexican Americans. In A. C. Gaw (Ed.), *Culture, ethnicity, and mental illness* (pp. 431–466). Washington, DC: American Psychiatric Press.

Martinez, R. E. (1993, August). Minority label "dehumanizing" [Letter to the editor]. *San Antonio Express News,* p. 5B.

Masuda, M., Matsumoto, G. H., & Meredith, G. M. (1970). Ethnic identity in three generations of Japanese Americans. *Journal of Social Psychology, 81,* 199–207.

Matheson, L. (1986). If you are not an Indian, how do you treat an Indian? In H. P. Lefley & P. B. Pedersen (Eds.), *Cross-cultural training for mental health professionals* (pp. 115–130). Springfield, IL: Charles C Thomas.

McAdoo, H. P. (1993a). Ethnic families: Strengths that are found in diversity. In H. P. McAdoo (Ed.), *Family ethnicity: Strength in diversity* (pp. 3–14). Newbury Park, CA: Sage.

McAdoo, H. P. (Ed.). (1993b). *Family ethnicity: Strength in diversity.* Newbury Park, CA: Sage.

Mendoza, R. H. (1989). An empirical scale to measure type and degree of acculturation in Mexican-American adolescents and adults. *Journal of Cross-Cultural Psychology, 20,* 372–385.

Mercer, J., & Lewis, J. (1978). *System of multicultural pluralistic assessment.* New York: Psychological Corporation.

Milliones, J. (1980). Construction of a Black consciousness measure: Psychotherapeutic implications. *Psychotherapy: Theory, Research, and Practice, 17,* 175–182.

Moffic, H. S., & Kinzie, J. D. (1996). The history and future of cross-cultural psychiatric services. *Community Mental Health Journal, 32,* 581–592.

Mollica, R. F. (1989). Developing effective mental health policies and services for traumatized refugee patients. In D. R. Koslow & E. P. Salett (Eds.), *Crossing cultures in mental health* (pp. 101–115). Washington, DC: International Counseling Center.

Mollica, R. F., & Lavelle, J. (1988). Southeast Asian refugees. In L. Comas-Diaz & E. E. H. Griffith (Eds.), *Clinical guidelines in cross-cultural mental health* (pp. 262–293). New York: John Wiley.

Montgomery, G. T., & Orozco, S. (1985). Mexican Americans' performance on the MMPI as a function of level of acculturation. *Journal of Clinical Psychology, 41,* 203–212.

Moyerman, D. R., & Forman, B. D. (1992). Acculturation and adjustment: A meta-analytic study. *Hispanic Journal of Behavioral Sciences, 14,* 163–200.

Mueller, J., Kiernan, R. J., & Langston, J. W. (1992). The mental status examination. In H. H. Goldman (Ed.), *Review of general psychiatry* (pp. 109–117). San Mateo, CA: Appleton & Lange.

Murase, K. (1992). Models of service delivery in Asian American communities. In A. M. Furuto, R. Biswas, D. K. Chung, K. Murase, & F. Ross-Sheriff (Eds.), *Social work practice with Asian Americans* (pp. 101–119). Newbury Park, CA: Sage.

Murphy, J. M. (2002). Symptom scales and diagnostic schedules in adult psychiatry. In M. T. Tsuang & M. Tohen (Eds.), *Textbook in psychiatric epidemiology* (2nd ed., pp. 273–332). New York: Wiley-Liss.

Musser-Granski, J., & Carrillo, D. F. (1997). The use of bilingual, bicultural professionals in mental health services: Issues for hiring, training, and supervision. *Community Mental Health Journal, 33,* 51–60.

Neff, J. A., & Hoppe, S. K. (1993). Race/ethnicity, acculturation, and psychological distress: Fatalism and religiosity as cultural resources. *Journal of Community Psychology, 21,* 3–20.

Negy, C., Shreve, T. L., Jensen, B. J., & Uddin, N. (2003). Ethnic identity, self-esteem, and ethnocentrism: A study of social identity versus multicultural theory of development. *Cultural Diversity and Ethnic Minority Psychology, 9,* 333–344.

Neighbors, H. W., & Lumpkin, S. (1990). The epidemiology of mental disorder in the Black population. In D. S. Ruiz (Ed.), *Handbook of mental health and mental disorder among Black Americans* (pp. 55–70). Westport, CT: Greenwood.

Norris, A. E., Ford, K., & Bova, C. A. (1996). Psychometrics of a brief acculturation scale for Hispanics in a probability sample of urban Hispanic adolescents and young adults. *Hispanic Journal of Behavioral Sciences, 18,* 29–38.

O'Brien, S. (1989). *American Indian tribal governments.* Norman: University of Oklahoma Press.

Okazaki, S. (2000). Assessing and treating Asian Americans: Recent advances. In I. Cuéllar & F. A. Paniagua (Eds.), *Handbook of multicultural mental health: Assessment and treatment of diverse populations* (pp. 171–193). New York: Academic Press.

Paniagua, F. A. (1994). *Assessing and treating culturally diverse clients: A practical guide.* Thousand Oaks, CA: Sage.

Paniagua, F. A. (1996). Cross-cultural guidelines in family therapy practice. *Family Journal: Counseling and Therapy for Couples and Families, 4,* 127–138.

Paniagua, F. A. (1998). *Assessing and treating culturally diverse clients: A practical guide* (2nd ed.). Thousand Oaks, CA: Sage.

Paniagua, F. A. (2000). Culture-bound syndromes, cultural variations, and psychopathology. In I. Cuéllar & F. A. Paniagua (Eds.), *Handbook of multicultural mental health: Assessment and treatment of diverse populations* (pp. 139–169). New York: Academic Press.

Paniagua, F. A. (2001a). *Diagnosis in a multicultural context: A casebook for mental health professionals.* Thousand Oaks, CA: Sage.

Paniagua, F. A. (2001b). Functional analysis and behavioral assessment of children and adolescents. In H. B. Vance & A. J. Pumariega (Eds.), *Clinical assessment of child and adolescent behavior* (pp. 32–85). New York: John Wiley.

Paniagua, F. A. (2004). Culturally sensitive mental health services for Latino or Hispanic families [Review of the book *Counseling Latinos and la familia: A practical guide*]. *Contemporary Psychology, 49,* 54–57.

Paniagua, F. A., & Baer, D. M. (1981). A procedural analysis of the symbolic forms of behavior therapy. *Behaviorism, 9,* 171–205.

Paniagua, F. A., & Black, S. A. (1990). Management and prevention of hyperactivity and conduct disorders in 8–10-year-old boys through correspondence training procedures. *Child and Family Behavior Therapy, 12,* 23–56.

Paniagua, F. A., O'Boyle, M., Tan, V. L., & Lew, A. S. (2000). Self-evaluation of unintended biases and prejudices. *Psychological Reports, 87,* 823–829.

Paniagua, F. A., Wassef, A., O'Boyle, M., Linares, S. A., & Cuéllar, I. (1993). What is a difficult mental health case? An empirical study of relationships among domain variables. *Journal of Contemporary Psychotherapy, 23,* 77–98.

Pedersen, P. B. (Ed.). (1987). *Handbook of cross-cultural counseling and therapy.* London: Greenwood.

Pedersen, P. B. (1997). *Culture-centered counseling interventions: Striving for accuracy.* Thousand Oaks, CA: Sage.

Pedersen, P. B., Draguns, J. G., Lonner, W. J., & Trimble, J. E. (Eds.). (1996). *Counseling across cultures* (4th ed.). Thousand Oaks, CA: Sage.

Phinney, J. S. (1992). The Multigroup Ethnic Identity Measure: A new scale for use with adolescents and young adults from diverse groups. *Journal of Adolescent Research, 7,* 156–176.

Phinney, J. S. (1996). When we talk about American ethnic groups, what do we mean? *American Psychologist, 51,* 918–927.

Pierce, R. C., Clark, M., & Kiefer, C. W. (1972). A "bootstrap" scaling technique. *Human Organization, 31,* 403–410.

Pitta, P., Marcos, L. R., & Alpert, M. (1978). Language switch as a treatment strategy with bilingual patients. *American Journal of Psychoanalysis, 38,* 255–258.

Ponterotto, J. G., Casas, J. M., Suzuki, L. A., & Alexander, C. M. (Eds.). (1995). *Handbook of multicultural counseling.* Thousand Oaks, CA: Sage.

Pope-Davis, D. B., & Coleman, H. L. K. (Eds.). (1997). *Multicultural counseling competencies: Assessment, education and training, and supervision.* Thousand Oaks, CA: Sage.

Pumariega, A. J., Nace, D., England, M. J., Diamond, J., Matson, A., Fallon, T., et al. (1997). Community-based systems approach to children's managed mental health services. *Journal of Child and Family Studies, 6,* 149–164.

Radloff, L. S. (1977). The CES-D Scale: A self-report depression scale for research in the general population. *Applied Psychological Measurement, 1,* 385–401.

Ramirez, M. (1984). Assessing and understanding biculturalism-multiculturalism in Mexican-American adults. In J. L. Martinez & R. H. Mendoza (Eds.), *Chicano psychology* (pp. 77–94). Orlando, FL: Academic Press.

Ramirez, S. Z., Paniagua, F. A., Linskey, A., & O'Boyle, M. (1993, August). *Diagnosing mental disorders in Hispanic children and youth: Cultural considerations.* Paper presented at the annual meeting of the American Psychological Association, Toronto.

Ramirez, S. Z., Wassef, A., Paniagua, F. A., & Linskey, A. O. (1993, November). *The significance of cultural evaluations of psychopathology in ethnic minority individuals.* Paper presented at the annual meeting of the Texas Psychological Association, Austin.

Ramirez, S. Z., Wassef, A., Paniagua, F. A., Linskey, A. O., & O'Boyle, M. (1994). Perceptions of mental health providers concerning cultural factors in the evaluation of Hispanic children and adolescents. *Hispanic Journal of Behavioral Sciences, 16,* 28–42.

Ramos-McKay, J. M., Comas-Diaz, L., & Rivera, L. A. (1988). Puerto Ricans. In L. Comas-Diaz & E. E. H. Griffith (Eds.), *Clinical guidelines in cross-cultural mental health* (pp. 204–232). New York: John Wiley.

Reyhner, J., & Eder, J. (1988). A history of Indian education. In J. Reyhner (Ed.), *Teaching American Indian students* (2nd ed., pp. 33–58). Norman: University of Oklahoma Press.

Richardson, E. H. (1981). Cultural and historical perspectives in counseling American Indians. In D. W. Sue (Ed.), *Counseling the culturally different: Theory and practice* (pp. 216–255). New York: John Wiley.

Robins, L. N., Helzer, J. E., Weissman, M. M., Orvasche, H., Gruenberg, E., Burke, J. D., et al. (1984). Lifetime prevalence of specific psychiatric disorders in three sites. *Archives of General Psychiatry, 41,* 949–958.

Robins, L. N., & Regier, D. A. (Eds.). (1991). *Psychiatric disorders in America: The Epidemiologic Catchment Area Study.* New York: Free Press.

Rogler, L. H. (1993). Culture in psychiatric diagnosis: An issue of scientific accuracy. *Psychiatry, 56,* 324–327.

Root, M., Ho, C., & Sue, S. (1986). Issues in the training of counselors for Asian Americans. In H. P. Lefley & P. B. Pedersen (Eds.), *Cross-cultural training for mental health professionals* (pp. 199–209). Springfield, IL: Charles C Thomas.

Rubel, A. J., O'Nell, C. W., & Collado-Ardón, R. (1991). *Susto: A folk illness* (Repr. ed.). Berkeley: University of California Press.

Ruiz, R. A. (1981). Cultural and historical perspectives in counseling Hispanics. In D. W. Sue (Ed.), *Counseling the culturally different: Theory and practice* (pp. 186–215). New York: John Wiley.

Ruiz, R. A., & Padilla, A. M. (1977). Counseling Latinos. *Personnel and Guidance Journal, 55,* 401–408.

Russell, D. M. (1988). Language and psychotherapy: The influence of nonstandard English in clinical practice. In L. Comas-Diaz & E. E. H. Griffith (Eds.), *Clinical guidelines in cross-cultural mental health* (pp. 33–68). New York: John Wiley.

Russo, N. F., Olmedo, E. L., Stapp, J., & Fulcher, R. (1981). Women and minorities in psychology. *American Psychologist, 36,* 1315–1363.

Rutter, M., Tuma, A. H., & Lann, I. S. (1988). *Assessment and diagnosis in child psychopathology.* New York: Guilford.

Sadock, B. J., & Sadock, V. A. (2003). *Synopsis of psychiatry: Behavioral sciences/clinical psychiatry* (9th ed.). Philadelphia: Lippincott Williams & Wilkins.

Sandoval, M. C., & De La Roza, M. C. (1986). A cultural perspective for serving Hispanic clients. In H. P. Lefley & P. B. Pedersen (Eds.), *Cross-cultural training for mental health professionals* (pp. 151–181). Springfield, IL: Charles C Thomas.

Santiago-Rivera, A., Arredondo, P., & Gallardo-Cooper, M. (2002). *Counseling Latinos and la familia: A practical guide.* Thousand Oaks, CA: Sage.

Scholl, L., Upshaw, V. M., Rashid, A., Jackson, E. B., & Bethea, K. (2004). Person factors associated with suicidal behavior among African American women and men. *Cultural Diversity and Ethnic Minority Psychology, 10,* 5–22.

Seijo, R., Gomez, H., & Freidenberg, J. (1991). Language as a communication barrier in medical care for Hispanic patients. *Hispanic Journal of Behavioral Sciences, 13,* 363–376.

Sevig, T. D., Highlen, P. S., & Adams, E. M. (2000). Development and validation of the Self-Identity Inventory (SII): A multicultural identity development instrument. *Cultural Diversity and Ethnic Minority Psychology, 6,* 168–182.

Silver, B., Poland, R. E., & Lin, K. (1993). Ethnicity and the pharmacology of tricyclic antidepressants. In K. Lin, R. E. Poland, & G. Nakasaki (Eds.), *Psychopharmacology and psychobiology of ethnicity* (pp. 61–89). Washington, DC: American Psychiatric Press.

Simons, R. C., & Hughes, C. C. (1993). Culture-bound syndromes. In A. C. Gaw (Ed.), *Culture, ethnicity, and mental illness* (pp. 75–93). Washington, DC: American Psychiatric Press.

Smart, D. W., & Smart, J. F. (1997). *DSM-IV* and culturally sensitive diagnosis: Some observations for counselors. *Journal of Counseling and Development, 75,* 392–398.

Smedley, B. D., Stith, A. Y., & Nelson, A. R. (Eds.). (2003). *Unequal treatment: Confronting racial and ethnic disparities in health care.* Washington, DC: National Academies Press.

Smith, E. J. (1981). Cultural and historical perspectives in counseling Blacks. In D. W. Sue (Ed.), *Counseling the culturally different: Theory and practice* (pp. 141–185). New York: John Wiley.

Smith, T. W. (1992). Changing racial labels: From "colored" to "Negro" to "Black" to "African American." *Public Opinion Quarterly, 56,* 496–544.

Smither, R., & Rodriguez-Giegling, M. (1982). Personality, demographics, and acculturation of Vietnamese and Nicaraguan refugees to the United States. *International Journal of Psychology, 17,* 19–25.

Smitherman, G. (1995). *Black talk.* Boston: Houghton Mifflin.

Sodowsky, G. R., Kwan, K. L., & Pannu, R. (1995). Ethnic identity of Asians in the United States. In J. G. Ponterotto, J. M. Casas, L. A. Suzuki, & C. M. Alexander (Eds.), *Handbook of multicultural counseling* (pp. 123–154). Thousand Oaks, CA: Sage.

Soto, E. (1983). Sex-role traditionalism and assertiveness in Puerto Rican women living in the United States. *Journal of Community Psychology, 11,* 346–354.

Spitzer, R. L., & Endicott, J. (1978). *The schedule for affective disorders and schizophrenia* (3rd ed.). New York: New York State Psychiatric Institute.

Sue, D., & Sundberg, N. D. (1996). Research and research hypotheses about effectiveness in intercultural counseling. In P. B. Pedersen, J. G. Draguns, W. J. Lonner, & J. E. Trimble (Eds.), *Counseling across cultures* (4th ed., pp. 323–352). Thousand Oaks, CA: Sage.

Sue, D. W., & Sue, D. (1987). Asian-Americans and Pacific Islanders. In P. B. Pedersen (Ed.), *Handbook of cross-cultural counseling and therapy* (pp. 141–146). London: Greenwood.

Sue, D. W., & Sue, D. (Eds.). (2003). *Counseling the culturally different: Theory and practice* (4th ed.). New York: John Wiley.

Sue, S. (1988). Psychotherapy services for ethnic minorities: Two decades of research findings. *American Psychologist, 43,* 301–308.

Sue, S., Fujino, D. C., Hu, L., Takeuchi, D. T., & Zane, N. W. S. (1991). Community mental health services for ethnic minority groups: A test of the cultural responsiveness hypothesis. *Journal of Consulting and Clinical Psychology, 59,* 533–540.

Sue, S. & Zane, N. W. S. (1987). The role of culture and cultural techniques in psychotherapy: A critique and reformulation. *American Psychologist, 42,* 37–45.

Suinn, R. M., Ahuna, C., & Khoo, G. (1992). The Suinn-Lew Asian Self-Identification Acculturation Scale: Concurrent and factorial validation. *Educational and Psychological Measurement, 52,* 1041–1046.

Suinn, R. M., Rickard-Figueroa, K., Lew, S., & Vigil, P. (1987). The Suinn-Lew Asian Self-Identity Acculturation Scale: An initial report. *Educational and Psychological Measurement, 47,* 401–407.

Szalacha, L. A., Erkut, S., García Coll, C., Alarcón, O., Fields, J. P., & Ceder, I. (2003). Discrimination and Puerto Rican children's and adolescents' mental health. *Cultural Diversity and Ethnic Minority Psychology, 9,* 141–155.

Szapocznik, J., Scopetta, M. A., Arnalde, M., & Kurtines, W. (1978). Cuban value structure: Treatment implications. *Journal of Consulting and Clinical Psychology, 46,* 961–970.

Tanaka-Matsumi, J., & Higginbotham, H. N. (1996). Behavioral approaches to counseling across cultures. In P. B. Pedersen, J. G. Draguns, W. J. Lonner, & J. E. Trimble (Eds.), *Counseling across cultures* (4th ed., pp. 266–292). Thousand Oaks, CA: Sage.

Taylor, R. J., & Chatters, L. M. (1986). Church-based informal support among elderly Blacks. *Gerontologist, 26,* 637–642.

Tharp, R. G. (1991). Cultural diversity and treatment of children. *Journal of Consulting and Clinical Psychology, 59,* 799–812.

Thompson, J., Walker, R. D., & Silk-Walker, P. (1993). Psychiatric care of American Indians and Alaska Natives. In A. C. Gaw (Ed.), *Culture, ethnicity, and mental illness* (pp. 189–243). Washington, DC: American Psychiatric Press.

Trimble, J. E., & Fleming, C. M. (1989). Providing counseling services for Native American Indians: Client, counselor, and community characteristics. In P. B. Pedersen, J. G. Draguns, W. J. Lonner, & J. E. Trimble (Eds.), *Counseling across cultures* (3rd ed., pp. 177–204). Honolulu: University of Hawaii Press.

Tsui, A. M. (1985). Psychotherapeutic considerations in sexual counseling for Asian immigrants. *Psychotherapy, 22,* 357–362.

Turner, S. M., DeMers, S. T., Fox, H. R., & Reed, G. M. (2001). APA's guidelines for test user qualifications: An executive summary. *American Psychologist, 56,* 1099–1113.

U.S. Bureau of the Census. (1992). *Statistical abstract of the United States.* Washington, DC: Government Printing Office.

U.S. Bureau of the Census. (2000). *Summary File 1 and Summary File 3.* Washington, DC: Author.

U.S. Bureau of the Census. (2001). *Current population survey, March 2001.* Washington, DC: Author.

U.S. Bureau of the Census. (2002a). *Current population survey: Annual demographic supplements.* Washington, DC: Author.

U.S. Bureau of the Census. (2002b). *Current population survey, March 2002*. Washington, DC: Author.

U.S. Bureau of the Census. (2004). Income of household by race and Hispanic origin using 2- and 3-year averages: 2000–2002. In *Current population survey: 2001, 2001, and 2003 annual and social economic supplements*. Washington, DC: Author.

U.S. Department of Health and Human Services. (1991). *Health status of minorities and low-income groups* (3rd ed.). Washington, DC: Government Printing Office.

Utsey, S. O., Chae, M. H., Brown, C. F., & Kelly, D. (2002). Effect of ethnic group membership on ethnic identity, race-related stress, and quality of life. *Cultural Diversity and Ethnic Minority Psychology, 8,* 366–377.

Walker, R. D., & LaDue, R. (1986). An integrative approach to American Indian mental health. In C. B. Wilkinson (Ed.), *Ethnic psychiatry* (pp. 143–199). New York: Plenum Medical.

Wehrly, B., Kenney, K. R., & Kenney, M. E. (1999). *Counseling multiracial families*. Thousand Oaks, CA: Sage.

Westermeyer, J. J. (1993). Cross-cultural psychiatric assessment. In A. C. Gaw (Ed.), *Culture, ethnicity, and mental illness* (pp. 125–144). Washington, DC: American Psychiatric Press.

Whatley, P. R., Allen, J., & Dana, R. H. (2003). Racial identity and the MMPI in African American male college students. *Cultural Diversity and Ethnic Minority Psychology, 9,* 345–353.

Wilkinson, C. B. (1986). Introduction. In C. B. Wilkinson (Ed.), *Ethnic psychiatry* (pp. 1–11). New York: Plenum Medical.

Wilkinson, C. B., & Spurlock, J. (1986). The mental health of Black Americans: Psychiatric diagnosis and treatment. In C. B. Wilkinson (Ed.), *Ethnic psychiatry* (pp. 13–59). New York: Plenum Medical.

Wilkinson, D. (1993). Family ethnicity in America. In H. P. McAdoo (Ed.), *Family ethnicity: Strength in diversity* (pp. 15–59). Newbury Park, CA: Sage.

Wise, F., & Miller, N. B. (1983). The mental health of American Indian children. In G. J. Powell, J. Yamamoto, A. Romero, & A. Morales (Eds.), *The psychosocial development of minority group children* (pp. 344–361). New York: Brunner/Mazel.

Wolpe, J., & Lang, P. J. (1964). A fear survey schedule for use in behavior therapy. *Behaviour Research and Therapy, 2,* 27–30.

Wong-Rieger, D., & Quintana, D. (1987). Comparative acculturation of Southeast Asians and Hispanic immigrants and sojourners. *Journal of Cross-Cultural Psychology, 18,* 145–162.

Yamamoto, J. (1986). Therapy for Asian Americans and Pacific Islanders. In C. B. Wilkinson (Ed.), *Ethnic psychiatry* (pp. 89–141). New York: Plenum Medical.

Yamamoto, J., Silva, J. A., Justice, L. R., Chang, C. Y., & Leong, G. B. (1993). Cross-cultural psychotherapy. In A. C. Gaw (Ed.), *Culture, ethnicity, and mental illness* (pp. 101–124). Washington, DC: American Psychiatric Press.

Zea, M. C., Asner-Self, K. K., Birman, D., & Buki, L. P. (2003). The Abbreviated Multidimensional Acculturation Scale: Empirical validation with two Latino/Latina samples. *Cultural Diversity and Ethnic Minority Psychology, 9,* 107–126.

Author Index

Subject Index

About the Author

Freddy A. Paniagua (Ph.D., University of Kansas; postdoctoral training at Johns Hopkins University School of Medicine) is Professor in the Department of Psychiatry and Behavioral Sciences, University of Texas Medical Branch at Galveston, where he teaches cross-cultural mental health seminars with an emphasis on the assessment and treatment of African American, Hispanic, Asian, and American Indian clients. In 1989, he received a 6-year grant from the National Institute of Mental Health to provide training to mental health professionals representing culturally diverse groups, with emphasis on the assessment and treatment of emotionally disturbed clients. He has published more than 40 scientific articles, including reports on basic and applied research as well as theoretical contributions, and two textbooks on multicultural issues that are widely used in mental health training programs in the United States and abroad.